SUBURBAN GLAMOUR//

// STORY, ART & LETTERS - JAMIE McKELVIE / COLORS - MATTHEW WILSON / COVER ART - JAMIE McKELVIE / COLORS (ISSUE 1) - GUY MAJOR / LETTERS (ISSUE 2) - DREW GILL //

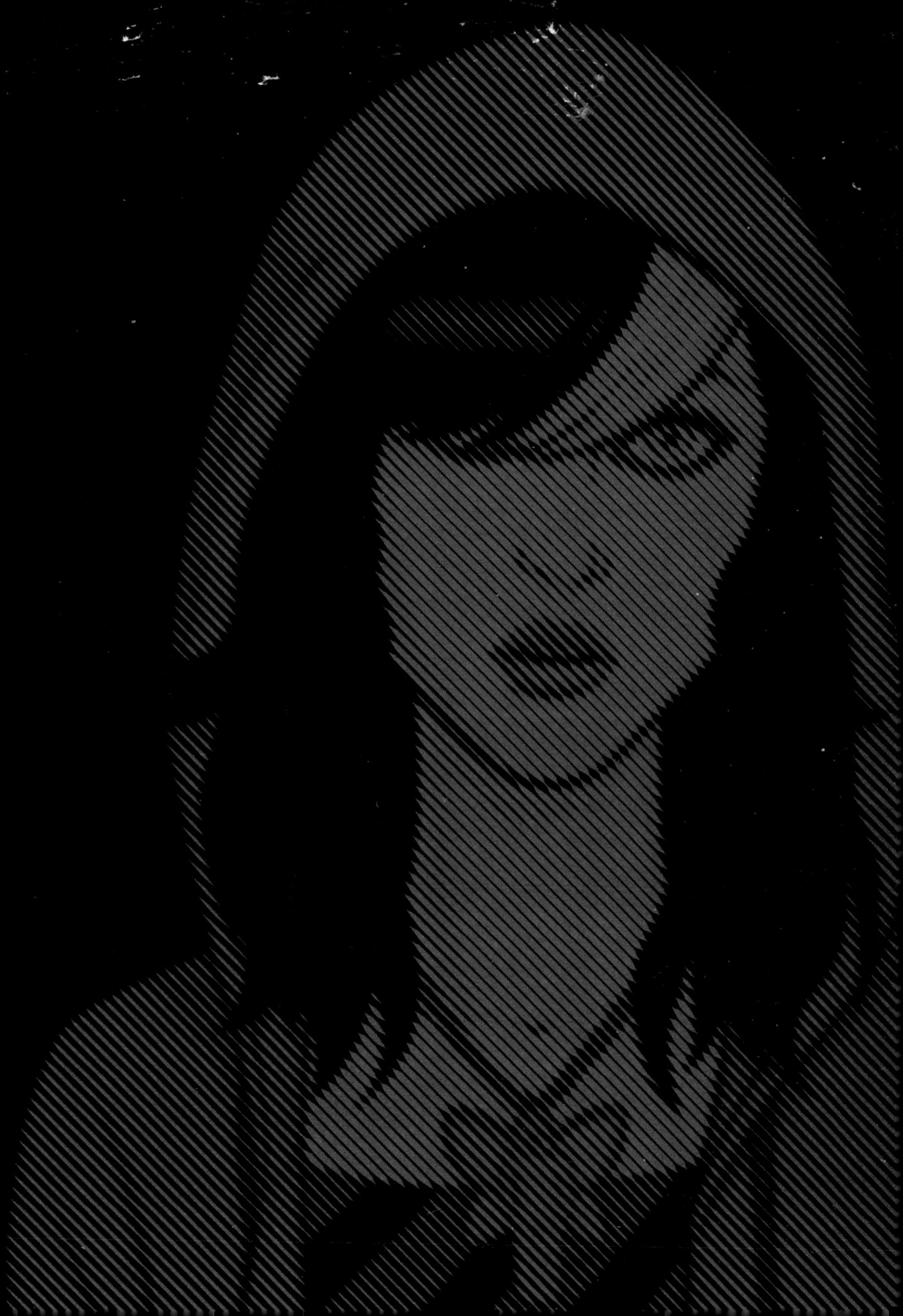

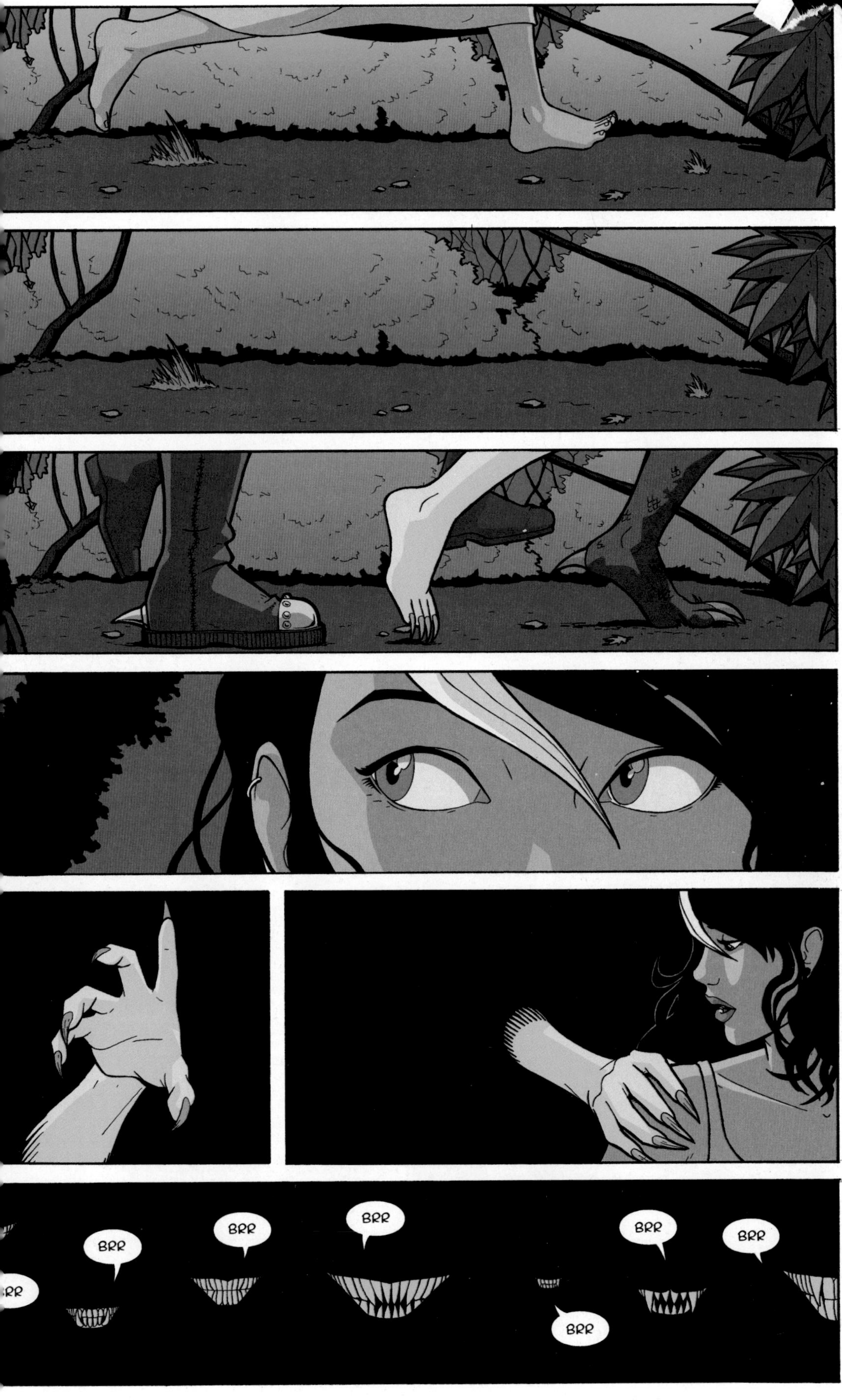
BRR
BRR
BRR
BRR
BRR
BRR
BRR

BRR BRR BRR BRR BRR BRR BRR BRR BRR BRR
BRR BRR BRR BRR
7:00
BRR BRR *
SIGH

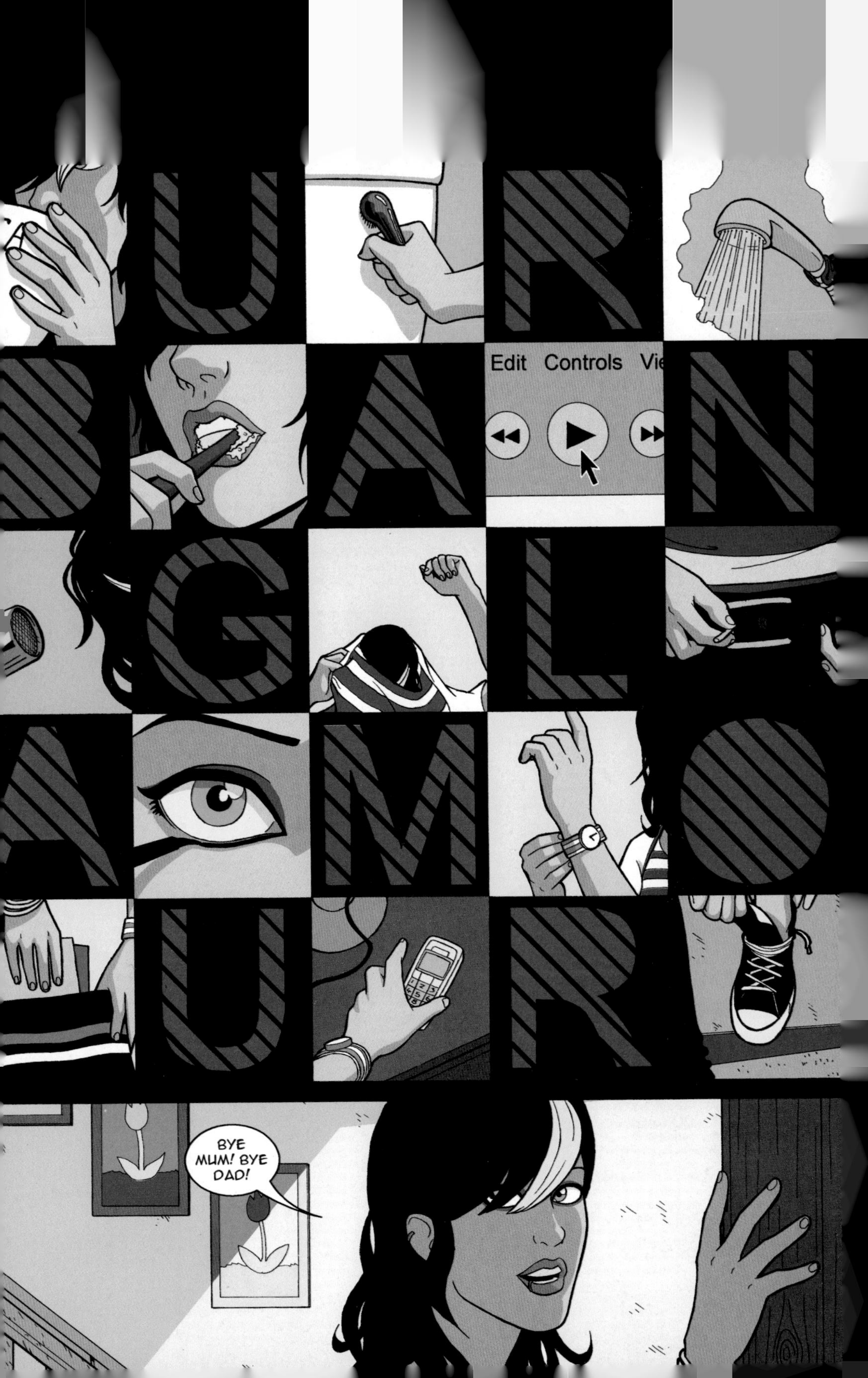
UR
BAN
GL
AMO
UR
Edit Controls Vie
BYE MUM! BYE DAD!

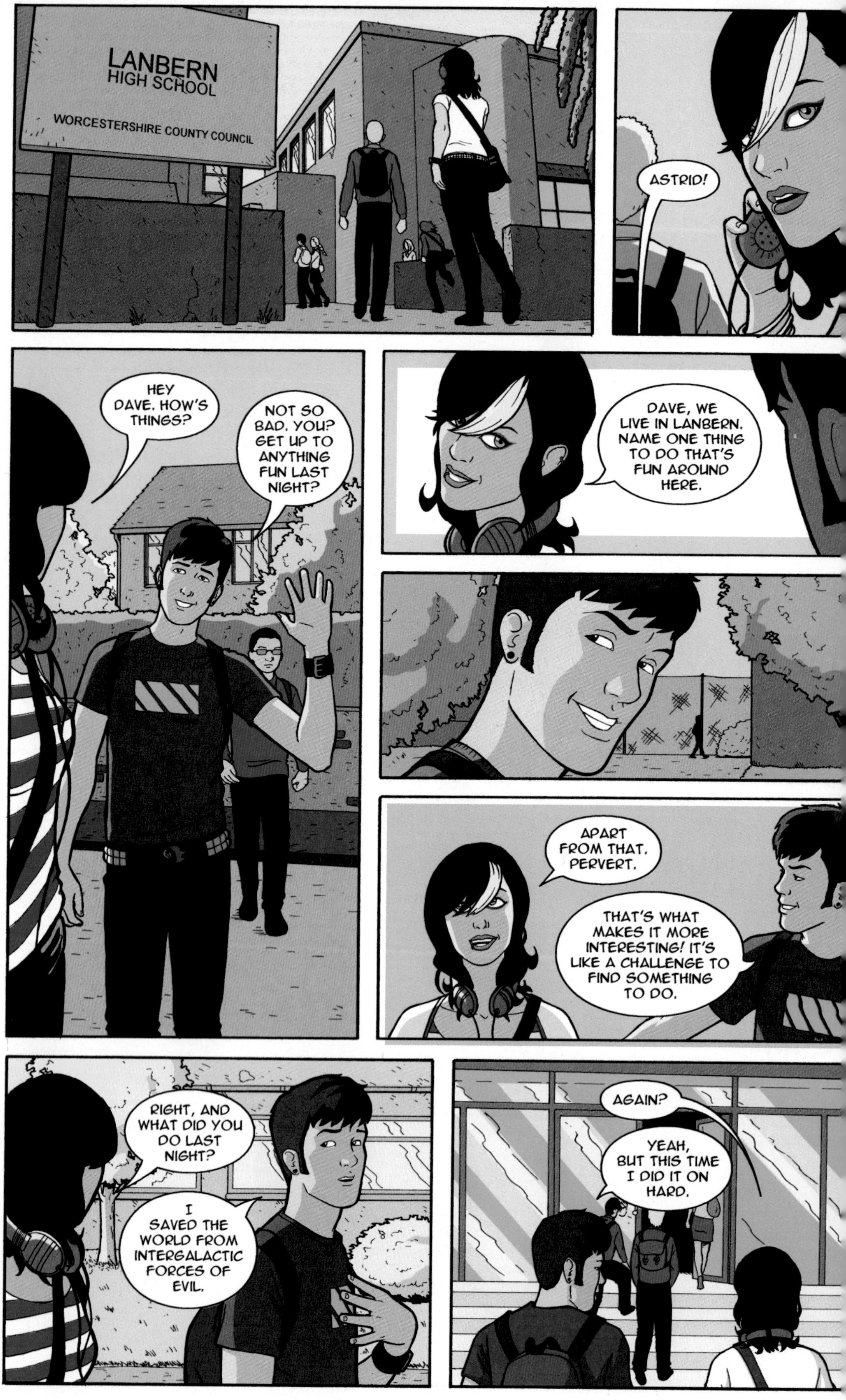
LANBERN
HIGH SCHOOL
WORCESTERSHIRE COUNTY COUNCIL
ASTRID!
HEY DAVE. HOW'S THINGS?
NOT SO BAD. YOU? GET UP TO ANYTHING FUN LAST NIGHT?
DAVE, WE LIVE IN LANBERN. NAME ONE THING TO DO THAT'S FUN AROUND HERE.
APART FROM THAT, PERVERT.
THAT'S WHAT MAKES IT MORE INTERESTING! IT'S LIKE A CHALLENGE TO FIND SOMETHING TO DO.
RIGHT, AND WHAT DID YOU DO LAST NIGHT?
I SAVED THE WORLD FROM INTERGALACTIC FORCES OF EVIL.
AGAIN?
YEAH, BUT THIS TIME I DID IT ON HARD.

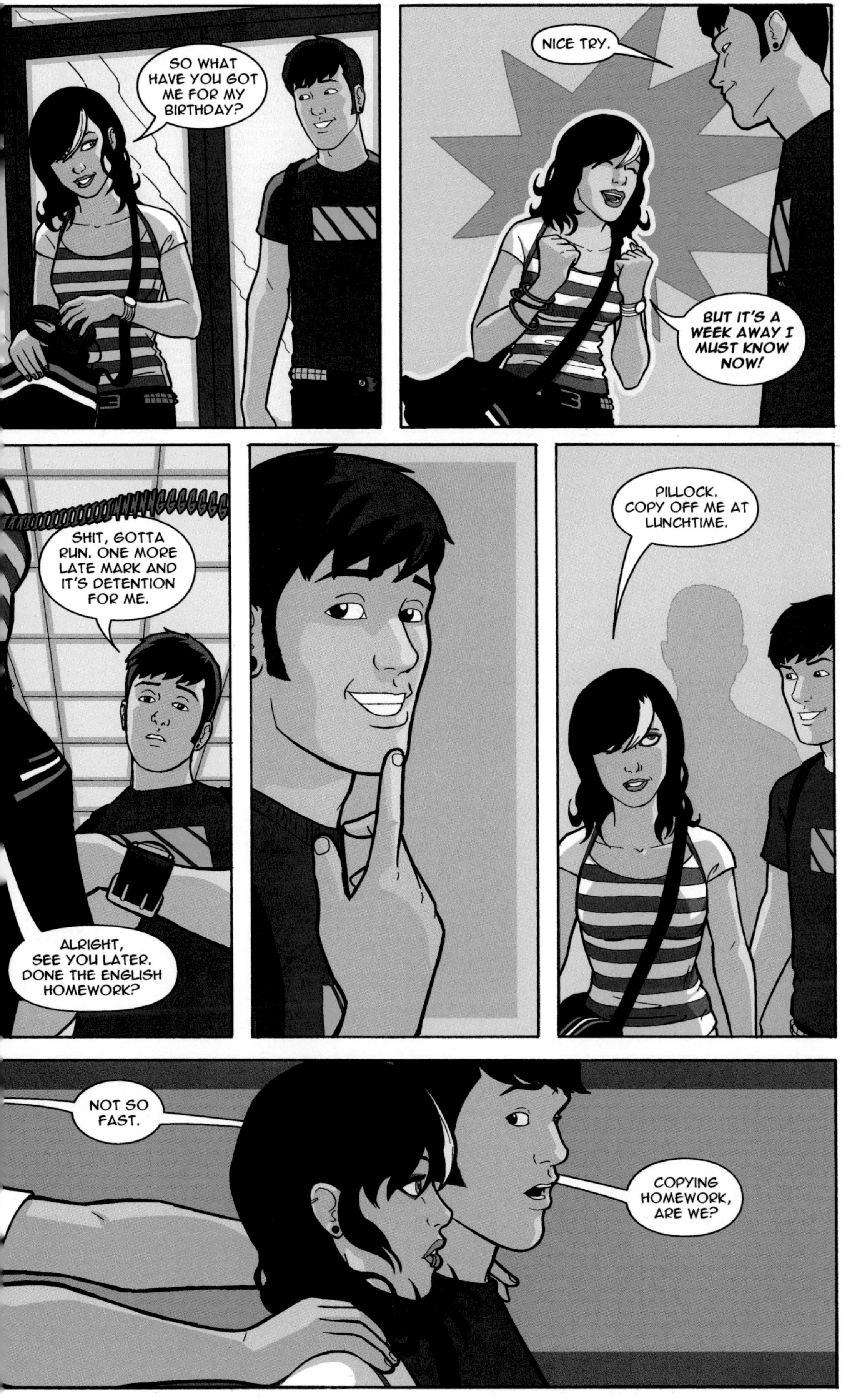
SO WHAT HAVE YOU GOT ME FOR MY BIRTHDAY?
NICE TRY.
BUT IT'S A WEEK AWAY I MUST KNOW NOW!
TTTTTTTTTTTTTTTTTTTTTTTTRRRRRRRRRRRRRRRRRRRRRRRRRIIIIIIIIIIIIIIIIINNNNNNNNNNNGGGGGGGGGGG
SHIT, GOTTA RUN. ONE MORE LATE MARK AND IT'S DETENTION FOR ME.
ALRIGHT, SEE YOU LATER. DONE THE ENGLISH HOMEWORK?
PILLOCK. COPY OFF ME AT LUNCHTIME.
NOT SO FAST.
COPYING HOMEWORK, ARE WE?

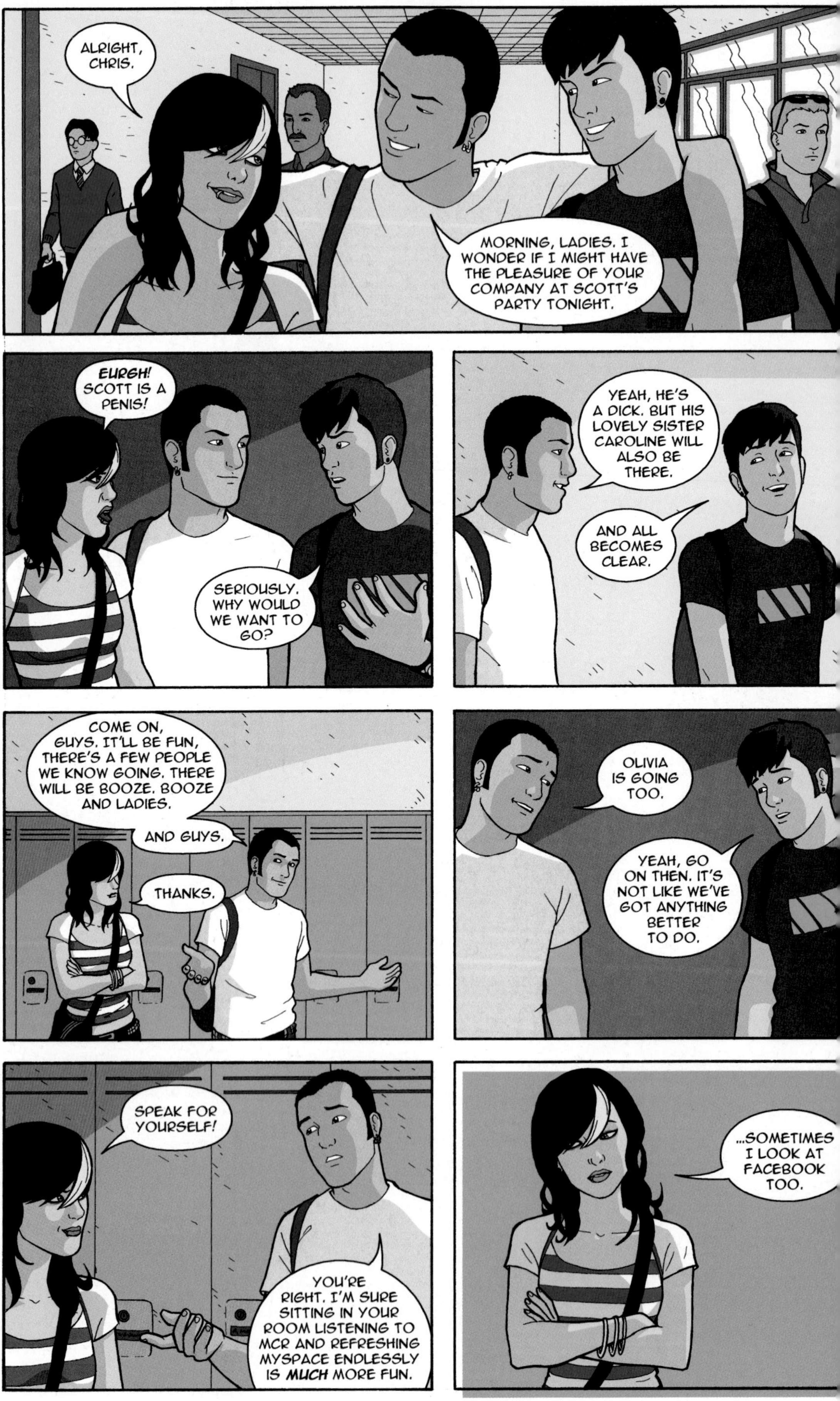
ALRIGHT, CHRIS.
MORNING, LADIES. I WONDER IF I MIGHT HAVE THE PLEASURE OF YOUR COMPANY AT SCOTT'S PARTY TONIGHT.
EURGH! SCOTT IS A PENIS!
SERIOUSLY. WHY WOULD WE WANT TO GO?
YEAH, HE'S A DICK. BUT HIS LOVELY SISTER CAROLINE WILL ALSO BE THERE.
AND ALL BECOMES CLEAR.
COME ON, GUYS. IT'LL BE FUN, THERE'S A FEW PEOPLE WE KNOW GOING. THERE WILL BE BOOZE. BOOZE AND LADIES.
AND GUYS.
THANKS.
OLIVIA IS GOING TOO.
YEAH, GO ON THEN. IT'S NOT LIKE WE'VE GOT ANYTHING BETTER TO DO.
SPEAK FOR YOURSELF!
YOU'RE RIGHT. I'M SURE SITTING IN YOUR ROOM LISTENING TO MCR AND REFRESHING MYSPACE ENDLESSLY IS MUCH MORE FUN.
...SOMETIMES I LOOK AT FACEBOOK TOO.

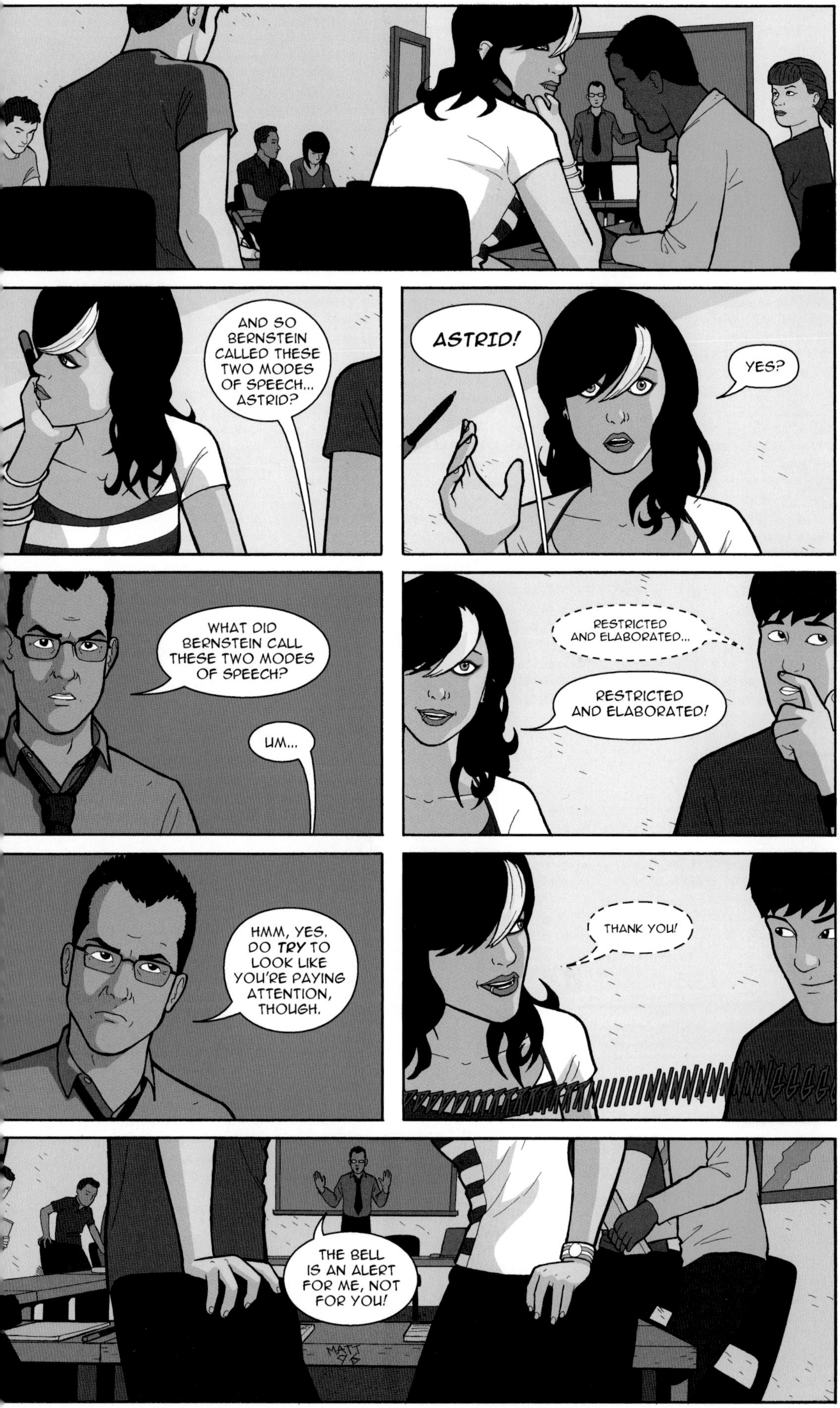
AND SO BERNSTEIN CALLED THESE TWO MODES OF SPEECH... ASTRID?
ASTRID!
YES?
WHAT DID BERNSTEIN CALL THESE TWO MODES OF SPEECH?
UM...
RESTRICTED AND ELABORATED...
RESTRICTED AND ELABORATED!
HMM, YES. DO TRY TO LOOK LIKE YOU'RE PAYING ATTENTION, THOUGH.
THANK YOU!
TTTTTTTTTTTTTTTTTTTTTTTTTTTTTTTTNIIIIIIIIIIIINNNNNNNNNNNNNGGGGG
THE BELL IS AN ALERT FOR ME, NOT FOR YOU!

CAFFÈNERO
CAFFÈNERO
CAFFÈ NERO
CAFFÈ NERO
HEY, IS THIS SEAT TAKEN?
NO, GO AHEAD.
YES?
I'M SORRY! I DIDN'T MEAN TO STARE, IT'S JUST, YOUR SLEEVES. THEY'RE **AWESOME**.
OH, THANK YOU!
WHO DID THEM?

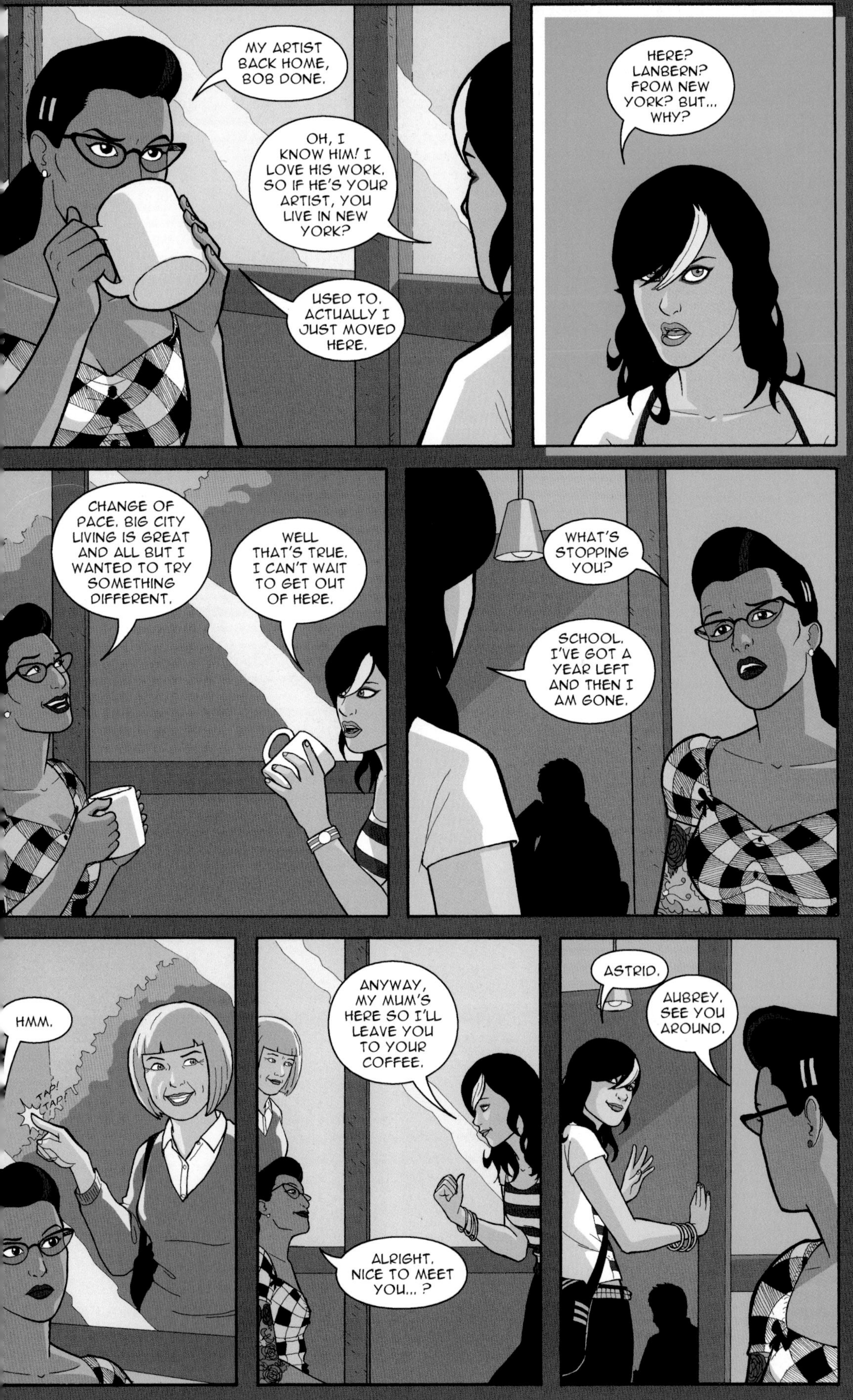
MY ARTIST BACK HOME, BOB DONE.
OH, I KNOW HIM! I LOVE HIS WORK. SO IF HE'S YOUR ARTIST, YOU LIVE IN NEW YORK?
USED TO. ACTUALLY I JUST MOVED HERE.
HERE? LANBERN? FROM NEW YORK? BUT... WHY?
CHANGE OF PACE. BIG CITY LIVING IS GREAT AND ALL BUT I WANTED TO TRY SOMETHING DIFFERENT.
WELL THAT'S TRUE. I CAN'T WAIT TO GET OUT OF HERE.
WHAT'S STOPPING YOU?
SCHOOL. I'VE GOT A YEAR LEFT AND THEN I AM GONE.
HMM.
TAP! TAP!
ANYWAY, MY MUM'S HERE SO I'LL LEAVE YOU TO YOUR COFFEE.
ALRIGHT. NICE TO MEET YOU... ?
ASTRID.
AUBREY. SEE YOU AROUND.

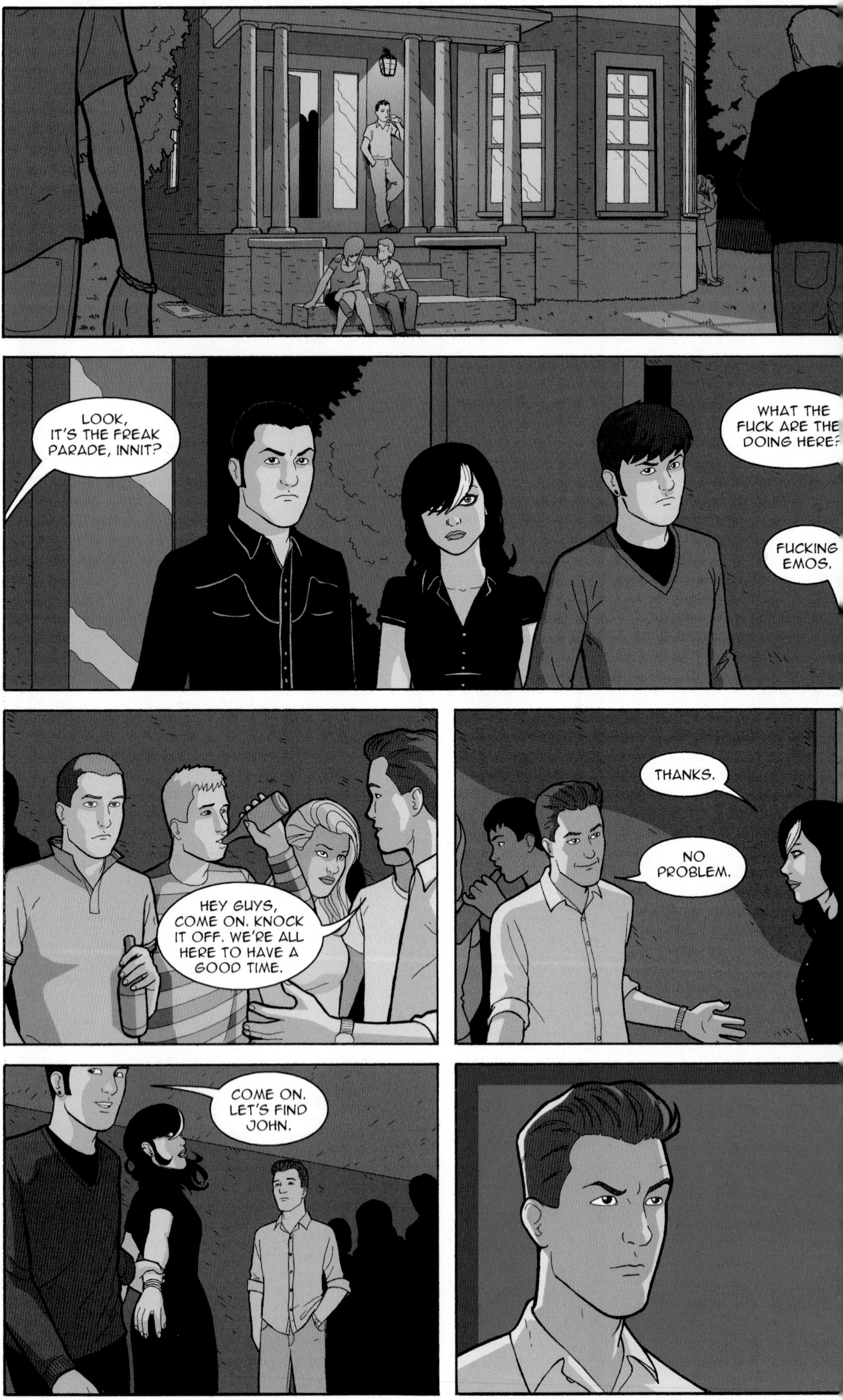
LOOK, IT'S THE FREAK PARADE, INNIT?
WHAT THE FUCK ARE THE DOING HERE?
FUCKING EMOS.
HEY GUYS, COME ON. KNOCK IT OFF. WE'RE ALL HERE TO HAVE A GOOD TIME.
THANKS.
NO PROBLEM.
COME ON. LET'S FIND JOHN.

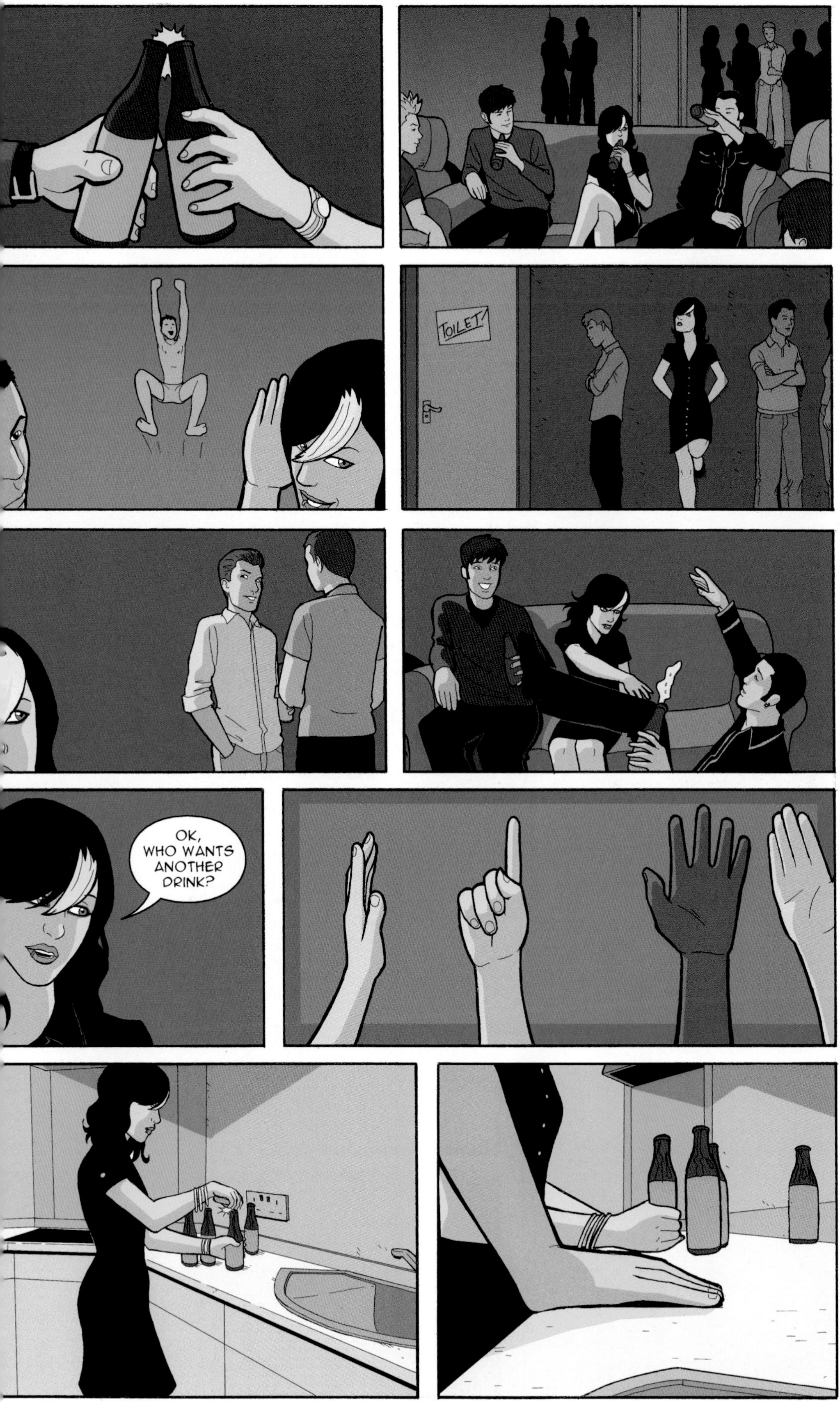
TOILET!
OK, WHO WANTS ANOTHER DRINK?

HEY.

OH, HI.

ASTRID, RIGHT. I'M NEIL.

I KNOW WHO YOU ARE.

I'M SORRY ABOUT MY FRIENDS. THEY CAN BE ARSEHOLES SOMETIMES.

HEY, I'M USED TO IT. NO WORRIES.

SO ARE YOU FRIENDS WITH SCOTT, THEN?

HAH! NO, MY FRIEND CHRIS KNOWS HIS SISTER.

WATCH OUT!

OOF!

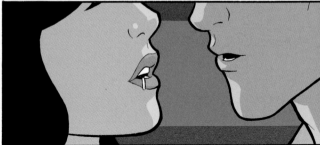

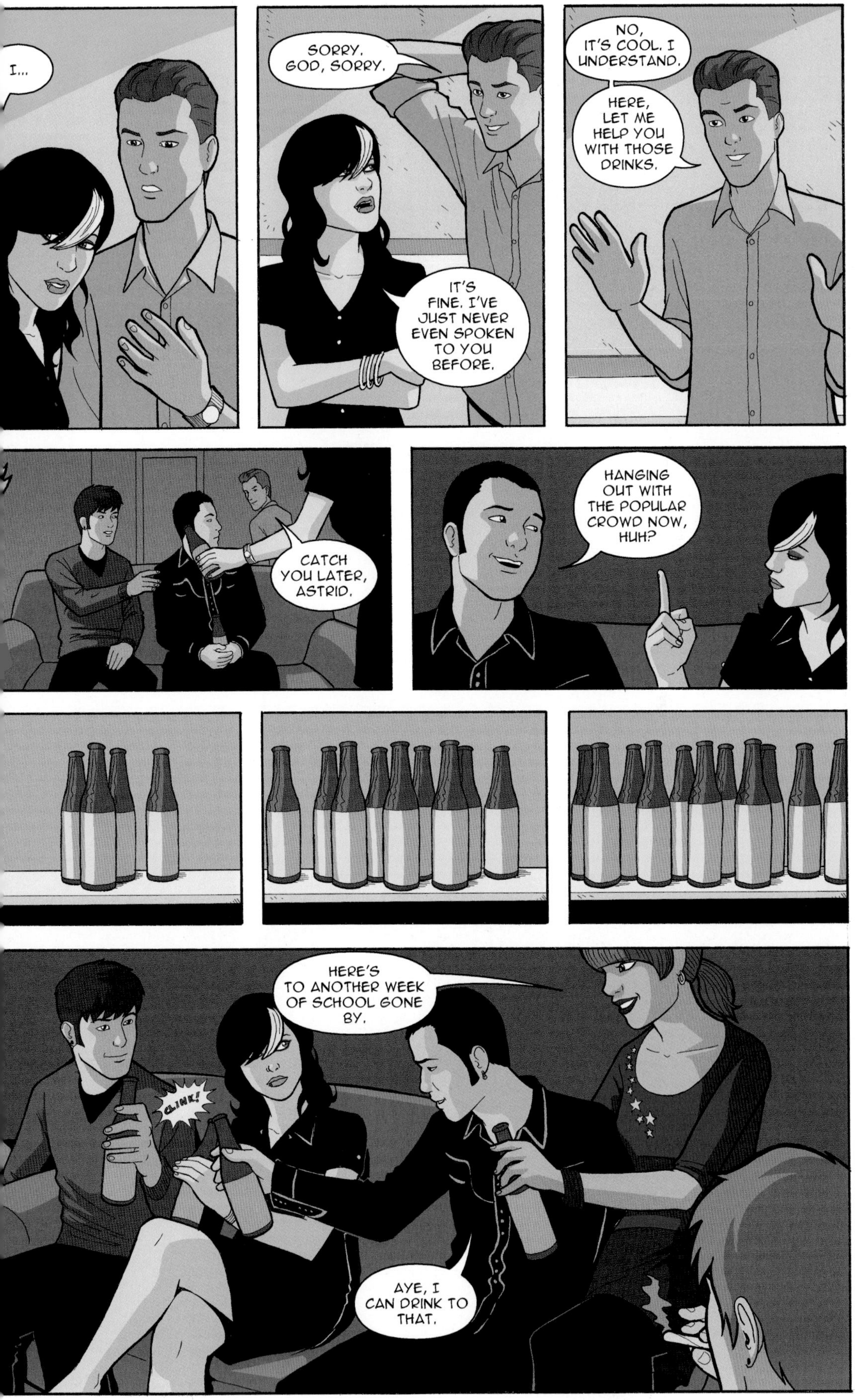
I...
SORRY. GOD, SORRY.
IT'S FINE. I'VE JUST NEVER EVEN SPOKEN TO YOU BEFORE.
NO, IT'S COOL. I UNDERSTAND.
HERE, LET ME HELP YOU WITH THOSE DRINKS.
CATCH YOU LATER, ASTRID.
HANGING OUT WITH THE POPULAR CROWD NOW, HUH?
HERE'S TO ANOTHER WEEK OF SCHOOL GONE BY.
CLINK!
AYE, I CAN DRINK TO THAT.

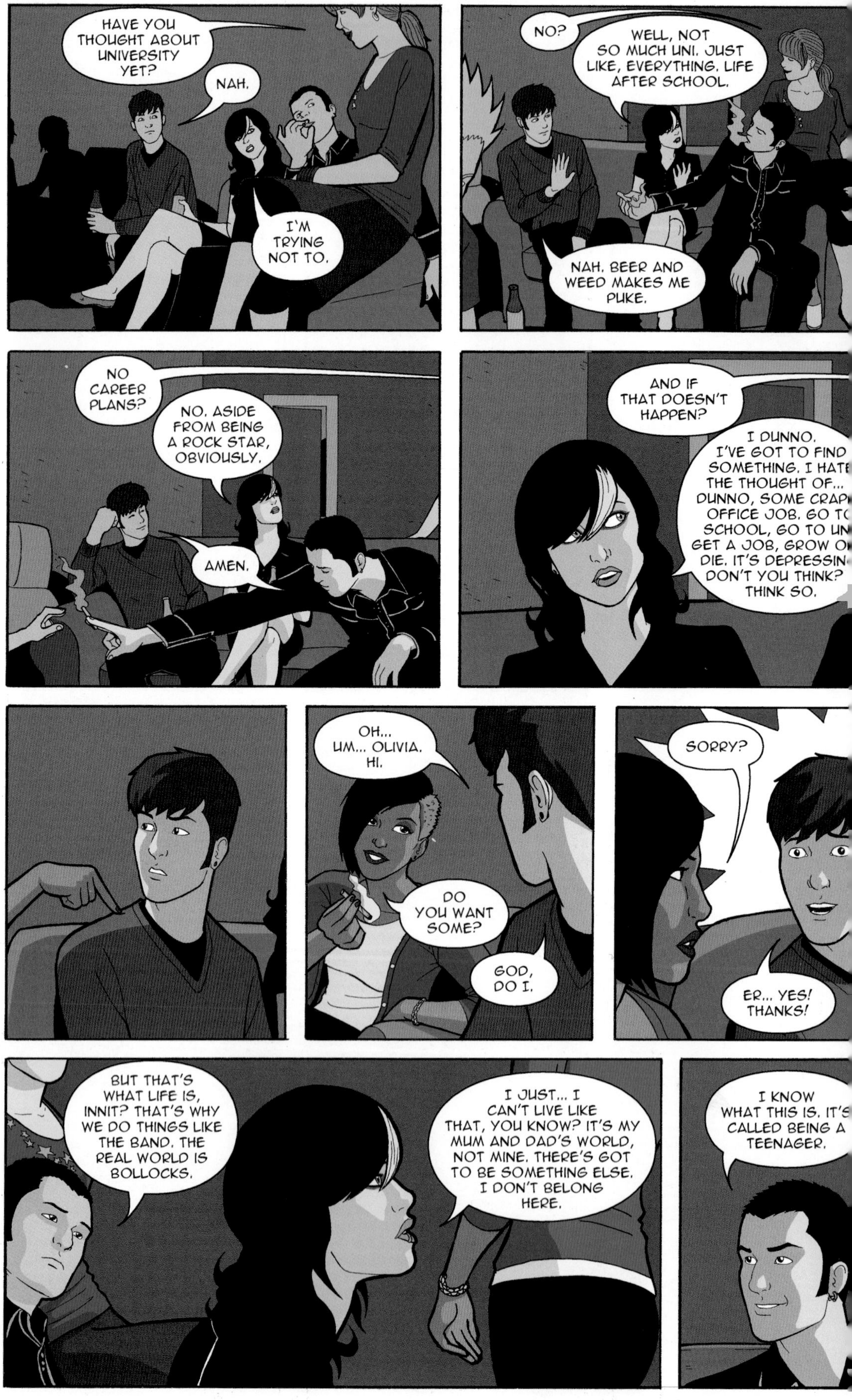
HAVE YOU THOUGHT ABOUT UNIVERSITY YET?
NAH.
I'M TRYING NOT TO.
NO?
WELL, NOT SO MUCH UNI. JUST LIKE, EVERYTHING. LIFE AFTER SCHOOL.
NAH. BEER AND WEED MAKES ME PUKE.
NO CAREER PLANS?
NO. ASIDE FROM BEING A ROCK STAR, OBVIOUSLY.
AMEN.
AND IF THAT DOESN'T HAPPEN?
I DUNNO. I'VE GOT TO FIND SOMETHING. I HATE THE THOUGHT OF... DUNNO, SOME CRAP OFFICE JOB. GO TO SCHOOL, GO TO UN GET A JOB, GROW O DIE. IT'S DEPRESSIN DON'T YOU THINK? THINK SO.
OH... UM... OLIVIA. HI.
DO YOU WANT SOME?
GOD, DO I.
SORRY?
ER... YES! THANKS!
BUT THAT'S WHAT LIFE IS, INNIT? THAT'S WHY WE DO THINGS LIKE THE BAND. THE REAL WORLD IS BOLLOCKS.
I JUST... I CAN'T LIVE LIKE THAT, YOU KNOW? IT'S MY MUM AND DAD'S WORLD, NOT MINE. THERE'S GOT TO BE SOMETHING ELSE. I DON'T BELONG HERE.
I KNOW WHAT THIS IS. IT'S CALLED BEING A TEENAGER.

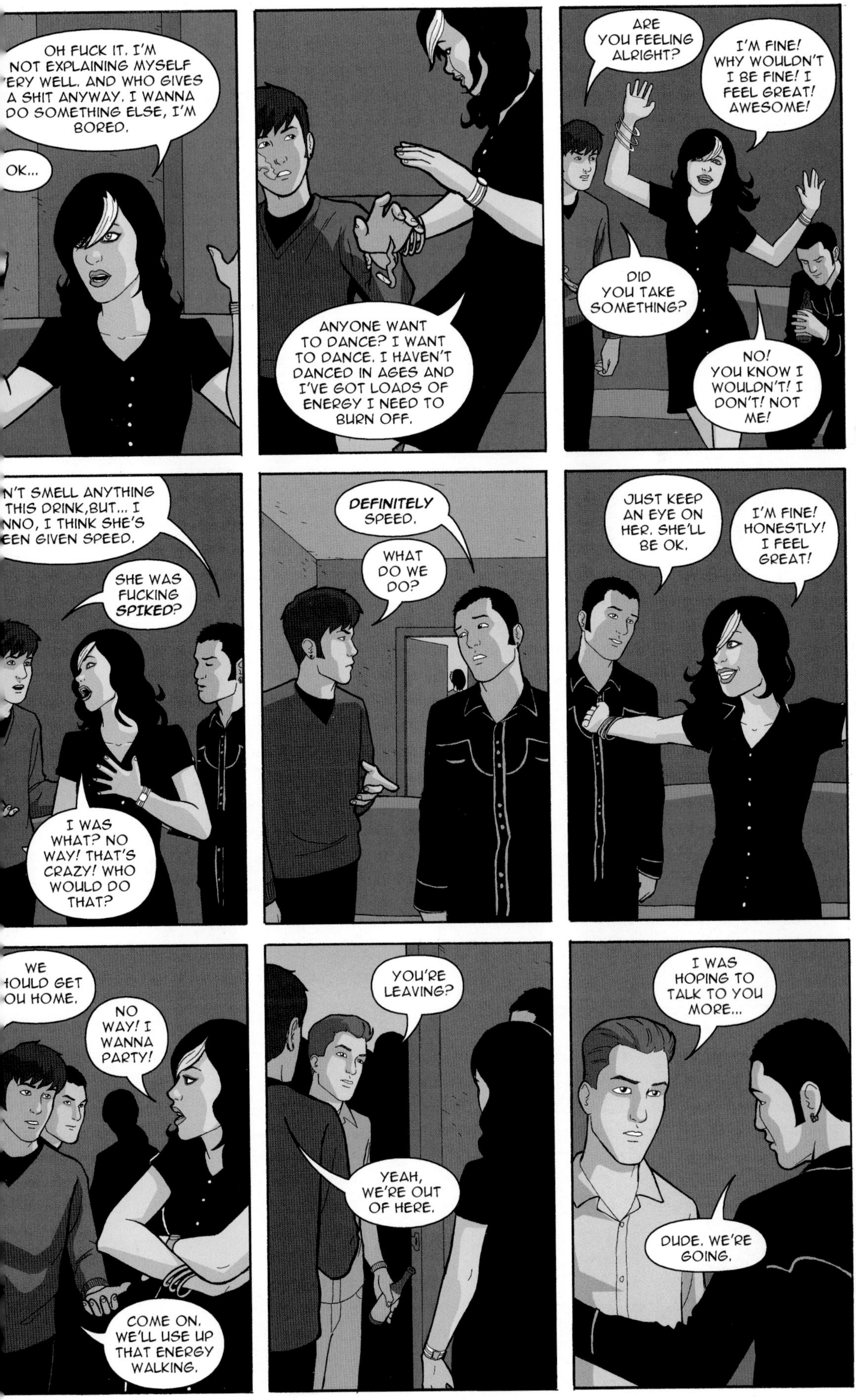
OH FUCK IT. I'M NOT EXPLAINING MYSELF 'ERY WELL. AND WHO GIVES A SHIT ANYWAY. I WANNA DO SOMETHING ELSE, I'M BORED.
OK...
ANYONE WANT TO DANCE? I WANT TO DANCE. I HAVEN'T DANCED IN AGES AND I'VE GOT LOADS OF ENERGY I NEED TO BURN OFF.
ARE YOU FEELING ALRIGHT?
I'M FINE! WHY WOULDN'T I BE FINE! I FEEL GREAT! AWESOME!
DID YOU TAKE SOMETHING?
NO! YOU KNOW I WOULDN'T! I DON'T! NOT ME!
N'T SMELL ANYTHING THIS DRINK,BUT... I NNO, I THINK SHE'S EEN GIVEN SPEED.
SHE WAS FUCKING *SPIKED*?
I WAS WHAT? NO WAY! THAT'S CRAZY! WHO WOULD DO THAT?
DEFINITELY SPEED.
WHAT DO WE DO?
JUST KEEP AN EYE ON HER. SHE'LL BE OK.
I'M FINE! HONESTLY! I FEEL GREAT!
WE HOULD GET OU HOME.
NO WAY! I WANNA PARTY!
COME ON. WE'LL USE UP THAT ENERGY WALKING.
YOU'RE LEAVING?
YEAH, WE'RE OUT OF HERE.
I WAS HOPING TO TALK TO YOU MORE...
DUDE. WE'RE GOING.

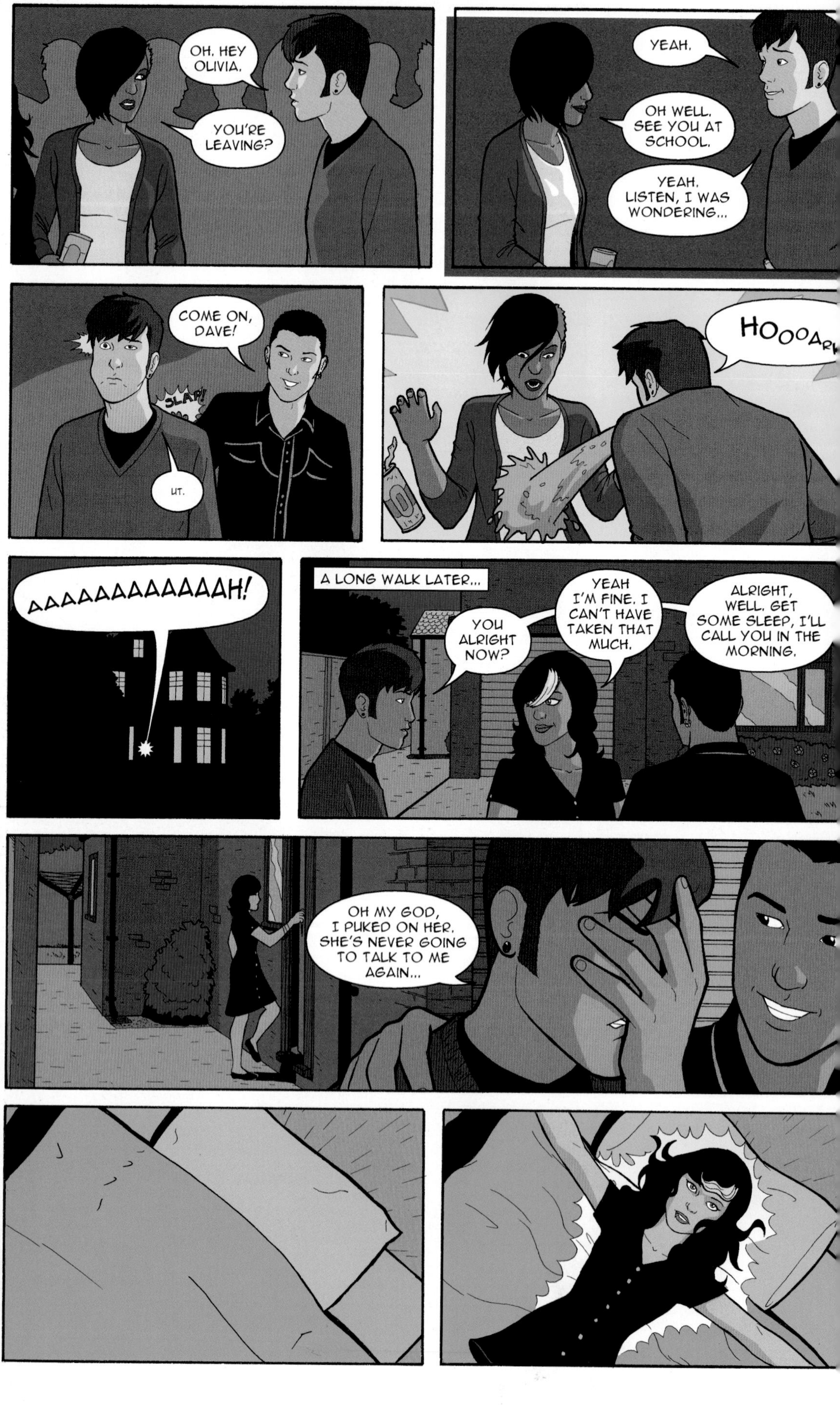
OH, HEY OLIVIA.
YOU'RE LEAVING?
YEAH.
OH WELL, SEE YOU AT SCHOOL.
YEAH. LISTEN, I WAS WONDERING...
COME ON, DAVE!
SLAP!
UT.
HOOOAR
AAAAAAAAAAAAH!
A LONG WALK LATER...
YOU ALRIGHT NOW?
YEAH I'M FINE. I CAN'T HAVE TAKEN THAT MUCH.
ALRIGHT, WELL, GET SOME SLEEP, I'LL CALL YOU IN THE MORNING.
OH MY GOD, I PUKED ON HER. SHE'S NEVER GOING TO TALK TO ME AGAIN...

ASTRID? ASTRID, WAKE UP.

AAAAAHHHH!

SHH, IT'S OK. SHH.

I... UH... WHAT?

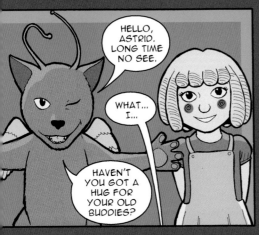

HELLO, ASTRID. LONG TIME NO SEE.

WHAT... I...

HAVEN'T YOU GOT A HUG FOR YOUR OLD BUDDIES?

OHHHH. I'M DREAMING AGAIN. OK.

NO, YOU'RE NOT.

YEAH BUT I AM.

DON'T YOU REMEMBER US?

SHOULD I?

BACK WHEN YOU ERE A CHILD. EBLIS AND MISS SALLY. YOUR FRIENDS.

OH SHIT! YEAH! I HAVEN'T THOUGHT ABOUT YOU GUYS IN YEA...

ALRIGHT, OK. LET'S GO ALONG WITH THIS. SO... YOU'RE MY IMAGINARY FRIENDS FROM MY CHILDHOOD. SO WHY ARE YOU HERE NOW?

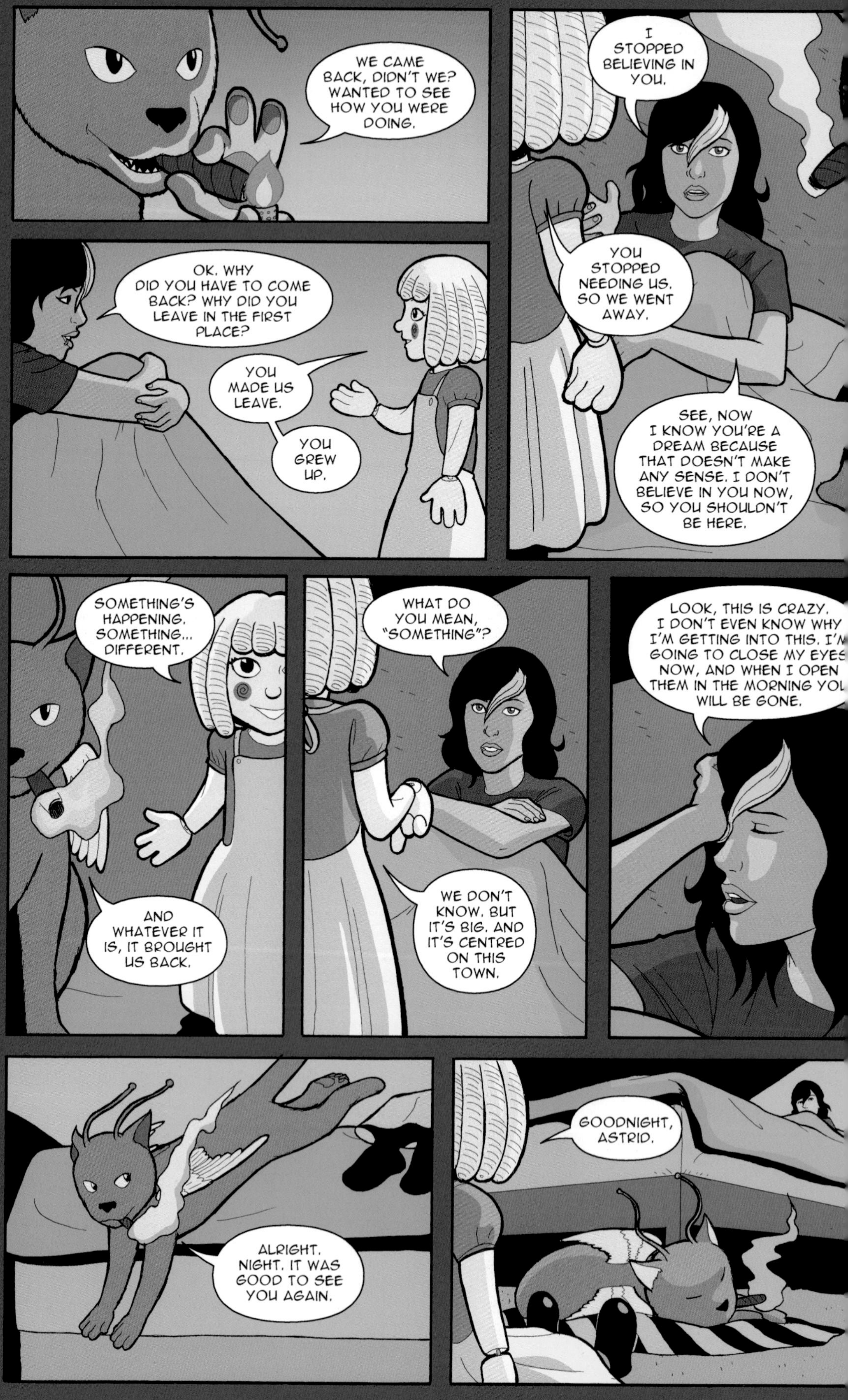
WE CAME BACK, DIDN'T WE? WANTED TO SEE HOW YOU WERE DOING.
I STOPPED BELIEVING IN YOU.
OK. WHY DID YOU HAVE TO COME BACK? WHY DID YOU LEAVE IN THE FIRST PLACE?
YOU MADE US LEAVE.
YOU GREW UP.
YOU STOPPED NEEDING US, SO WE WENT AWAY.
SEE, NOW I KNOW YOU'RE A DREAM BECAUSE THAT DOESN'T MAKE ANY SENSE. I DON'T BELIEVE IN YOU NOW, SO YOU SHOULDN'T BE HERE.
SOMETHING'S HAPPENING. SOMETHING... DIFFERENT.
AND WHATEVER IT IS, IT BROUGHT US BACK.
WHAT DO YOU MEAN, "SOMETHING"?
WE DON'T KNOW. BUT IT'S BIG. AND IT'S CENTRED ON THIS TOWN.
LOOK, THIS IS CRAZY. I DON'T EVEN KNOW WHY I'M GETTING INTO THIS. I'M GOING TO CLOSE MY EYES NOW, AND WHEN I OPEN THEM IN THE MORNING YOU WILL BE GONE.
ALRIGHT. NIGHT. IT WAS GOOD TO SEE YOU AGAIN.
GOODNIGHT, ASTRID.

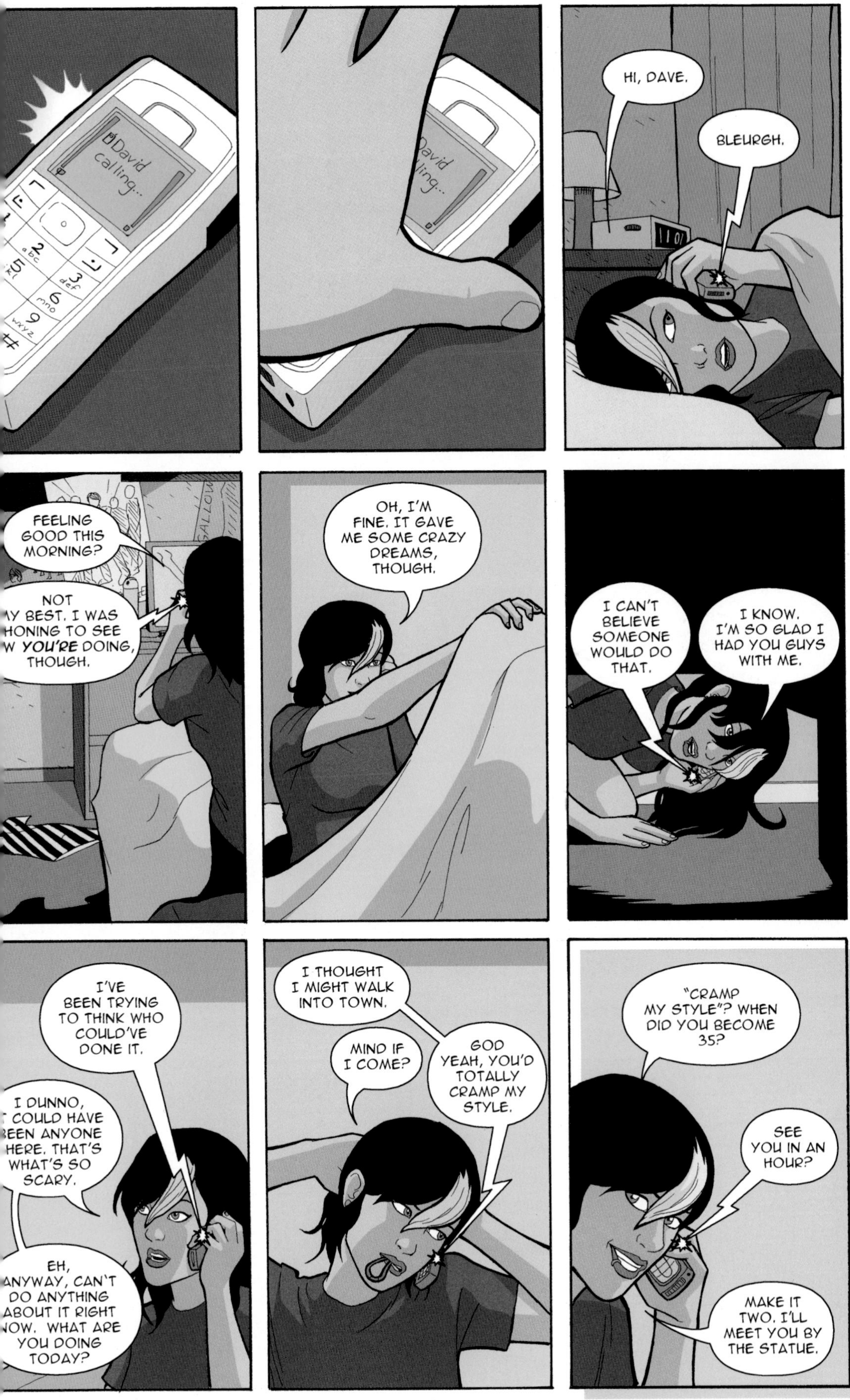
David calling...
HI, DAVE.
BLEURGH.
FEELING GOOD THIS MORNING?
NOT MY BEST. I WAS PHONING TO SEE HOW YOU'RE DOING, THOUGH.
OH, I'M FINE. IT GAVE ME SOME CRAZY DREAMS, THOUGH.
I CAN'T BELIEVE SOMEONE WOULD DO THAT.
I KNOW. I'M SO GLAD I HAD YOU GUYS WITH ME.
I'VE BEEN TRYING TO THINK WHO COULD'VE DONE IT.
I DUNNO, IT COULD HAVE BEEN ANYONE HERE. THAT'S WHAT'S SO SCARY.
EH, ANYWAY, CAN'T DO ANYTHING ABOUT IT RIGHT NOW. WHAT ARE YOU DOING TODAY?
I THOUGHT I MIGHT WALK INTO TOWN.
MIND IF I COME?
GOD YEAH, YOU'D TOTALLY CRAMP MY STYLE.
"CRAMP MY STYLE"? WHEN DID YOU BECOME 35?
SEE YOU IN AN HOUR?
MAKE IT TWO. I'LL MEET YOU BY THE STATUE.

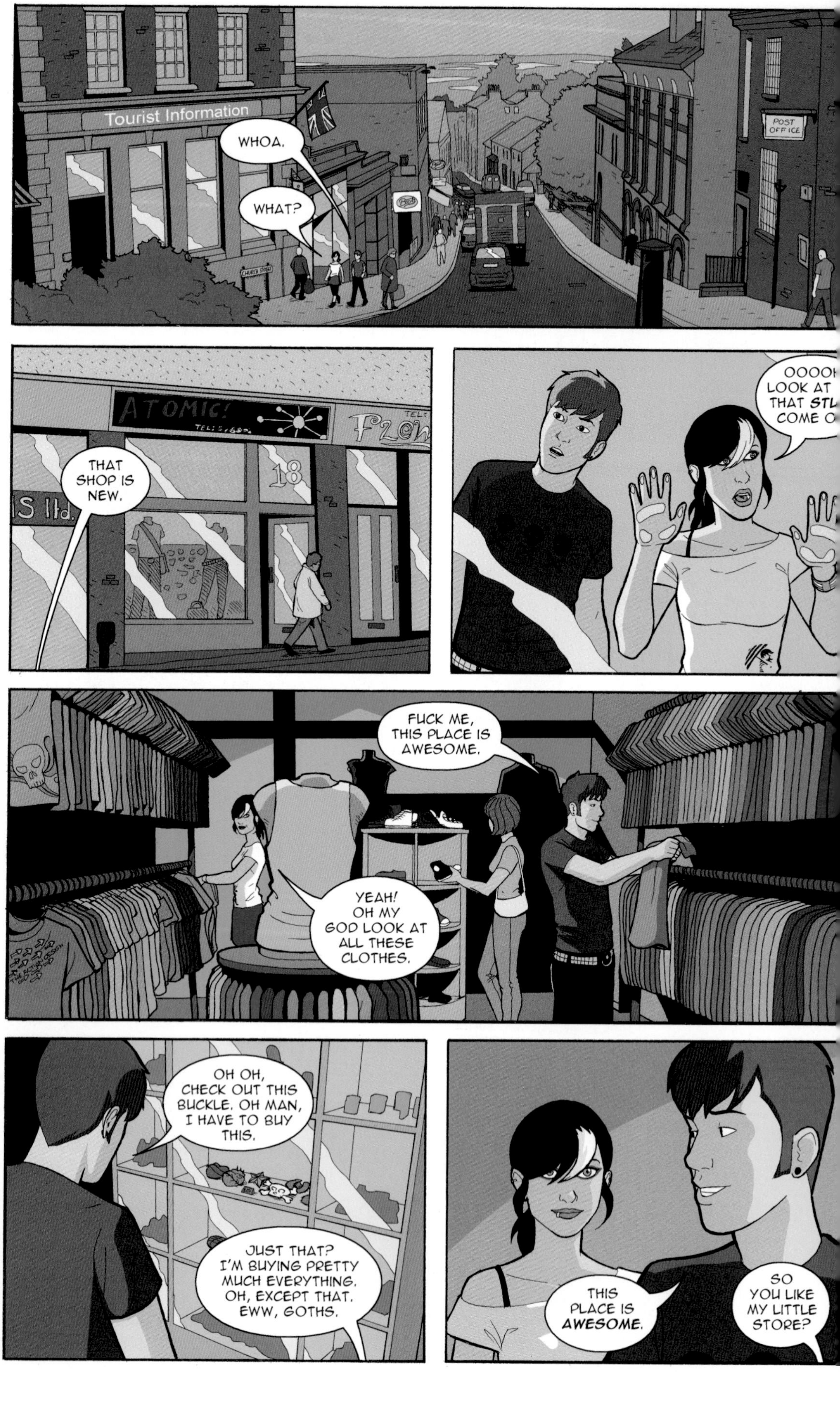
Tourist Information
POST OFFICE
WHOA.
WHAT?
ATOMIC!
18
THAT SHOP IS NEW.
LOOK AT THAT
FUCK ME, THIS PLACE IS AWESOME.
YEAH! OH MY GOD LOOK AT ALL THESE CLOTHES.
OH OH, CHECK OUT THIS BUCKLE. OH MAN, I HAVE TO BUY THIS.
JUST THAT? I'M BUYING PRETTY MUCH EVERYTHING. OH, EXCEPT THAT. EWW, GOTHS.
THIS PLACE IS AWESOME.
SO YOU LIKE MY LITTLE STORE?

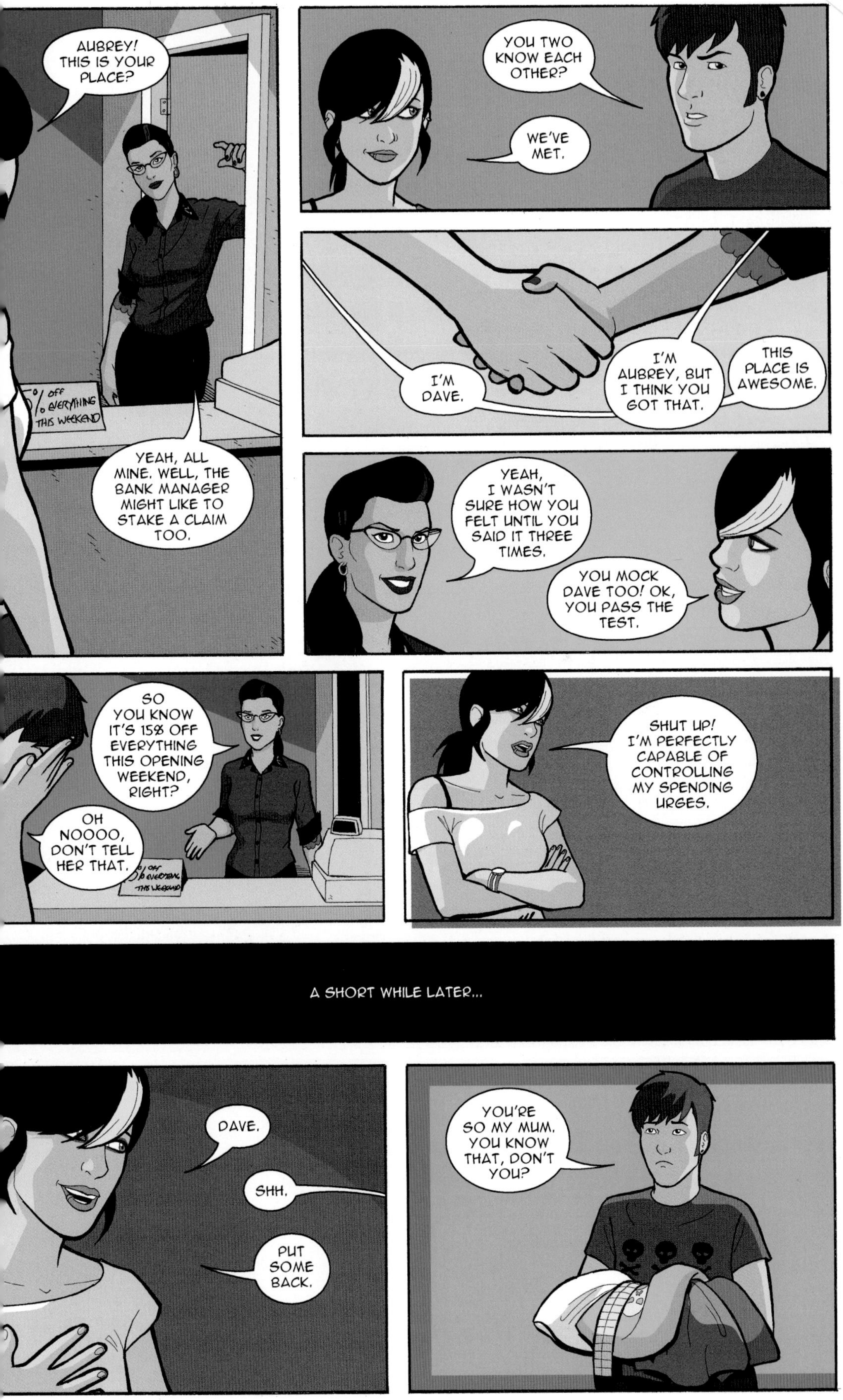
AUBREY! THIS IS YOUR PLACE?
5% OFF EVERYTHING THIS WEEKEND
YEAH, ALL MINE. WELL, THE BANK MANAGER MIGHT LIKE TO STAKE A CLAIM TOO.
YOU TWO KNOW EACH OTHER?
WE'VE MET.
I'M DAVE.
I'M AUBREY, BUT I THINK YOU GOT THAT.
THIS PLACE IS AWESOME.
YEAH, I WASN'T SURE HOW YOU FELT UNTIL YOU SAID IT THREE TIMES.
YOU MOCK DAVE TOO! OK, YOU PASS THE TEST.
SO YOU KNOW IT'S 15% OFF EVERYTHING THIS OPENING WEEKEND, RIGHT?
OH NOOOO, DON'T TELL HER THAT.
SHUT UP! I'M PERFECTLY CAPABLE OF CONTROLLING MY SPENDING URGES.
A SHORT WHILE LATER...
DAVE.
SHH.
PUT SOME BACK.
YOU'RE SO MY MUM. YOU KNOW THAT, DON'T YOU?

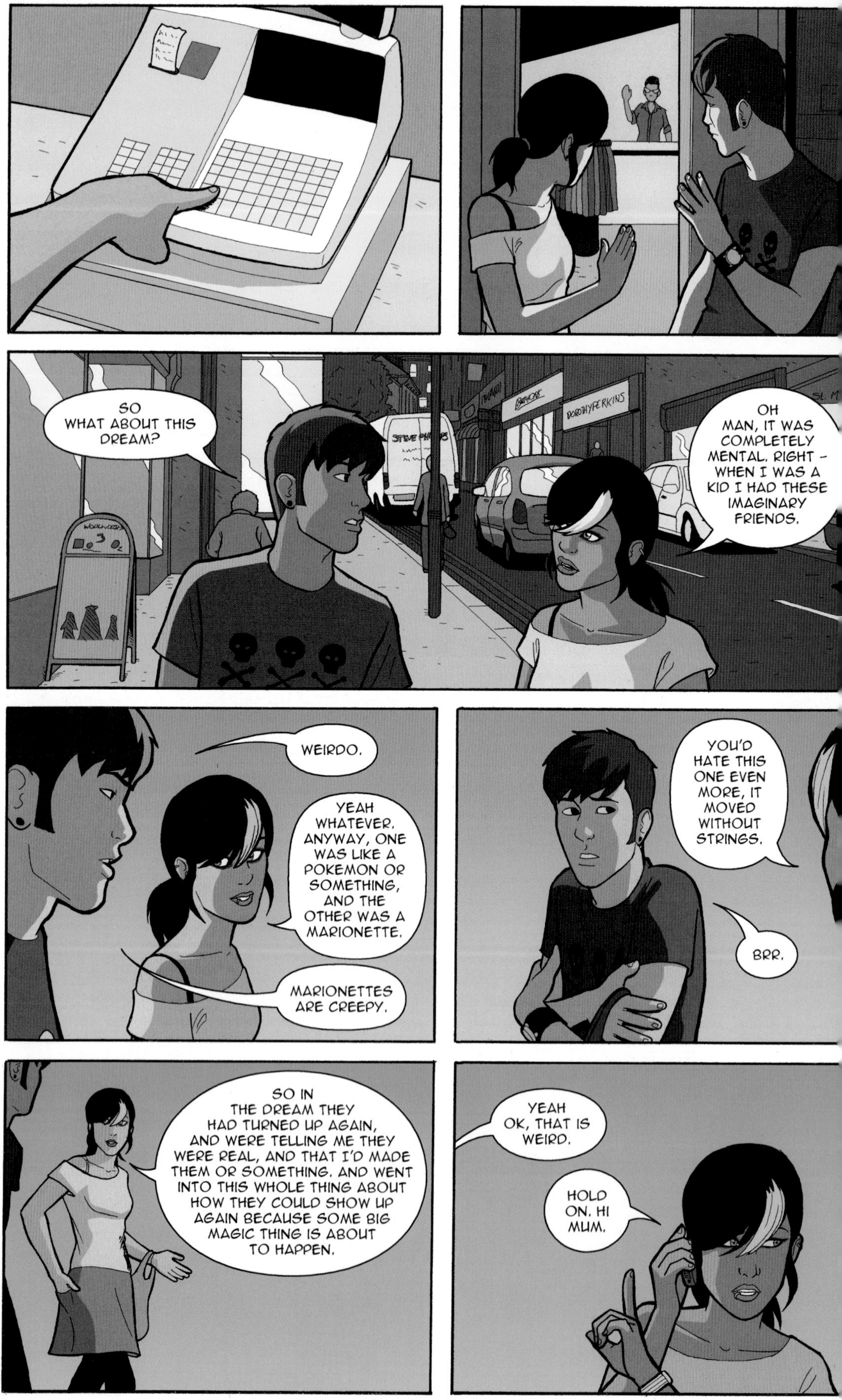
STEVE
DOROTHY PERKINS
SO WHAT ABOUT THIS DREAM?
OH MAN, IT WAS COMPLETELY MENTAL. RIGHT - WHEN I WAS A KID I HAD THESE IMAGINARY FRIENDS.
WEIRDO.
YEAH WHATEVER. ANYWAY, ONE WAS LIKE A POKEMON OR SOMETHING, AND THE OTHER WAS A MARIONETTE.
MARIONETTES ARE CREEPY.
YOU'D HATE THIS ONE EVEN MORE, IT MOVED WITHOUT STRINGS.
BRR.
SO IN THE DREAM THEY HAD TURNED UP AGAIN, AND WERE TELLING ME THEY WERE REAL, AND THAT I'D MADE THEM OR SOMETHING. AND WENT INTO THIS WHOLE THING ABOUT HOW THEY COULD SHOW UP AGAIN BECAUSE SOME BIG MAGIC THING IS ABOUT TO HAPPEN.
YEAH OK, THAT IS WEIRD.
HOLD ON. HI MUM.

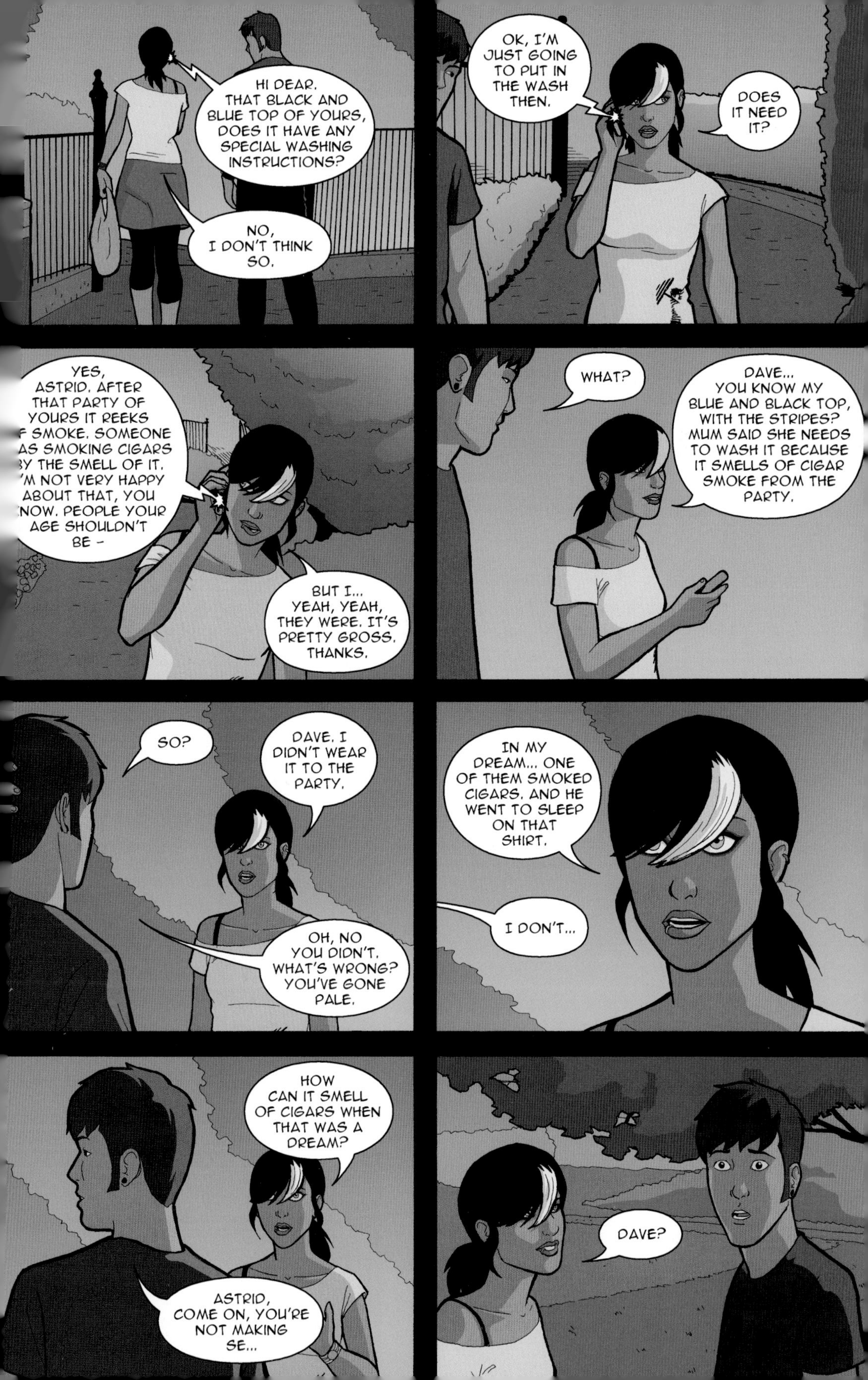
HI DEAR. THAT BLACK AND BLUE TOP OF YOURS, DOES IT HAVE ANY SPECIAL WASHING INSTRUCTIONS?
NO, I DON'T THINK SO.
OK, I'M JUST GOING TO PUT IN THE WASH THEN.
DOES IT NEED IT?
YES, ASTRID. AFTER THAT PARTY OF YOURS IT REEKS F SMOKE. SOMEONE AS SMOKING CIGARS BY THE SMELL OF IT. I'M NOT VERY HAPPY ABOUT THAT, YOU NOW. PEOPLE YOUR AGE SHOULDN'T BE -
BUT I... YEAH, YEAH, THEY WERE. IT'S PRETTY GROSS. THANKS.
WHAT?
DAVE... YOU KNOW MY BLUE AND BLACK TOP, WITH THE STRIPES? MUM SAID SHE NEEDS TO WASH IT BECAUSE IT SMELLS OF CIGAR SMOKE FROM THE PARTY.
SO?
DAVE. I DIDN'T WEAR IT TO THE PARTY.
OH, NO YOU DIDN'T. WHAT'S WRONG? YOU'VE GONE PALE.
IN MY DREAM... ONE OF THEM SMOKED CIGARS. AND HE WENT TO SLEEP ON THAT SHIRT.
I DON'T...
HOW CAN IT SMELL OF CIGARS WHEN THAT WAS A DREAM?
ASTRID, COME ON, YOU'RE NOT MAKING SE...
DAVE?

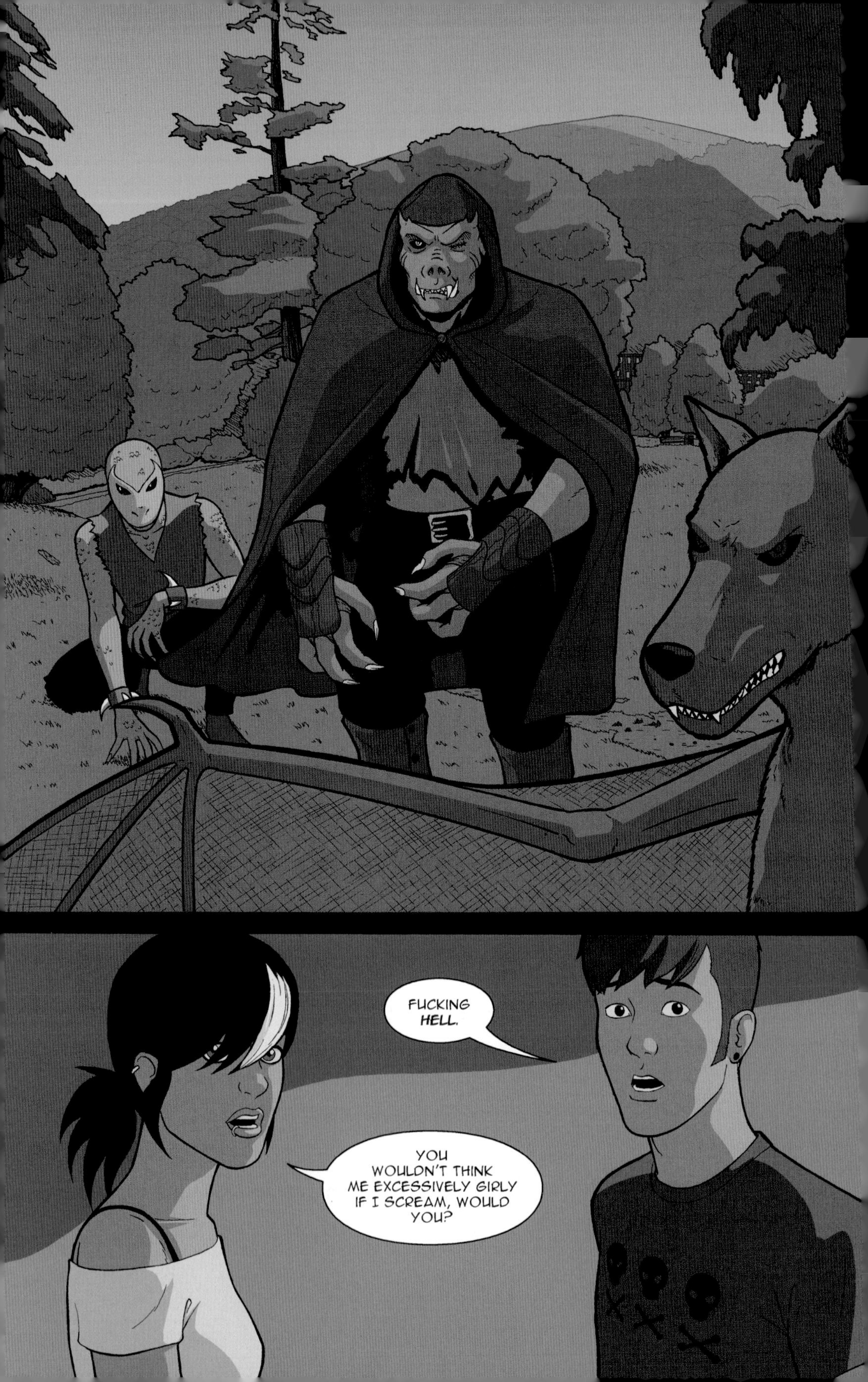
FUCKING **HELL**.
YOU WOULDN'T THINK ME EXCESSIVELY GIRLY IF I SCREAM, WOULD YOU?

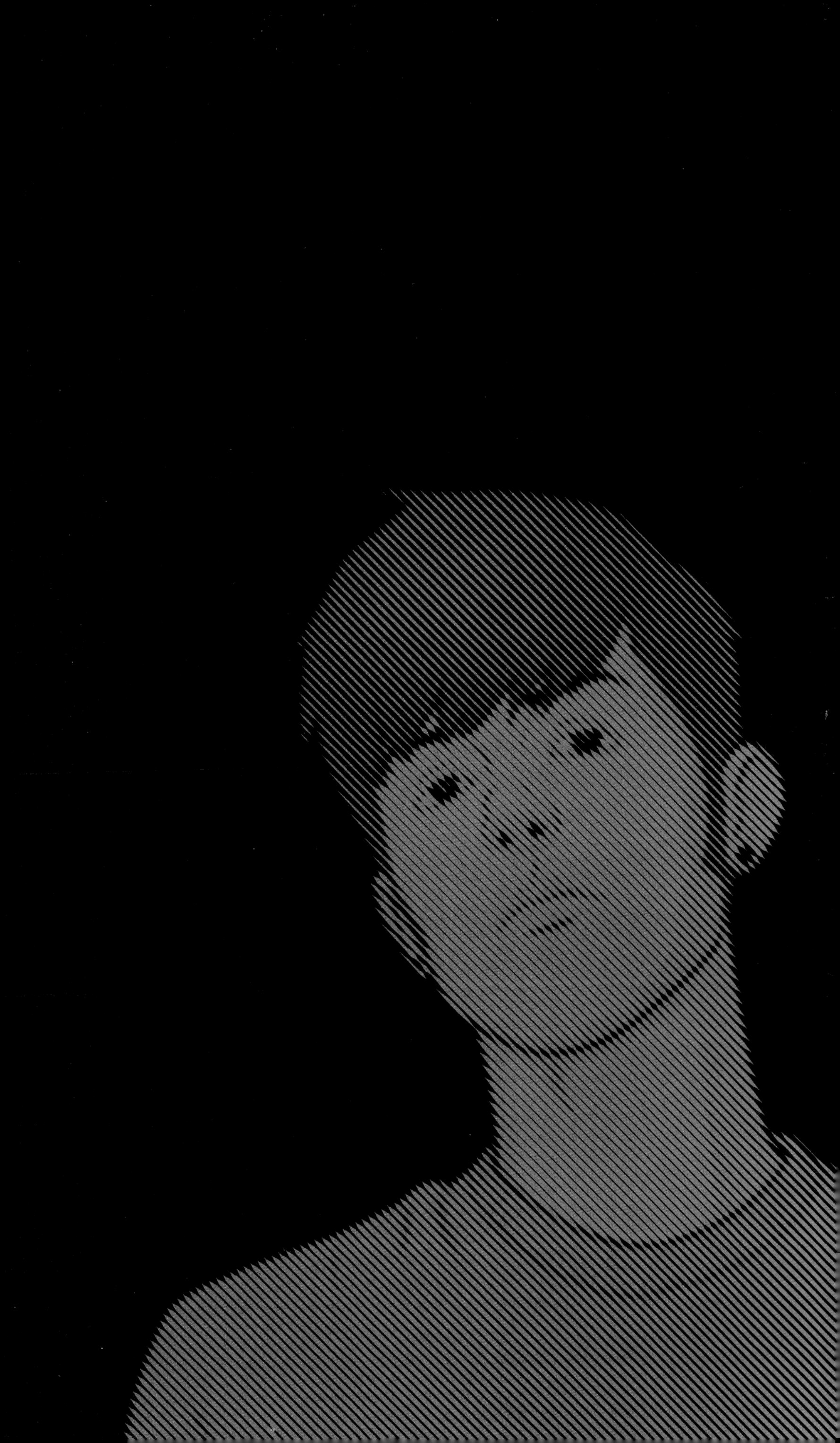

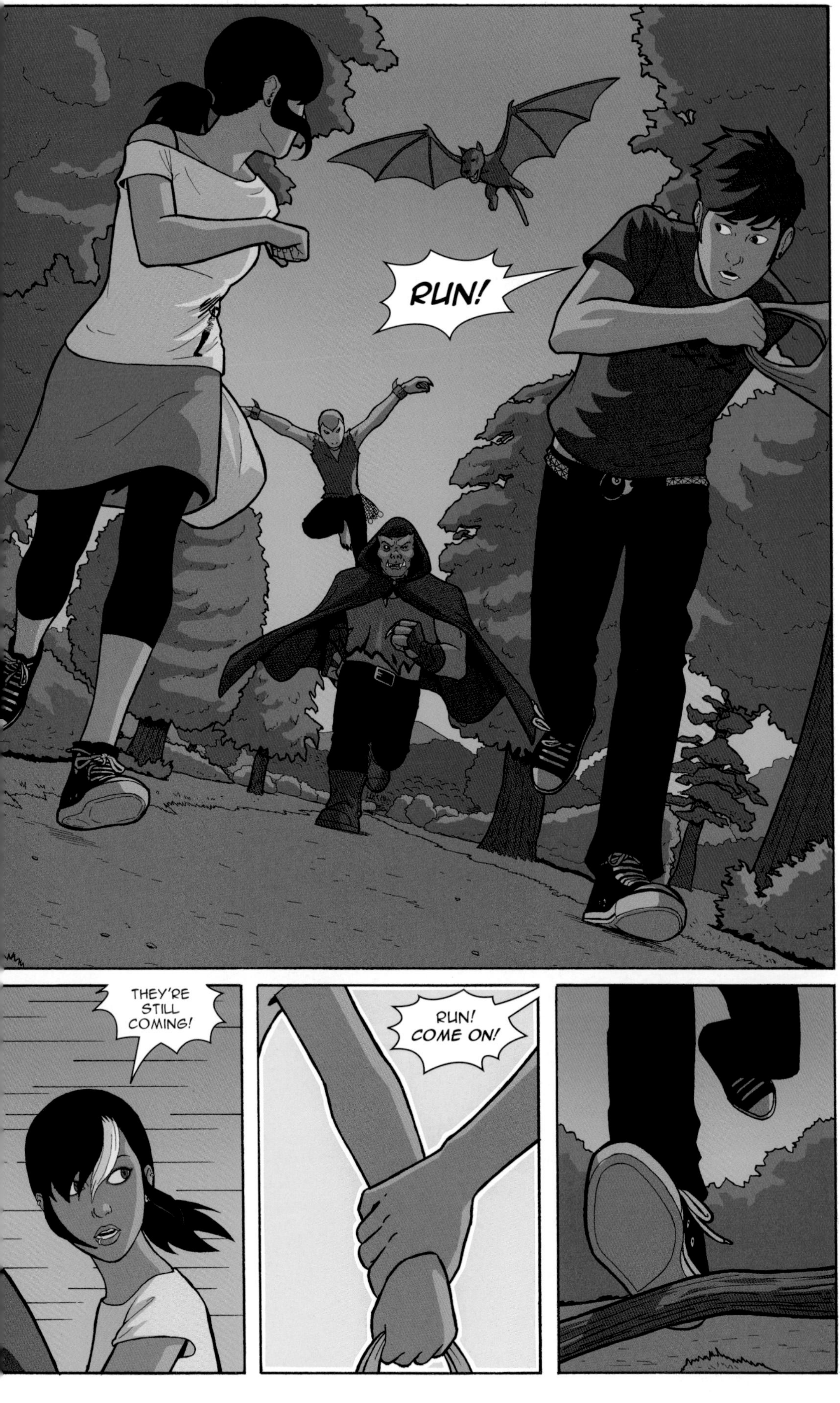
RUN!
THEY'RE STILL COMING!
RUN! COME ON!

DAVE!
AHH!
GET AWAY!
I'M NOT LEAVING YOU, YOU KNOB!
OOF!
DAVE!
WHAT'S GOING ON? *DAVE!*

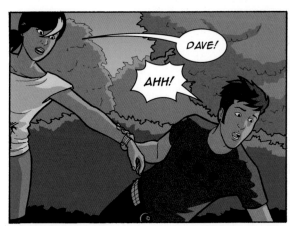

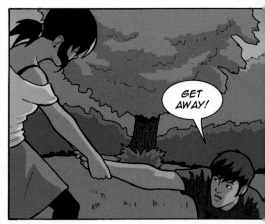

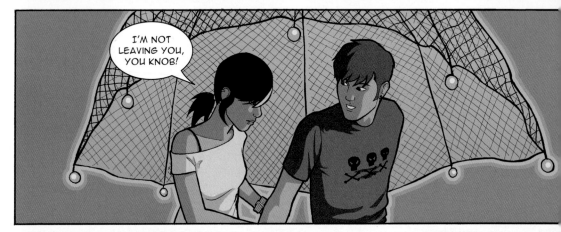

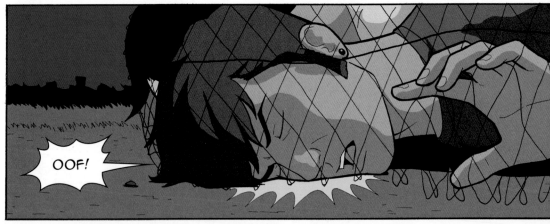

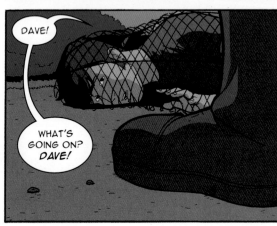

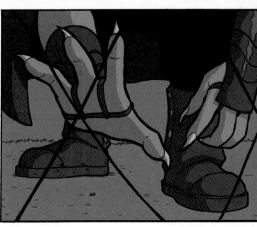

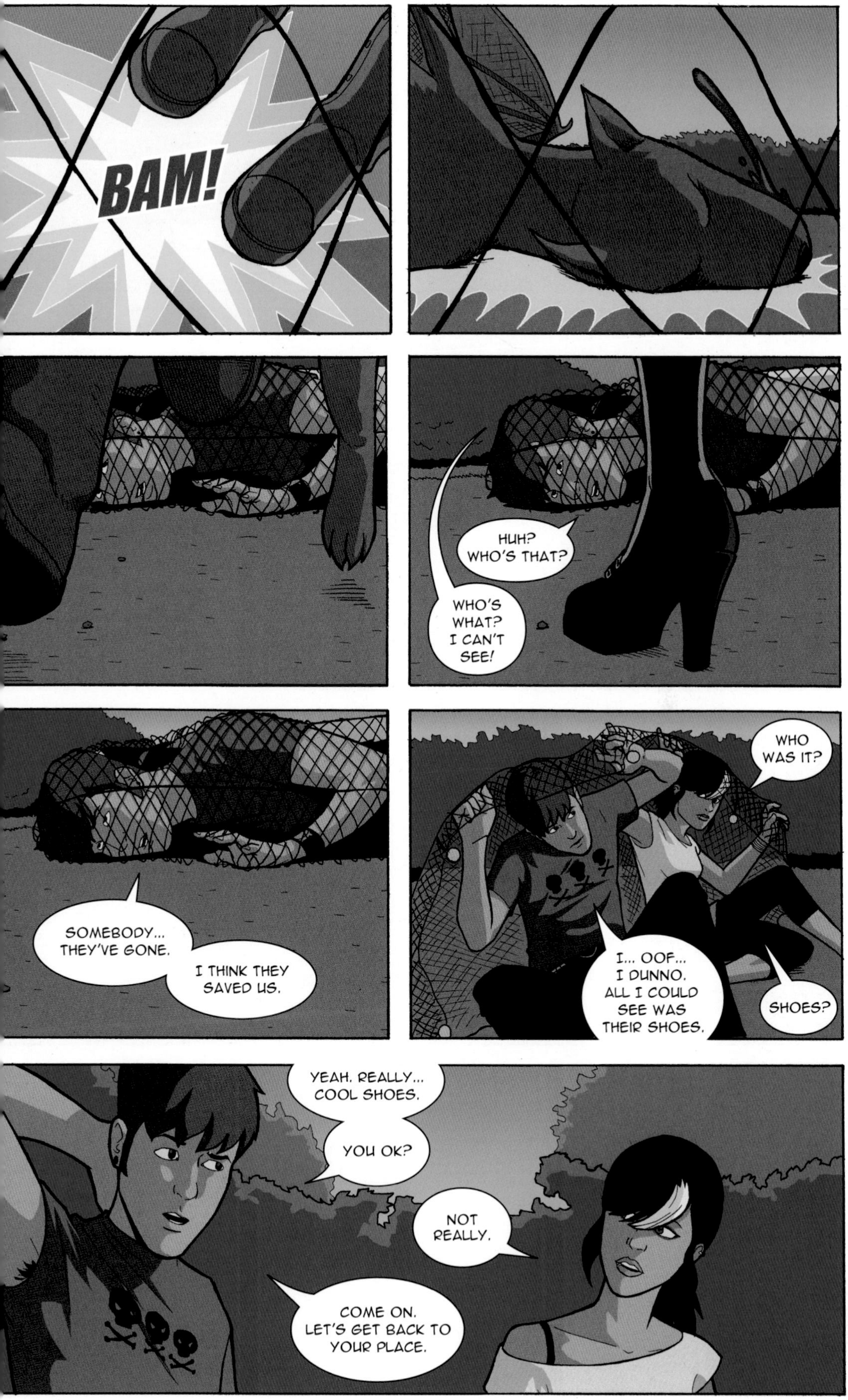
BAM!
HUH? WHO'S THAT?
WHO'S WHAT? I CAN'T SEE!
SOMEBODY... THEY'VE GONE.
I THINK THEY SAVED US.
WHO WAS IT?
I... OOF... I DUNNO. ALL I COULD SEE WAS THEIR SHOES.
SHOES?
YEAH. REALLY... COOL SHOES.
YOU OK?
NOT REALLY.
COME ON. LET'S GET BACK TO YOUR PLACE.

HI, DAD. CAN YOU COME PICK ME UP?

YEAH, I KNOW.

I KNOW.

I'M SORRY.

YEAH.

YEAH, I'M AT ASTRID'S.

THANKS.

JESUS. THOSE THINGS... I'VE DREAMT ABOUT THEM.

WHAT'S GOING ON? IT'S LIKE... THIS IS ALL COMING OUT OF MY HEAD.

ALL THESE THINGS I DREAMED AND THEY'RE CRAWLING OUT OF MY HEAD AND...

YOU DID SEE THEM?

WHAT? OF COURSE!

GOD. I FEEL LIKE I'M GOING INSANE.

I SAW THEM TOO. IT'S OK... WELL, IT'S NOT.

BUT I SAW THEM. I DID. IT'S NOT IN YOUR HEAD, I SWEAR.

I JUST DON'T KNOW...

COME ON. WE'LL STICK TOGETHER UNTIL WE FIGURE THIS OUT.

I'LL CALL 'RO FOR YOU IN T MORNING, WA YOU TO SCHO

IT'L BE O

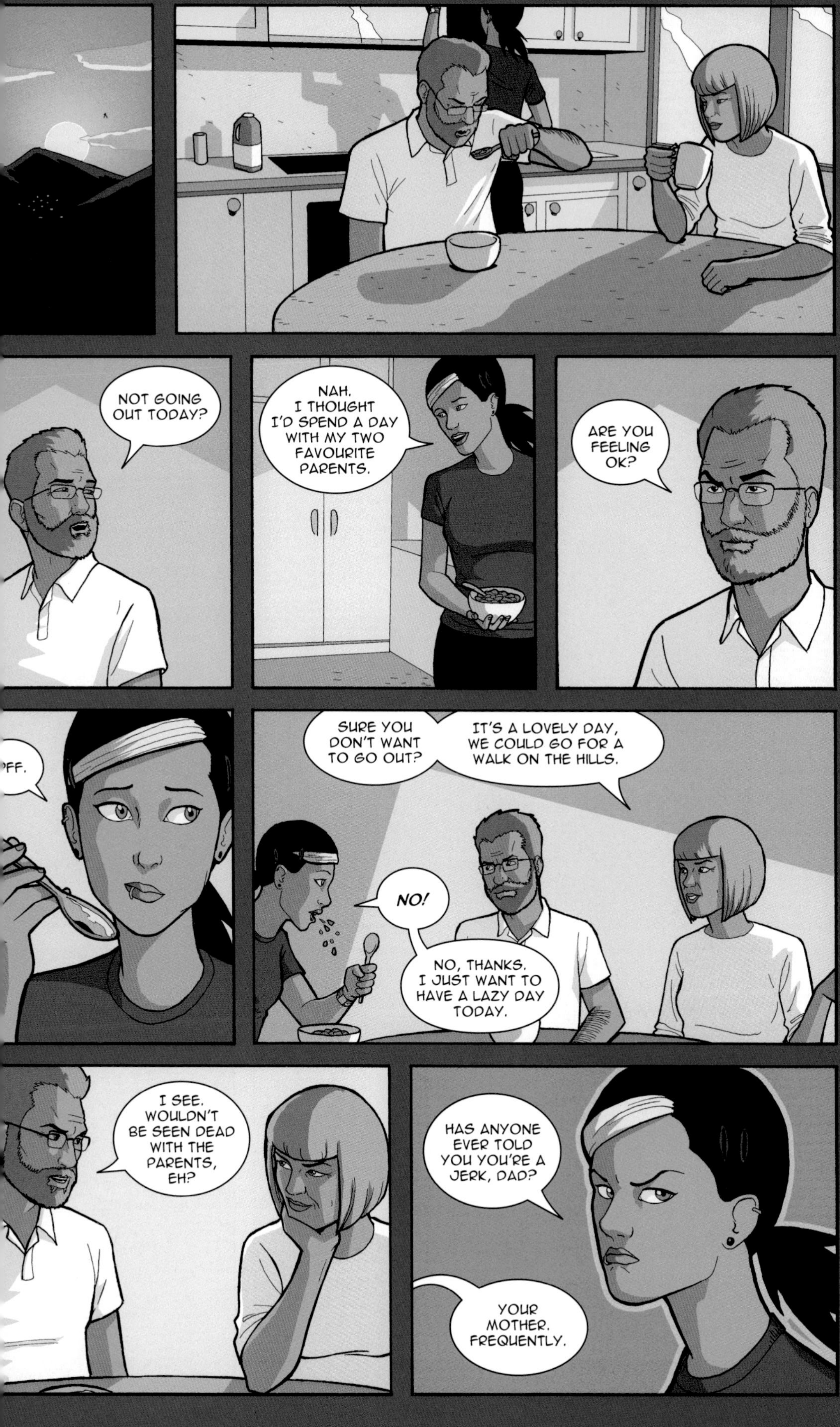
NOT GOING OUT TODAY?
NAH. I THOUGHT I'D SPEND A DAY WITH MY TWO FAVOURITE PARENTS.
ARE YOU FEELING OK?
SURE YOU DON'T WANT TO GO OUT?
IT'S A LOVELY DAY, WE COULD GO FOR A WALK ON THE HILLS.
NO!
NO, THANKS. I JUST WANT TO HAVE A LAZY DAY TODAY.
I SEE. WOULDN'T BE SEEN DEAD WITH THE PARENTS, EH?
HAS ANYONE EVER TOLD YOU YOU'RE A JERK, DAD?
YOUR MOTHER. FREQUENTLY.

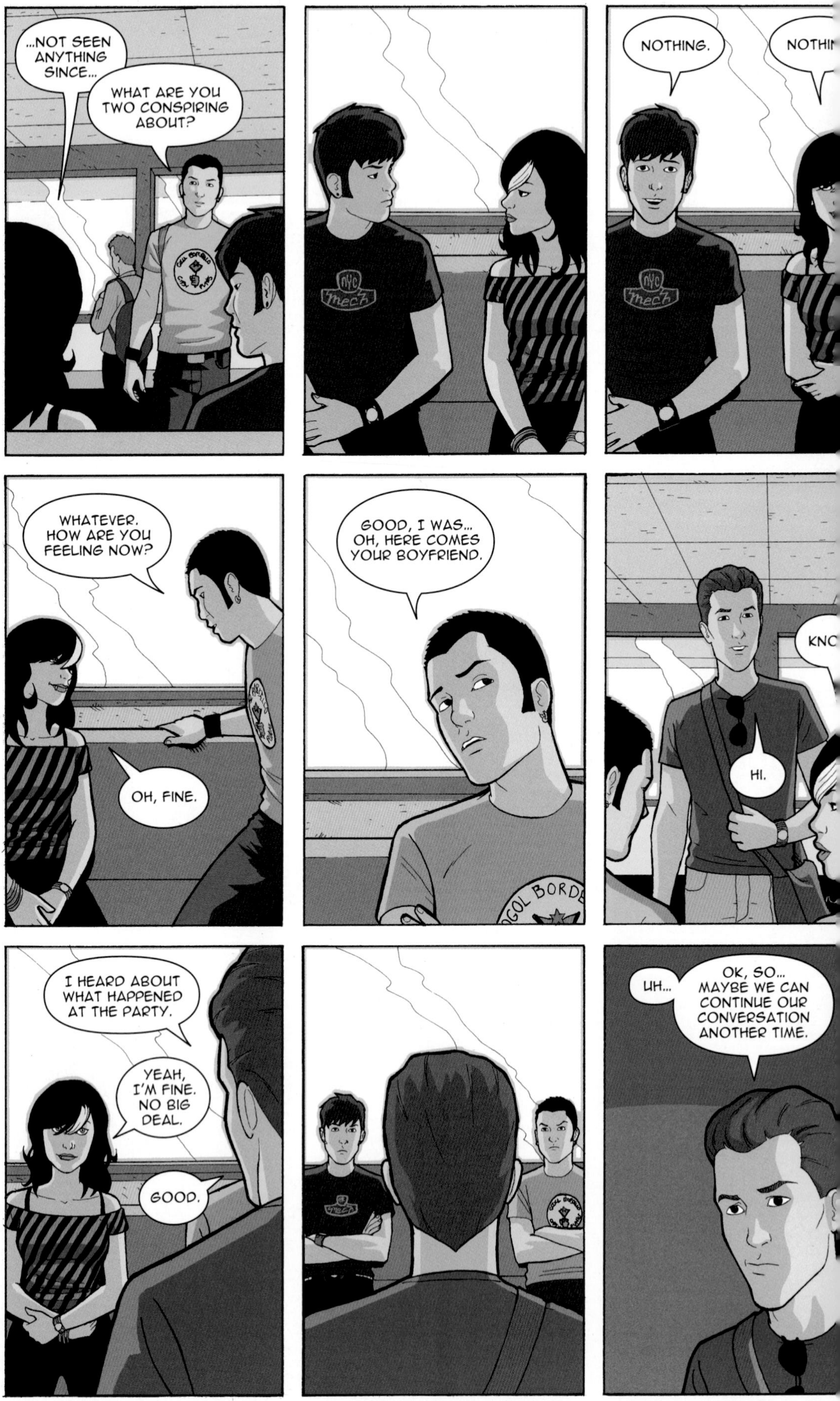
...NOT SEEN ANYTHING SINCE...
WHAT ARE YOU TWO CONSPIRING ABOUT?
NOTHING.
NOTHI
WHATEVER. HOW ARE YOU FEELING NOW?
OH, FINE.
GOOD, I WAS... OH, HERE COMES YOUR BOYFRIEND.
KNO
HI.
I HEARD ABOUT WHAT HAPPENED AT THE PARTY.
YEAH, I'M FINE. NO BIG DEAL.
GOOD.
UH...
OK, SO... MAYBE WE CAN CONTINUE OUR CONVERSATION ANOTHER TIME.

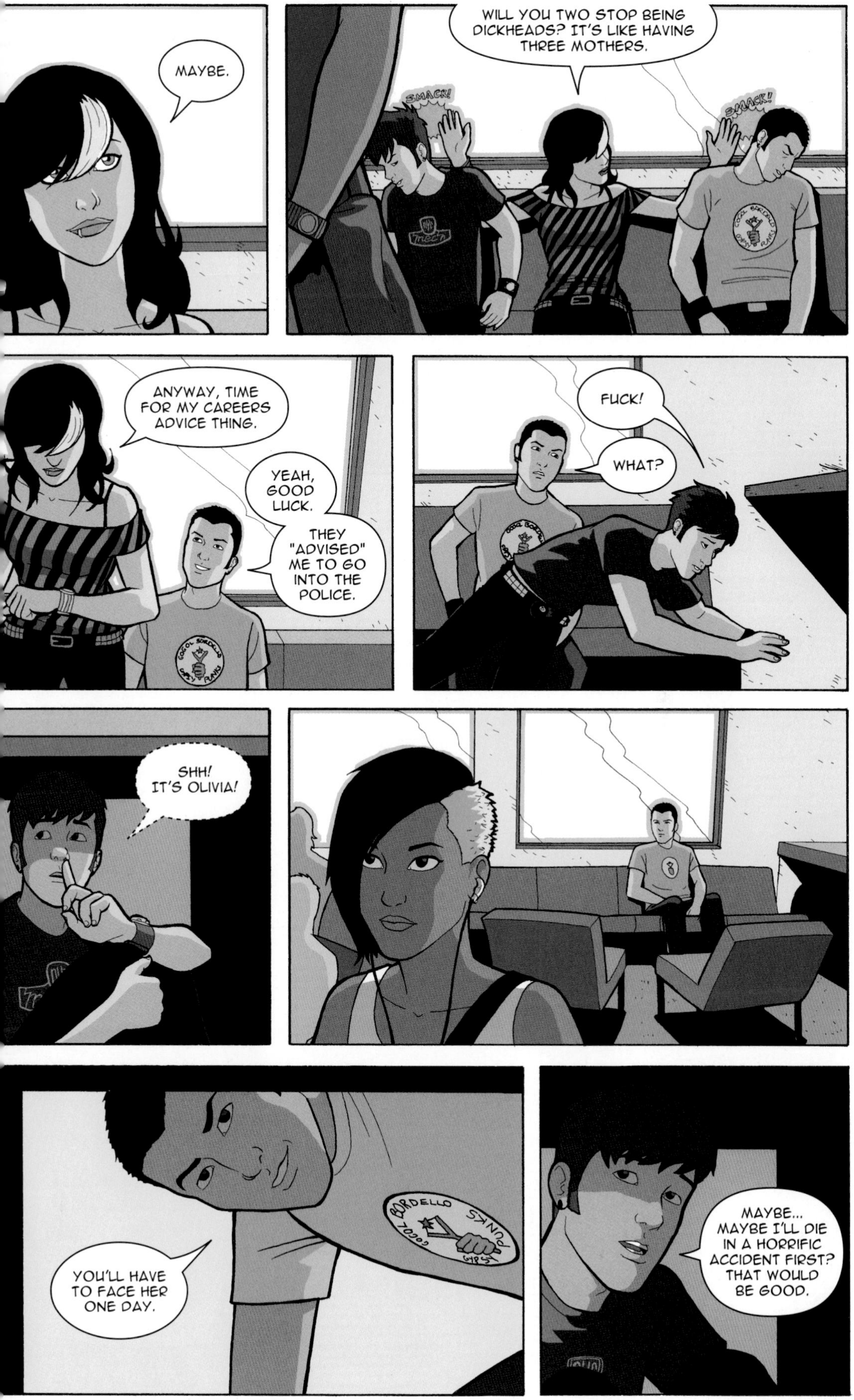
MAYBE.
WILL YOU TWO STOP BEING DICKHEADS? IT'S LIKE HAVING THREE MOTHERS.
SMACK!
SMACK!
ANYWAY, TIME FOR MY CAREERS ADVICE THING.
YEAH, GOOD LUCK.
THEY "ADVISED" ME TO GO INTO THE POLICE.
FUCK!
WHAT?
SHH! IT'S OLIVIA!
YOU'LL HAVE TO FACE HER ONE DAY.
MAYBE... MAYBE I'LL DIE IN A HORRIFIC ACCIDENT FIRST? THAT WOULD BE GOOD.

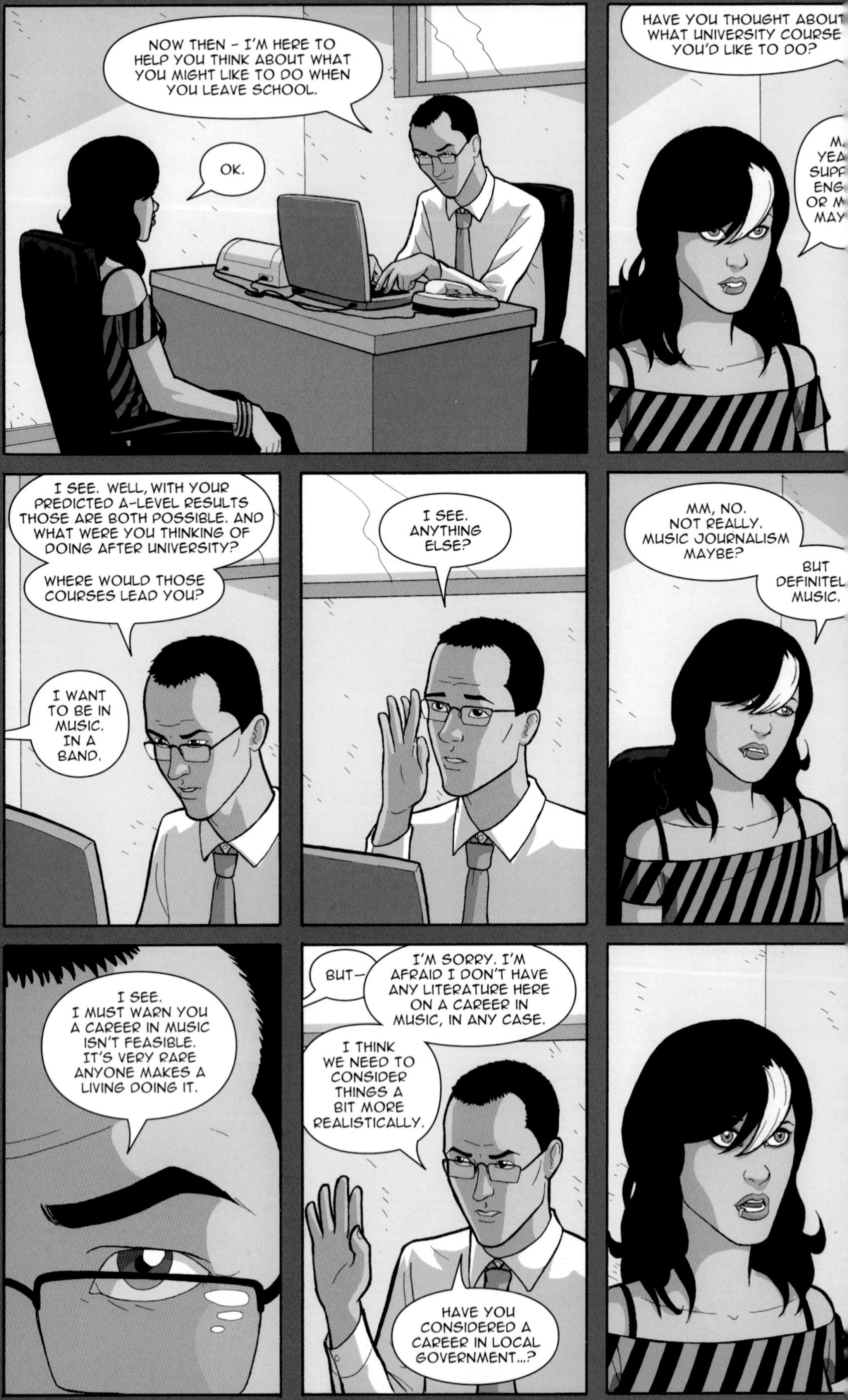

NOW THEN - I'M HERE TO HELP YOU THINK ABOUT WHAT YOU MIGHT LIKE TO DO WHEN YOU LEAVE SCHOOL.
OK.
HAVE YOU THOUGHT ABOUT WHAT UNIVERSITY COURSE YOU'D LIKE TO DO?
I SEE. WELL, WITH YOUR PREDICTED A-LEVEL RESULTS THOSE ARE BOTH POSSIBLE. AND WHAT WERE YOU THINKING OF DOING AFTER UNIVERSITY?
WHERE WOULD THOSE COURSES LEAD YOU?
I WANT TO BE IN MUSIC. IN A BAND.
I SEE. ANYTHING ELSE?
MM, NO. NOT REALLY. MUSIC JOURNALISM MAYBE?
BUT DEFINITEL MUSIC.
I SEE. I MUST WARN YOU A CAREER IN MUSIC ISN'T FEASIBLE. IT'S VERY RARE ANYONE MAKES A LIVING DOING IT.
BUT—
I'M SORRY. I'M AFRAID I DON'T HAVE ANY LITERATURE HERE ON A CAREER IN MUSIC, IN ANY CASE.
I THINK WE NEED TO CONSIDER THINGS A BIT MORE REALISTICALLY.
HAVE YOU CONSIDERED A CAREER IN LOCAL GOVERNMENT...?

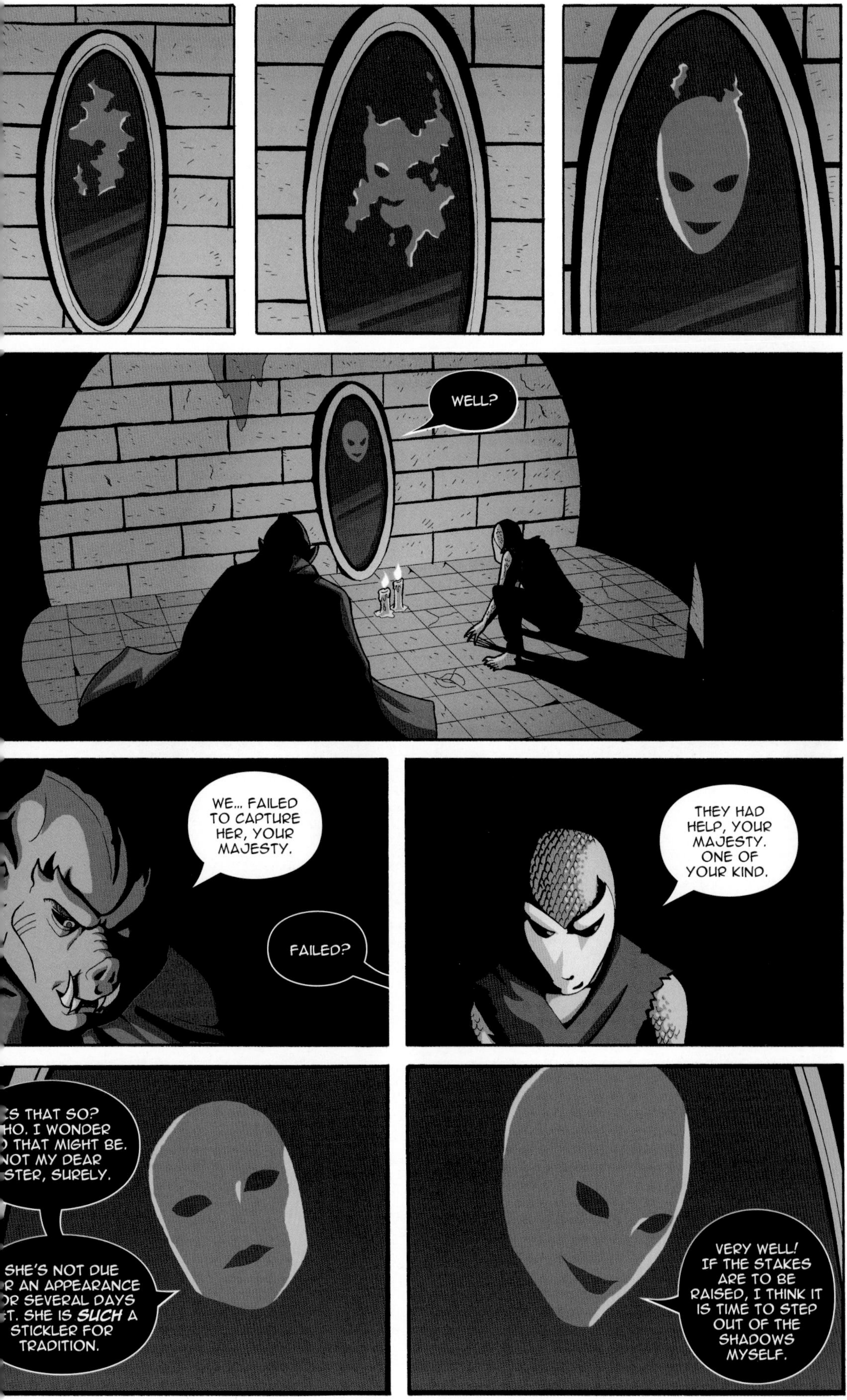
WELL?
WE... FAILED TO CAPTURE HER, YOUR MAJESTY.
FAILED?
THEY HAD HELP, YOUR MAJESTY. ONE OF YOUR KIND.
S THAT SO? HO. I WONDER THAT MIGHT BE. NOT MY DEAR STER, SURELY.
SHE'S NOT DUE R AN APPEARANCE OR SEVERAL DAYS T. SHE IS *SUCH* A STICKLER FOR TRADITION.
VERY WELL! IF THE STAKES ARE TO BE RAISED, I THINK IT IS TIME TO STEP OUT OF THE SHADOWS MYSELF.

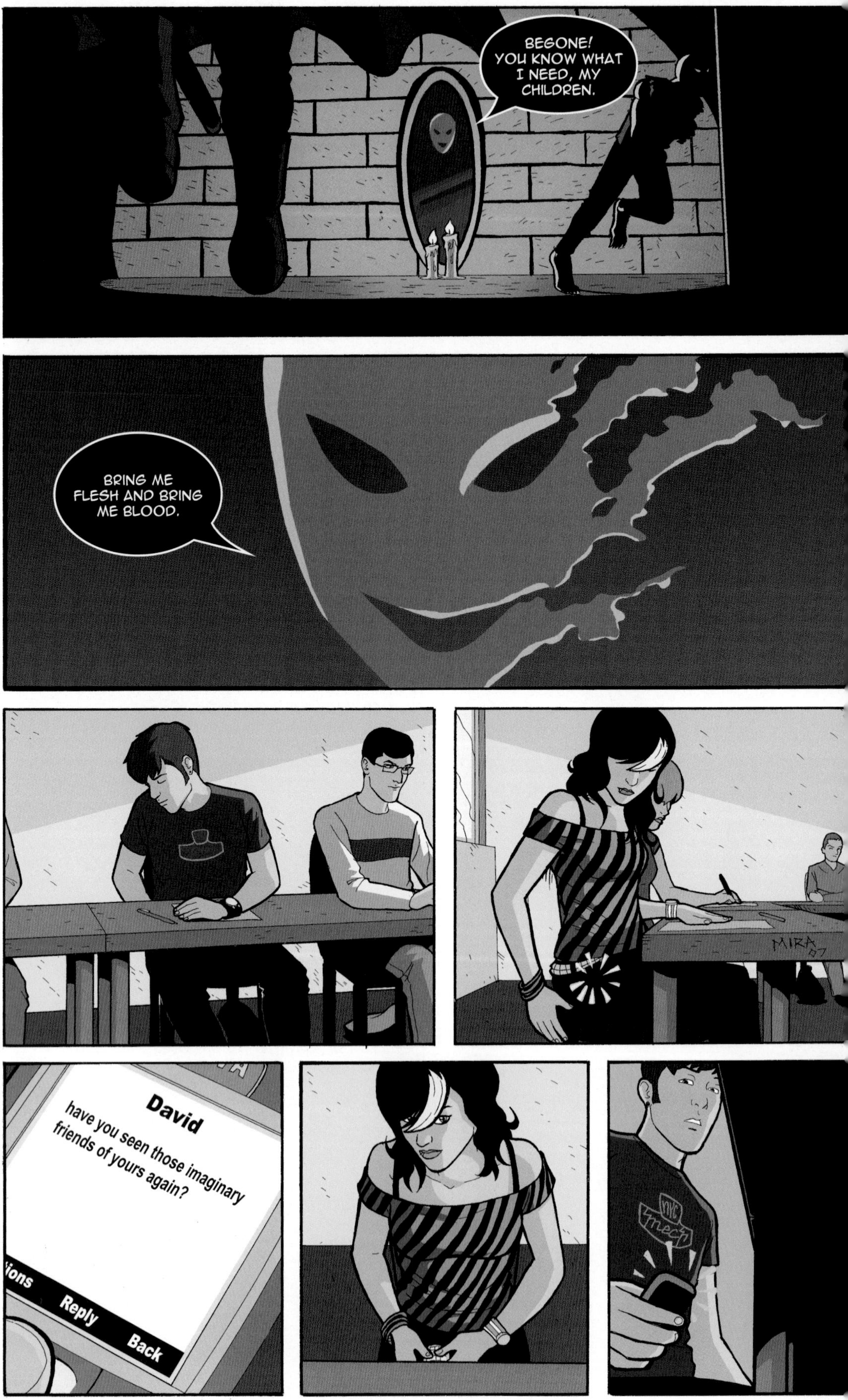
BEGONE! YOU KNOW WHAT I NEED, MY CHILDREN.
BRING ME FLESH AND BRING ME BLOOD.
MIRA 07
David
have you seen those imaginary friends of yours again?
Reply
Back
NYC mech

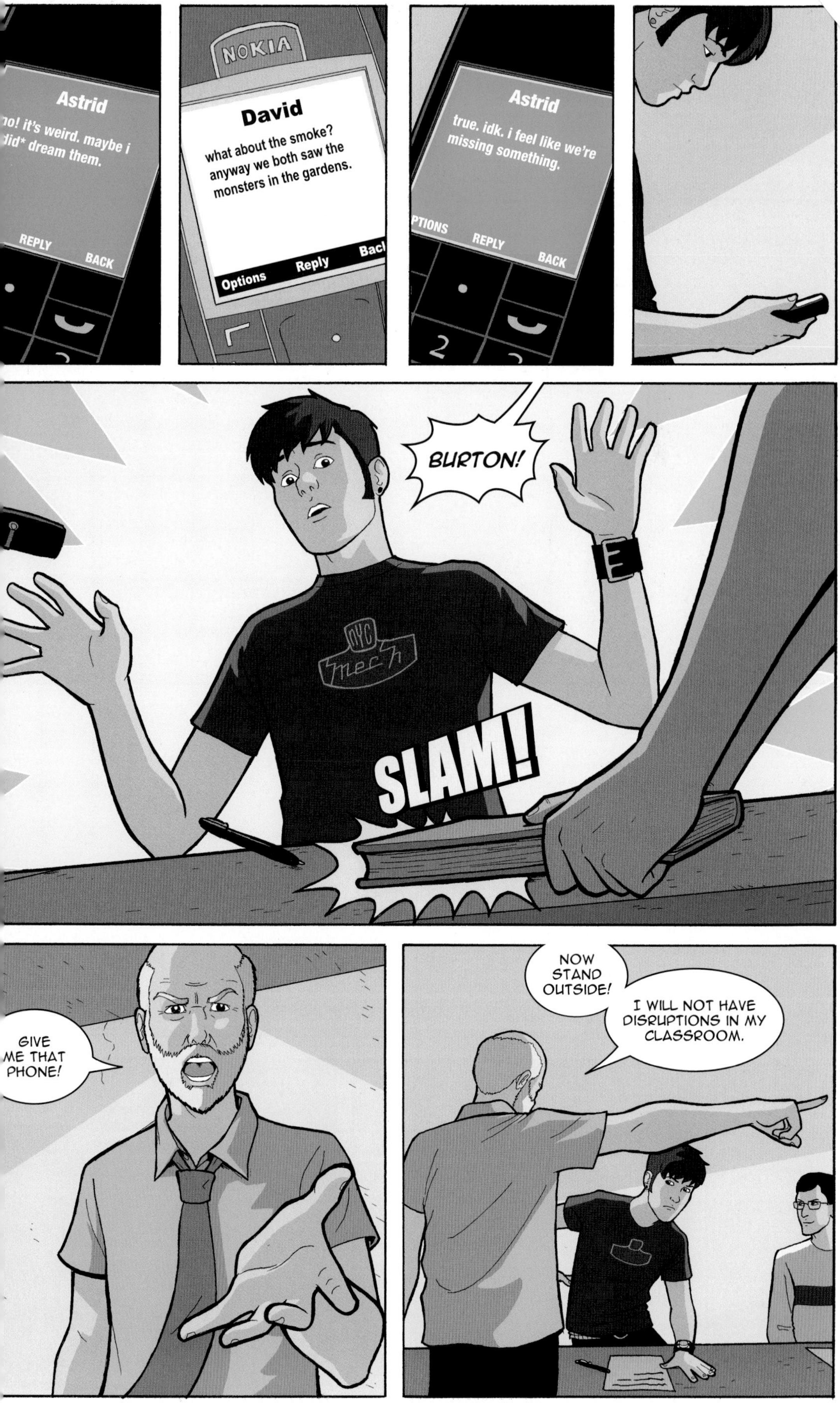
Astrid
no! it's weird. maybe i
did* dream them.
REPLY
BACK
NOKIA
David
what about the smoke?
anyway we both saw the
monsters in the gardens.
Options
Reply
Back
Astrid
true. idk. i feel like we're
missing something.
OPTIONS
REPLY
BACK
BURTON!
SLAM!
GIVE ME THAT PHONE!
NOW STAND OUTSIDE!
I WILL NOT HAVE DISRUPTIONS IN MY CLASSROOM.

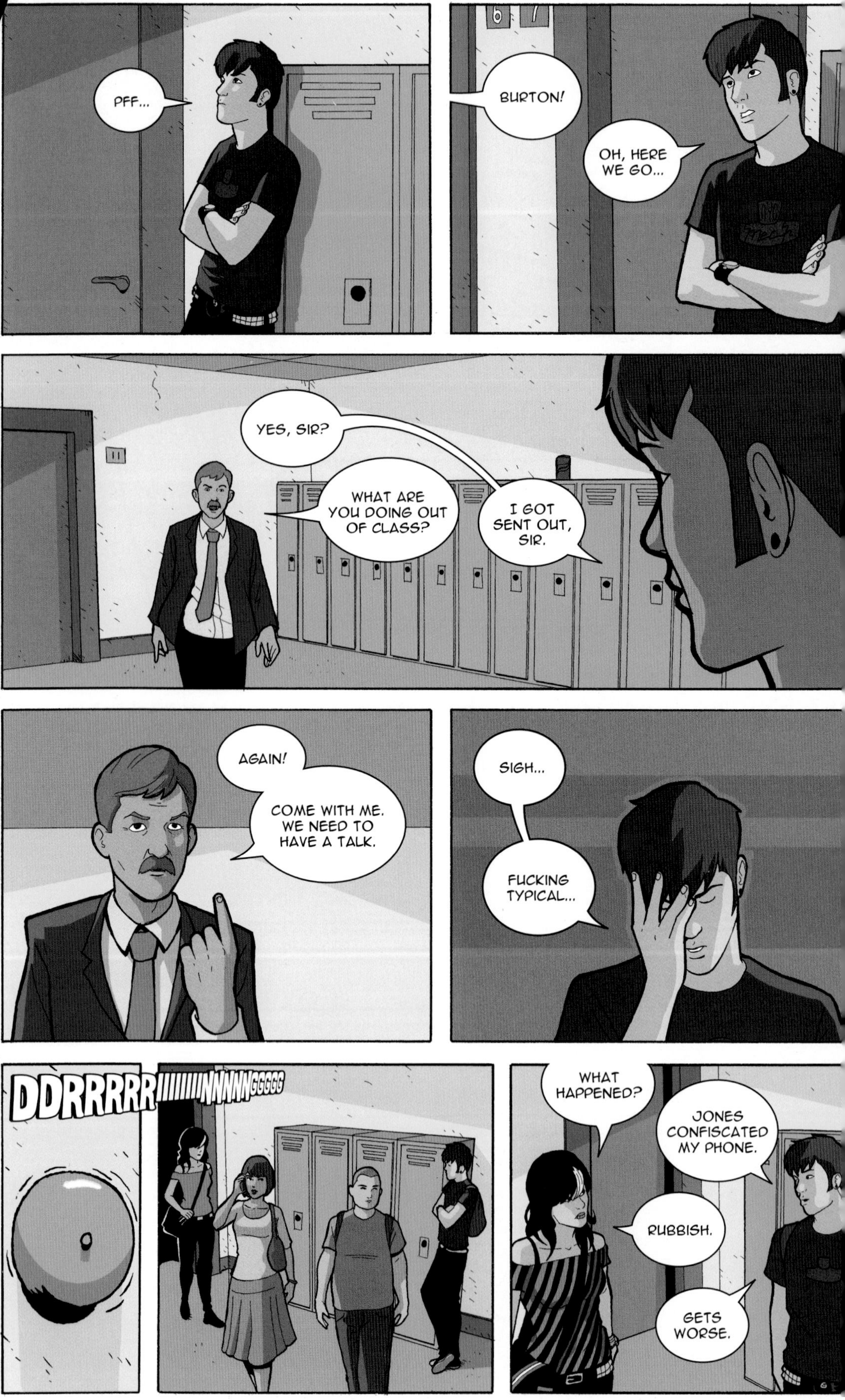
PFF...
BURTON!
OH, HERE WE GO...
YES, SIR?
WHAT ARE YOU DOING OUT OF CLASS?
I GOT SENT OUT, SIR.
AGAIN!
COME WITH ME. WE NEED TO HAVE A TALK.
SIGH...
FUCKING TYPICAL...
DDRRRRRRIIIIIIIINNNNNGGGGG
WHAT HAPPENED?
JONES CONFISCATED MY PHONE.
RUBBISH.
GETS WORSE.

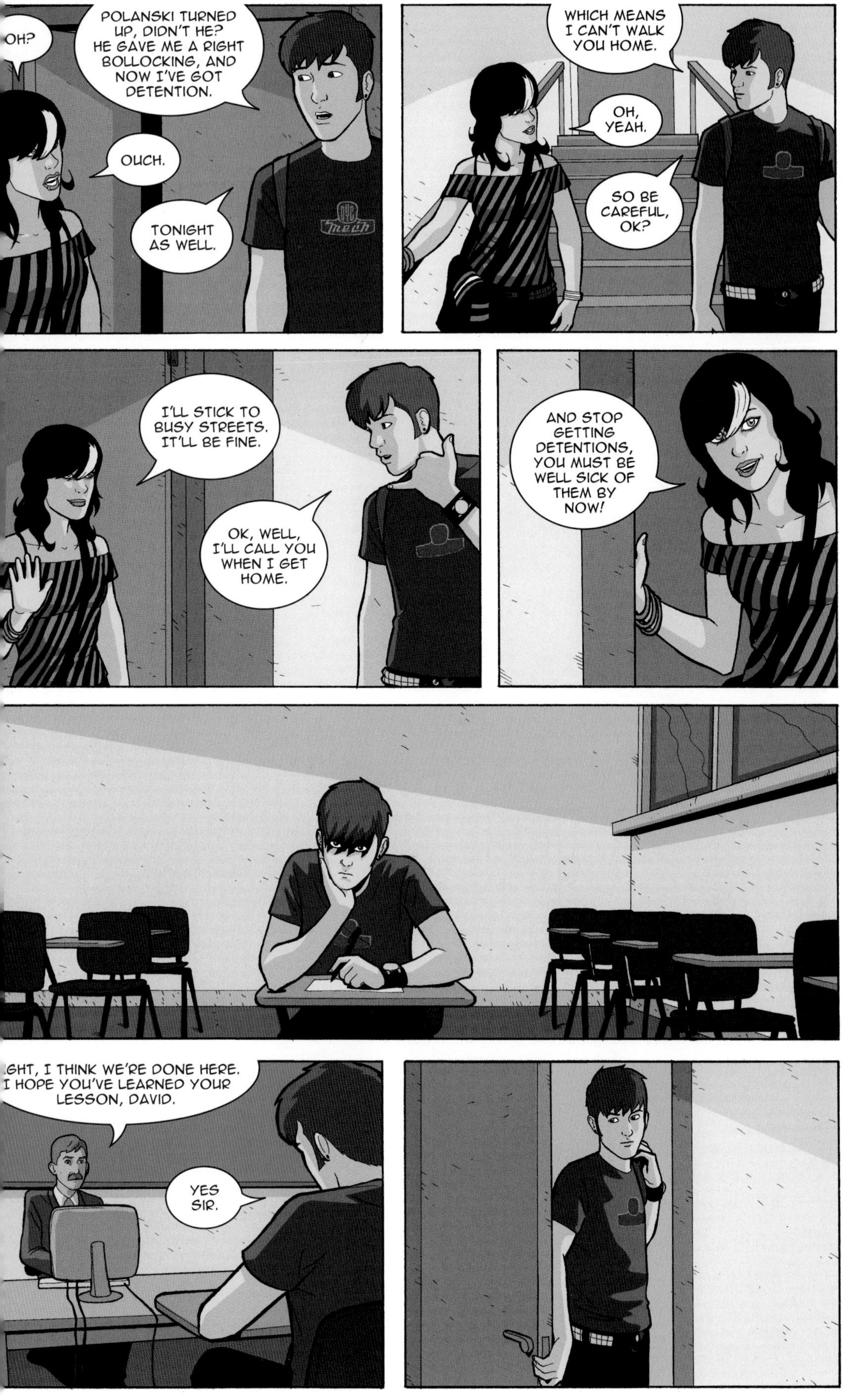
OH?
POLANSKI TURNED UP, DIDN'T HE? HE GAVE ME A RIGHT BOLLOCKING, AND NOW I'VE GOT DETENTION.
OUCH.
TONIGHT AS WELL.
WHICH MEANS I CAN'T WALK YOU HOME.
OH, YEAH.
SO BE CAREFUL, OK?
I'LL STICK TO BUSY STREETS. IT'LL BE FINE.
OK, WELL, I'LL CALL YOU WHEN I GET HOME.
AND STOP GETTING DETENTIONS, YOU MUST BE WELL SICK OF THEM BY NOW!
GHT, I THINK WE'RE DONE HERE. I HOPE YOU'VE LEARNED YOUR LESSON, DAVID.
YES SIR.

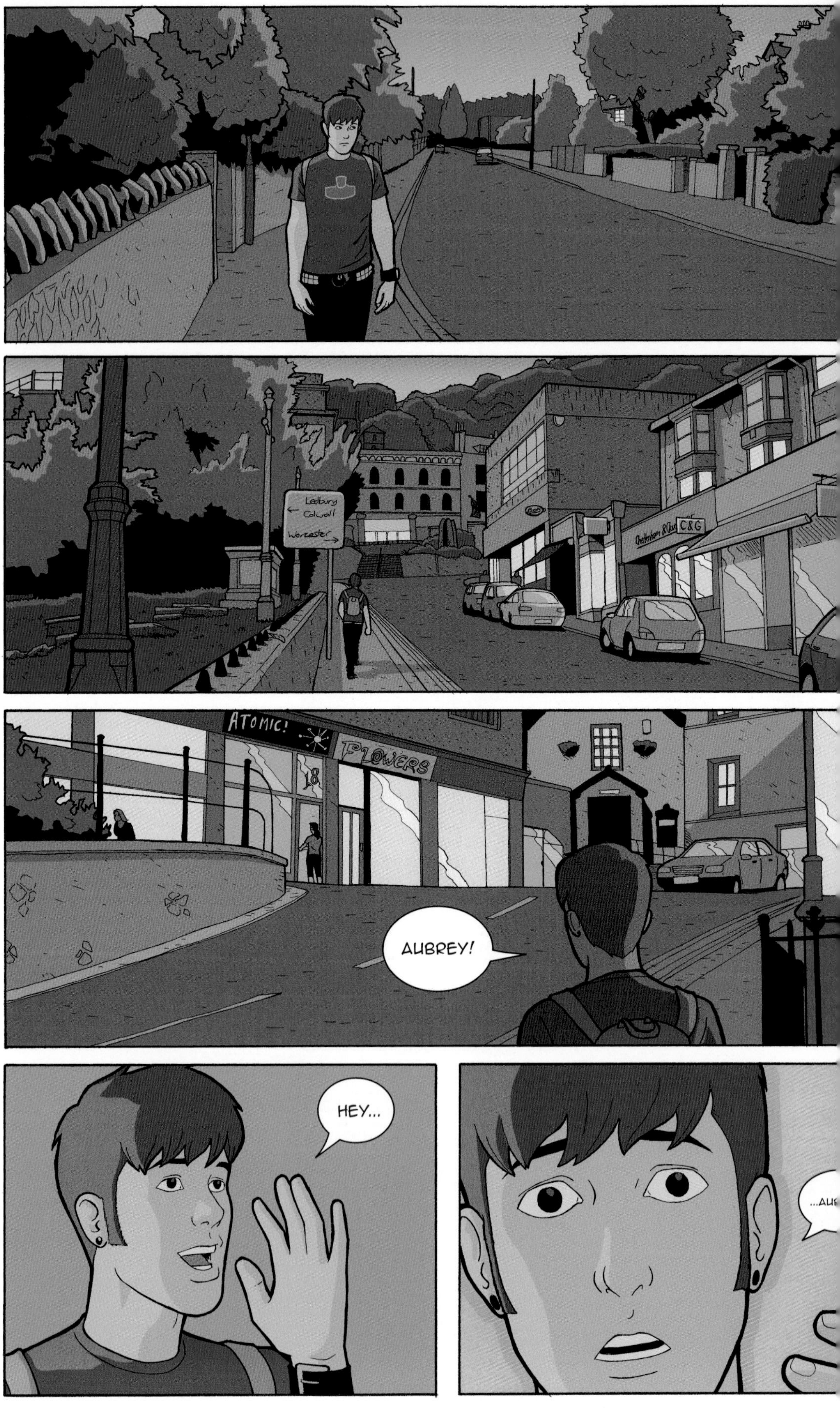
Ledbury
Colwall
Worcester
C&G
ATOMIC!
FLOWERS
18
AUBREY!
HEY...
...AU

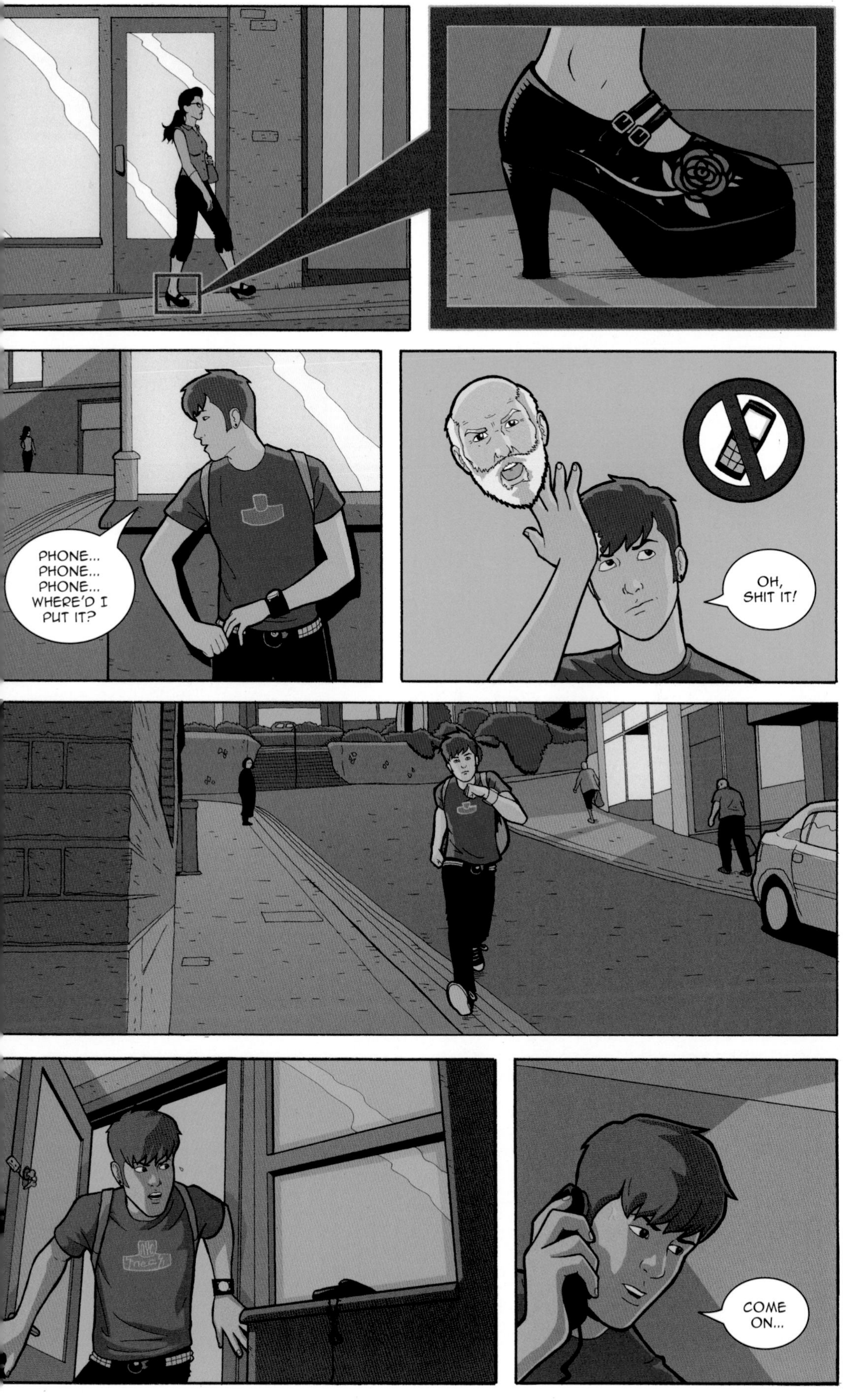
PHONE... PHONE... PHONE... WHERE'D I PUT IT?
OH, SHIT IT!
COME ON...

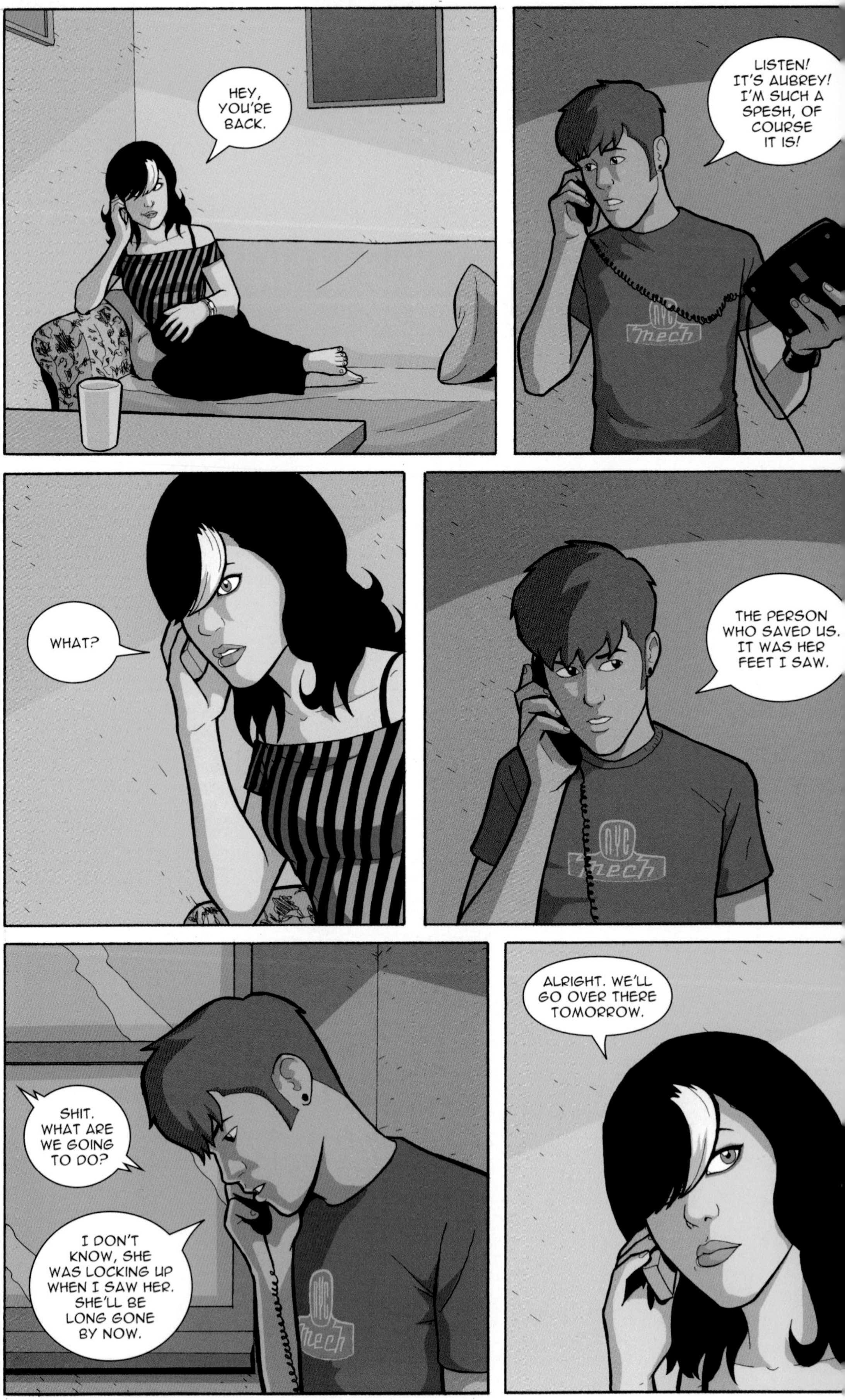
HEY, YOU'RE BACK.
LISTEN! IT'S AUBREY! I'M SUCH A SPESH, OF COURSE IT IS!
WHAT?
THE PERSON WHO SAVED US. IT WAS HER FEET I SAW.
SHIT. WHAT ARE WE GOING TO DO?
I DON'T KNOW, SHE WAS LOCKING UP WHEN I SAW HER. SHE'LL BE LONG GONE BY NOW.
ALRIGHT. WE'LL GO OVER THERE TOMORROW.

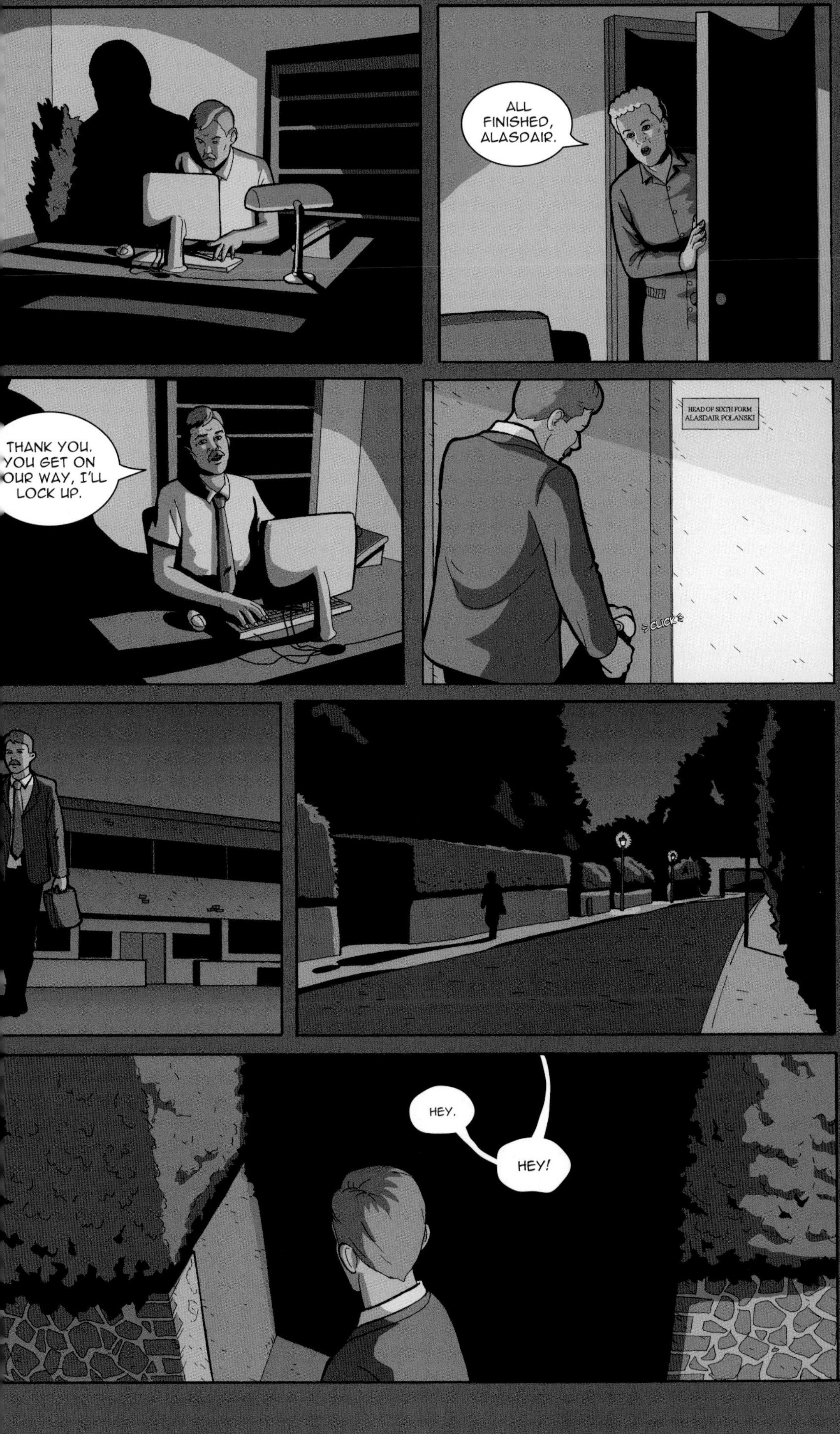
ALL FINISHED, ALASDAIR.
THANK YOU. YOU GET ON OUR WAY, I'LL LOCK UP.
HEAD OF SIXTH FORM ALASDAIR POLANSKI
CLICK
HEY.
HEY!

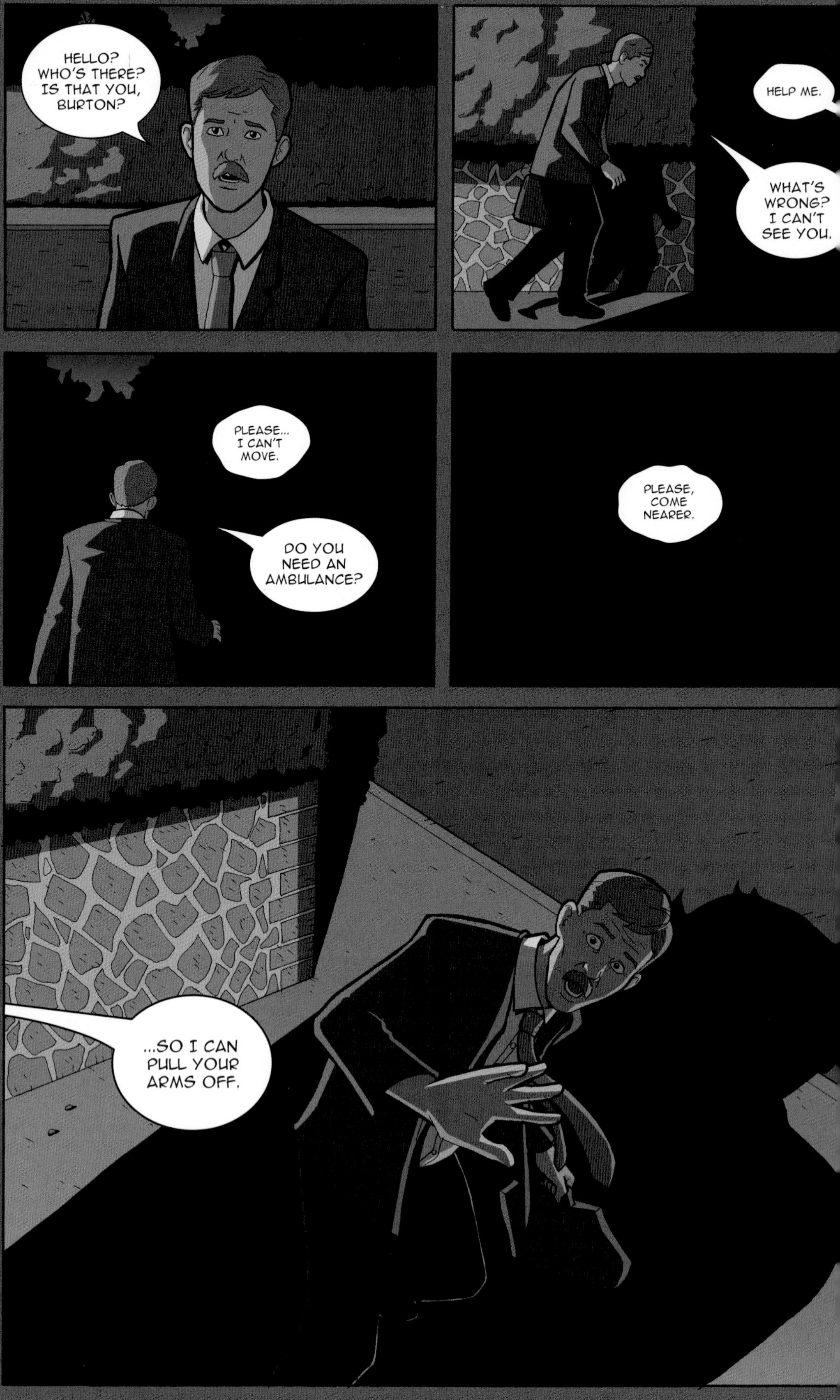
HELLO? WHO'S THERE? IS THAT YOU, BURTON?
HELP ME.
WHAT'S WRONG? I CAN'T SEE YOU.
PLEASE... I CAN'T MOVE.
DO YOU NEED AN AMBULANCE?
PLEASE, COME NEARER.
...SO I CAN PULL YOUR ARMS OFF.

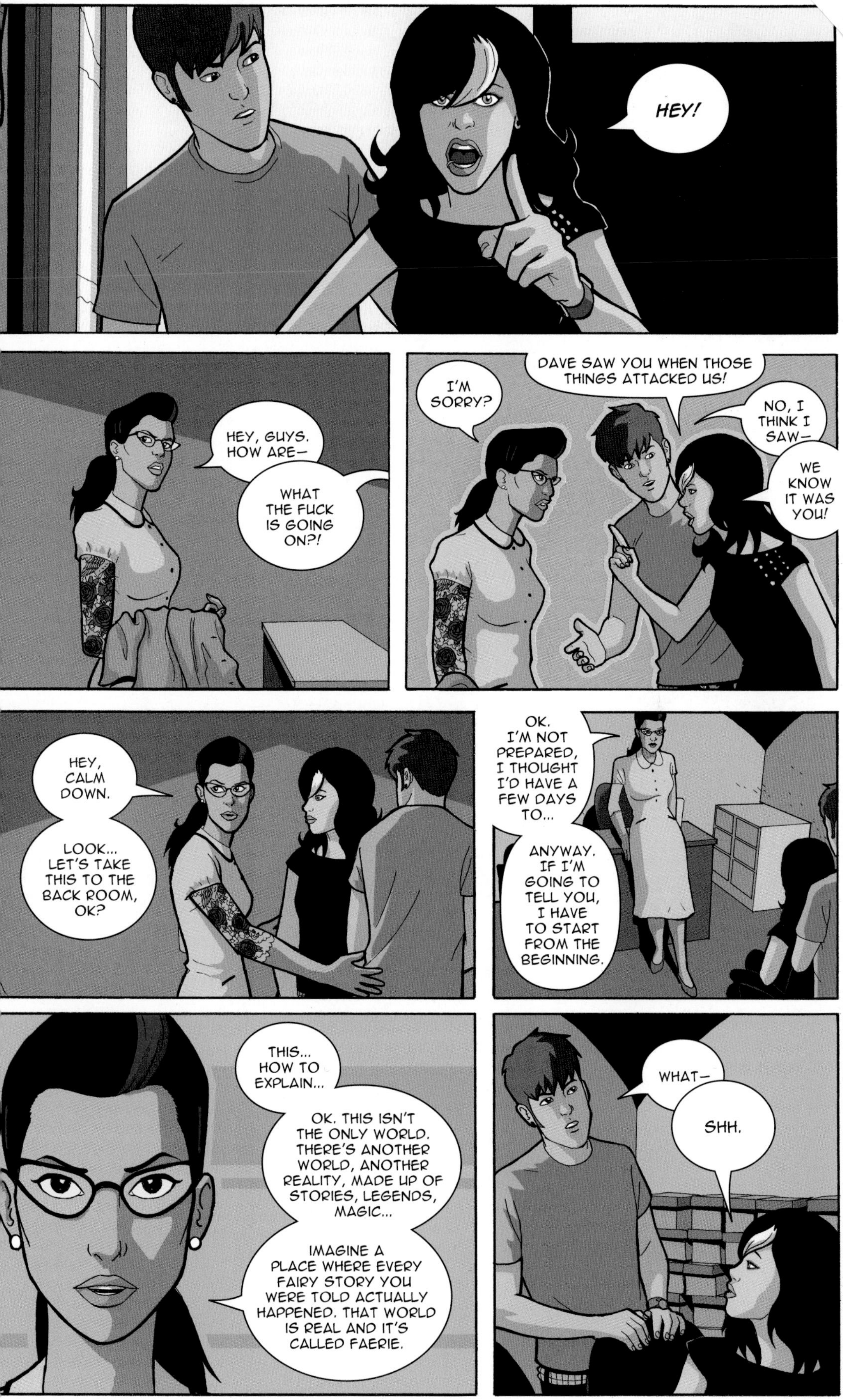
HEY!
HEY, GUYS. HOW ARE—
WHAT THE FUCK IS GOING ON?!
I'M SORRY?
DAVE SAW YOU WHEN THOSE THINGS ATTACKED US!
NO, I THINK I SAW—
WE KNOW IT WAS YOU!
HEY, CALM DOWN.
LOOK... LET'S TAKE THIS TO THE BACK ROOM, OK?
OK. I'M NOT PREPARED, I THOUGHT I'D HAVE A FEW DAYS TO...
ANYWAY. IF I'M GOING TO TELL YOU, I HAVE TO START FROM THE BEGINNING.
THIS... HOW TO EXPLAIN...
OK. THIS ISN'T THE ONLY WORLD. THERE'S ANOTHER WORLD, ANOTHER REALITY, MADE UP OF STORIES, LEGENDS, MAGIC...
IMAGINE A PLACE WHERE EVERY FAIRY STORY YOU WERE TOLD ACTUALLY HAPPENED. THAT WORLD IS REAL AND IT'S CALLED FAERIE.
WHAT—
SHH.

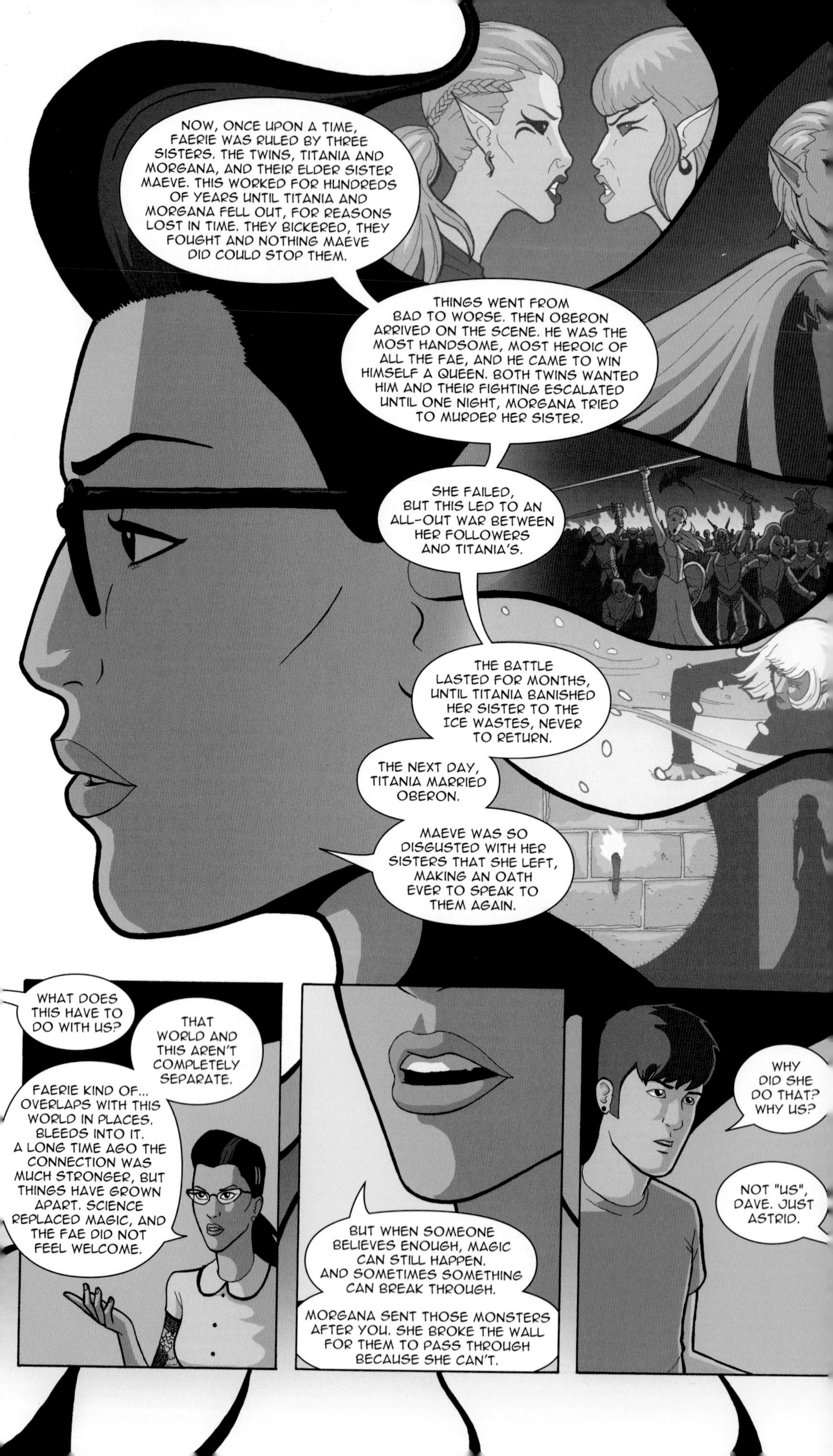
NOW, ONCE UPON A TIME, FAERIE WAS RULED BY THREE SISTERS. THE TWINS, TITANIA AND MORGANA, AND THEIR ELDER SISTER MAEVE. THIS WORKED FOR HUNDREDS OF YEARS UNTIL TITANIA AND MORGANA FELL OUT, FOR REASONS LOST IN TIME. THEY BICKERED, THEY FOUGHT AND NOTHING MAEVE DID COULD STOP THEM.
THINGS WENT FROM BAD TO WORSE. THEN OBERON ARRIVED ON THE SCENE. HE WAS THE MOST HANDSOME, MOST HEROIC OF ALL THE FAE, AND HE CAME TO WIN HIMSELF A QUEEN. BOTH TWINS WANTED HIM AND THEIR FIGHTING ESCALATED UNTIL ONE NIGHT, MORGANA TRIED TO MURDER HER SISTER.
SHE FAILED, BUT THIS LED TO AN ALL-OUT WAR BETWEEN HER FOLLOWERS AND TITANIA'S.
THE BATTLE LASTED FOR MONTHS, UNTIL TITANIA BANISHED HER SISTER TO THE ICE WASTES, NEVER TO RETURN.
THE NEXT DAY, TITANIA MARRIED OBERON.
MAEVE WAS SO DISGUSTED WITH HER SISTERS THAT SHE LEFT, MAKING AN OATH EVER TO SPEAK TO THEM AGAIN.
WHAT DOES THIS HAVE TO DO WITH US?
THAT WORLD AND THIS AREN'T COMPLETELY SEPARATE.
FAERIE KIND OF... OVERLAPS WITH THIS WORLD IN PLACES. BLEEDS INTO IT. A LONG TIME AGO THE CONNECTION WAS MUCH STRONGER, BUT THINGS HAVE GROWN APART. SCIENCE REPLACED MAGIC, AND THE FAE DID NOT FEEL WELCOME.
BUT WHEN SOMEONE BELIEVES ENOUGH, MAGIC CAN STILL HAPPEN. AND SOMETIMES SOMETHING CAN BREAK THROUGH.
MORGANA SENT THOSE MONSTERS AFTER YOU. SHE BROKE THE WALL FOR THEM TO PASS THROUGH BECAUSE SHE CAN'T.
WHY DID SHE DO THAT? WHY US?
NOT "US", DAVE. JUST ASTRID.

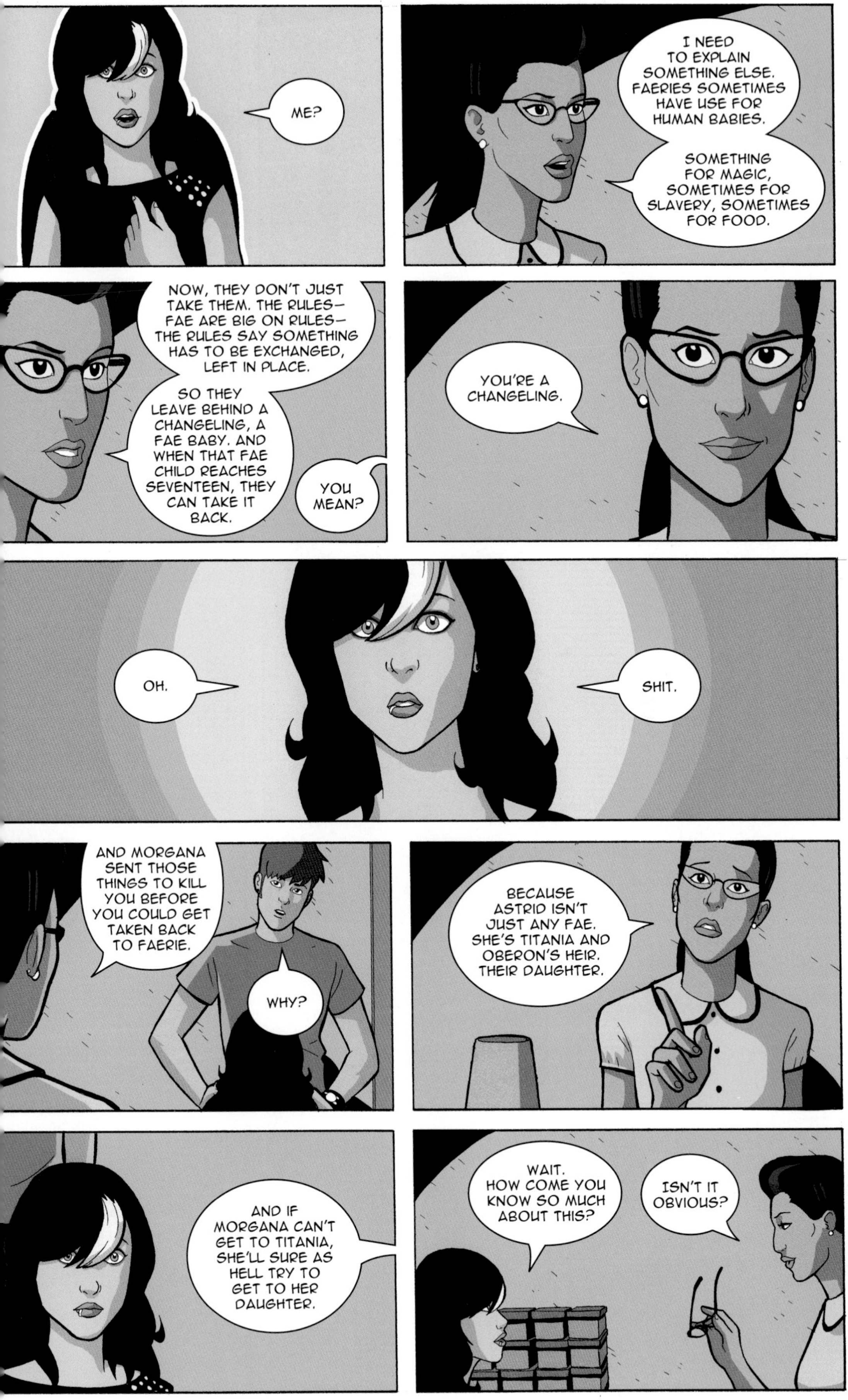
ME?
I NEED TO EXPLAIN SOMETHING ELSE. FAERIES SOMETIMES HAVE USE FOR HUMAN BABIES.
SOMETHING FOR MAGIC, SOMETIMES FOR SLAVERY, SOMETIMES FOR FOOD.
NOW, THEY DON'T JUST TAKE THEM. THE RULES— FAE ARE BIG ON RULES— THE RULES SAY SOMETHING HAS TO BE EXCHANGED, LEFT IN PLACE.
SO THEY LEAVE BEHIND A CHANGELING, A FAE BABY. AND WHEN THAT FAE CHILD REACHES SEVENTEEN, THEY CAN TAKE IT BACK.
YOU MEAN?
YOU'RE A CHANGELING.
OH.
SHIT.
AND MORGANA SENT THOSE THINGS TO KILL YOU BEFORE YOU COULD GET TAKEN BACK TO FAERIE.
WHY?
BECAUSE ASTRID ISN'T JUST ANY FAE. SHE'S TITANIA AND OBERON'S HEIR. THEIR DAUGHTER.
AND IF MORGANA CAN'T GET TO TITANIA, SHE'LL SURE AS HELL TRY TO GET TO HER DAUGHTER.
WAIT. HOW COME YOU KNOW SO MUCH ABOUT THIS?
ISN'T IT OBVIOUS?

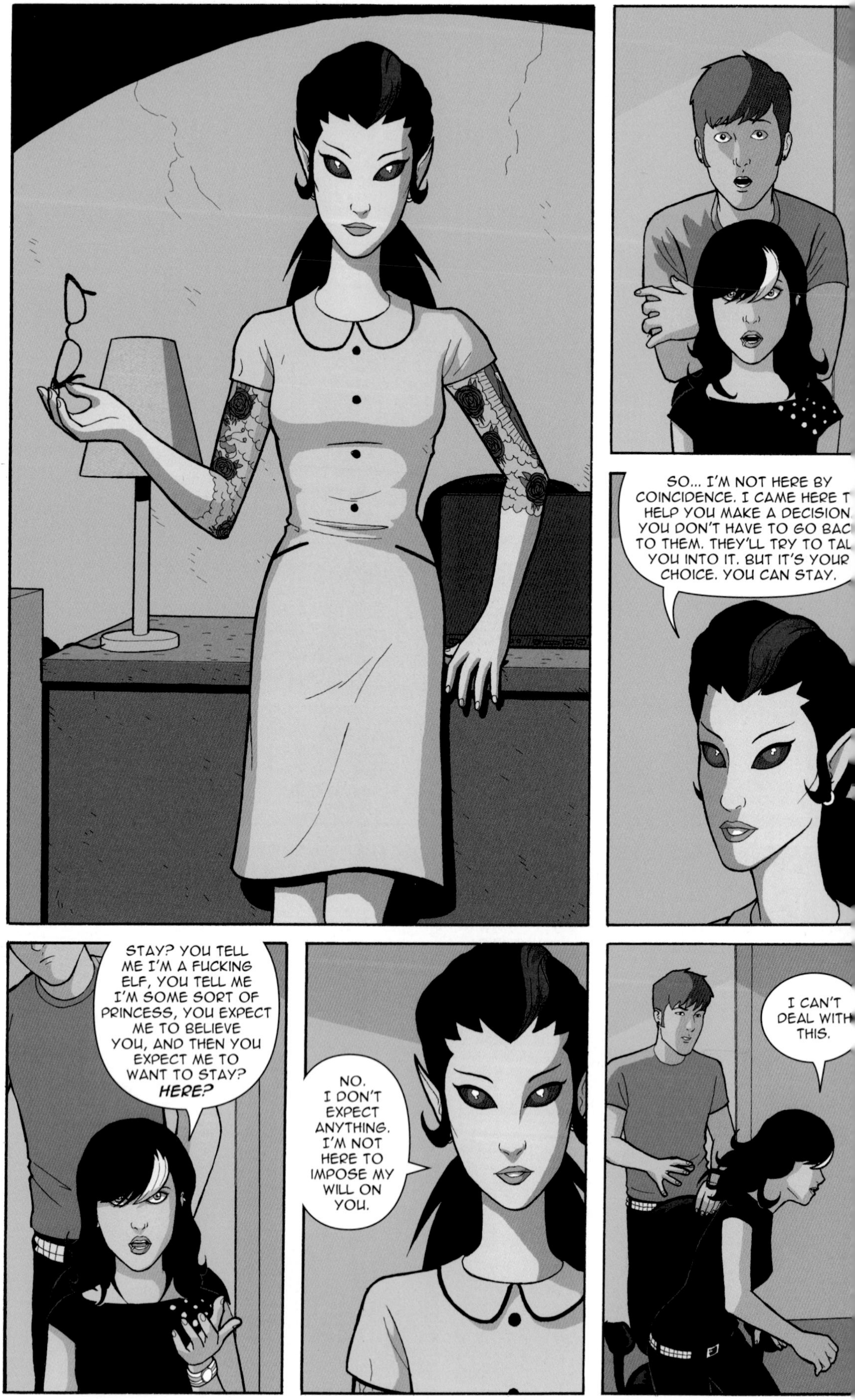
SO... I'M NOT HERE BY COINCIDENCE. I CAME HERE T HELP YOU MAKE A DECISION YOU DON'T HAVE TO GO BAC TO THEM. THEY'LL TRY TO TAL YOU INTO IT. BUT IT'S YOUR CHOICE. YOU CAN STAY.
STAY? YOU TELL ME I'M A FUCKING ELF, YOU TELL ME I'M SOME SORT OF PRINCESS, YOU EXPECT ME TO BELIEVE YOU, AND THEN YOU EXPECT ME TO WANT TO STAY? *HERE?*
NO. I DON'T EXPECT ANYTHING. I'M NOT HERE TO IMPOSE MY WILL ON YOU.
I CAN'T DEAL WITH THIS.

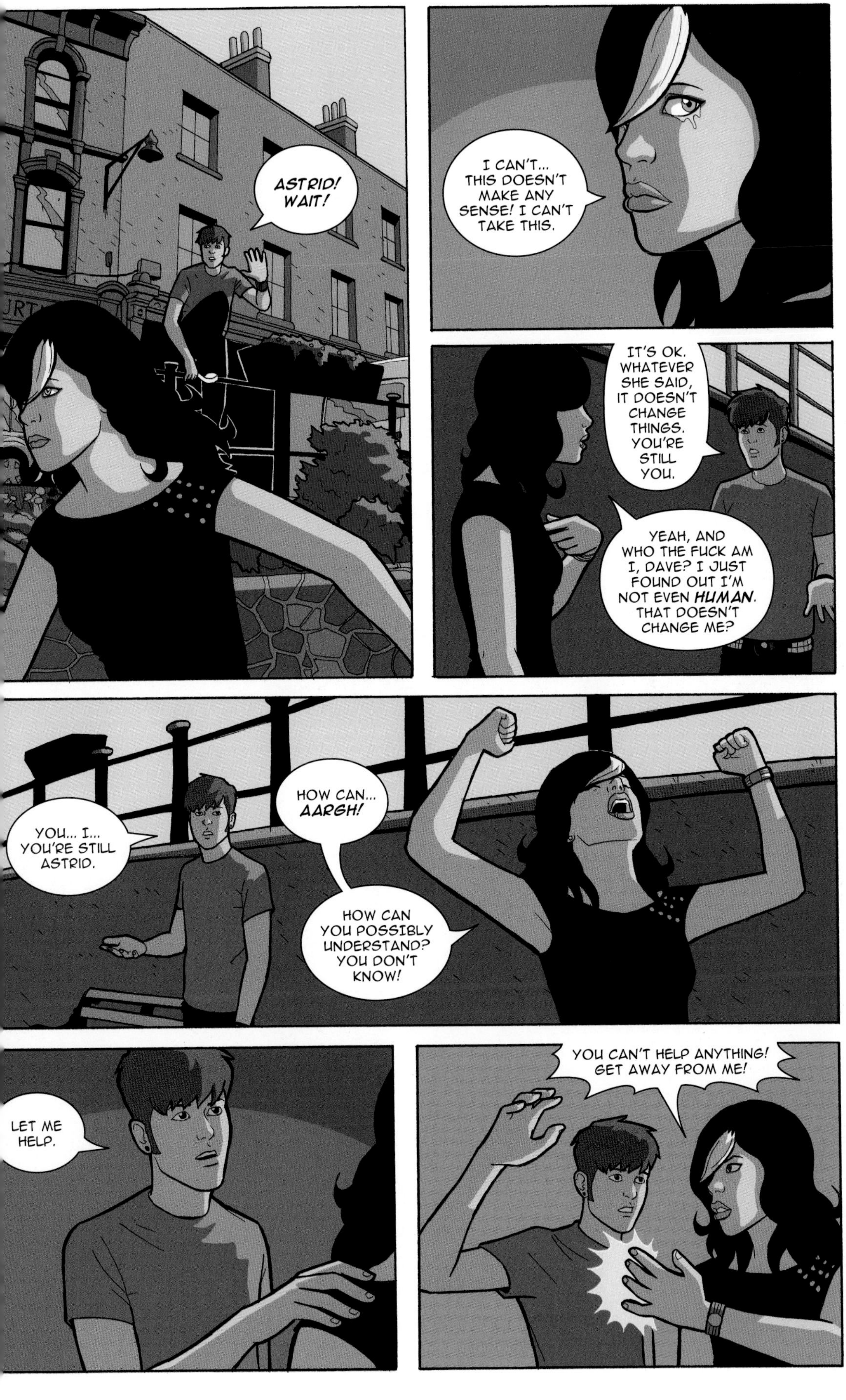
ASTRID! WAIT!
I CAN'T... THIS DOESN'T MAKE ANY SENSE! I CAN'T TAKE THIS.
IT'S OK. WHATEVER SHE SAID, IT DOESN'T CHANGE THINGS. YOU'RE STILL YOU.
YEAH, AND WHO THE FUCK AM I, DAVE? I JUST FOUND OUT I'M NOT EVEN *HUMAN*. THAT DOESN'T CHANGE ME?
YOU... I... YOU'RE STILL ASTRID.
HOW CAN... *AARGH!*
HOW CAN YOU POSSIBLY UNDERSTAND? YOU DON'T KNOW!
LET ME HELP.
YOU CAN'T HELP ANYTHING! GET AWAY FROM ME!

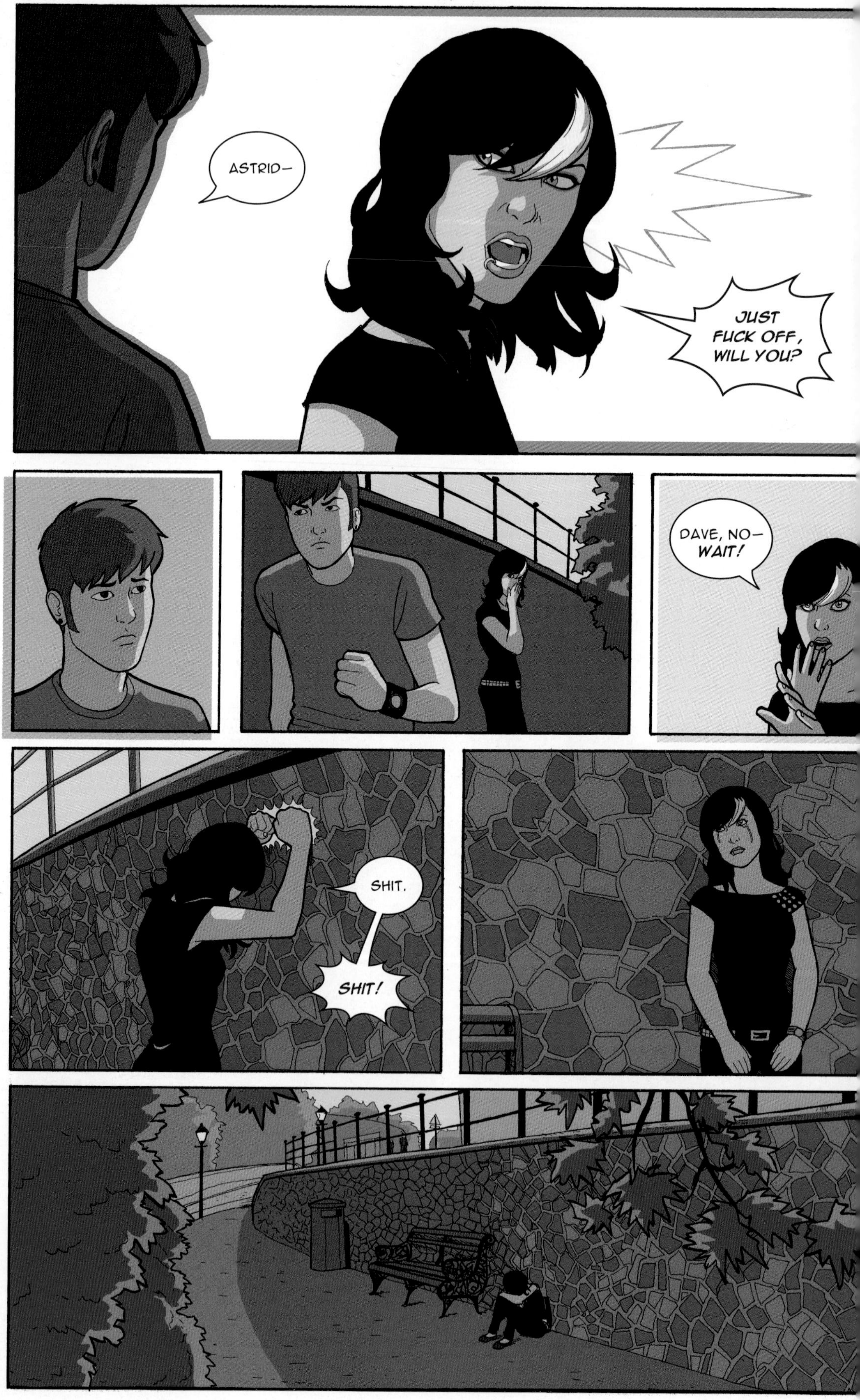
ASTRID—
JUST FUCK OFF, WILL YOU?
DAVE, NO— WAIT!
SHIT.
SHIT!

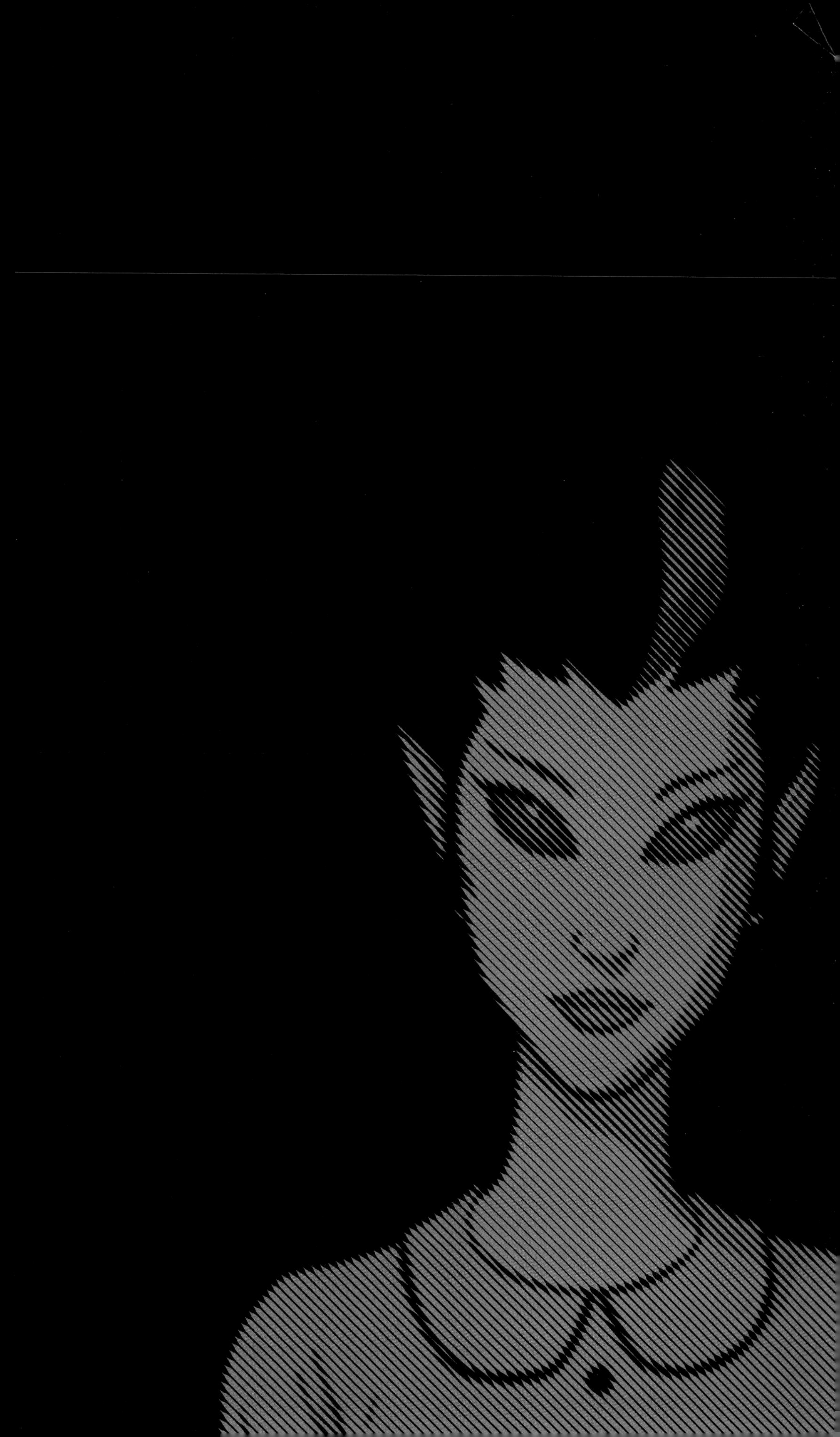

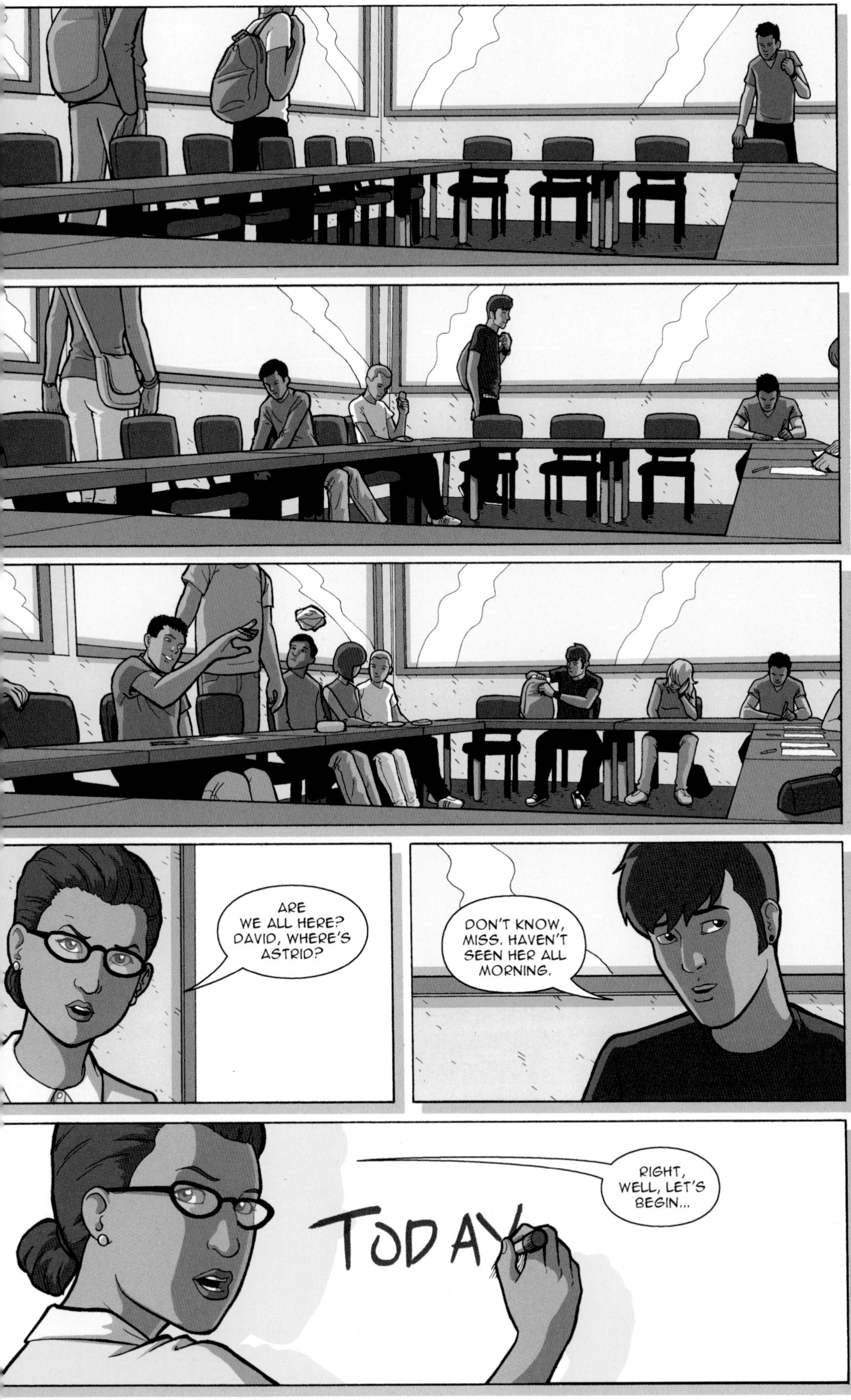
ARE WE ALL HERE? DAVID, WHERE'S ASTRID?
DON'T KNOW, MISS. HAVEN'T SEEN HER ALL MORNING.
RIGHT, WELL, LET'S BEGIN...
TODAY

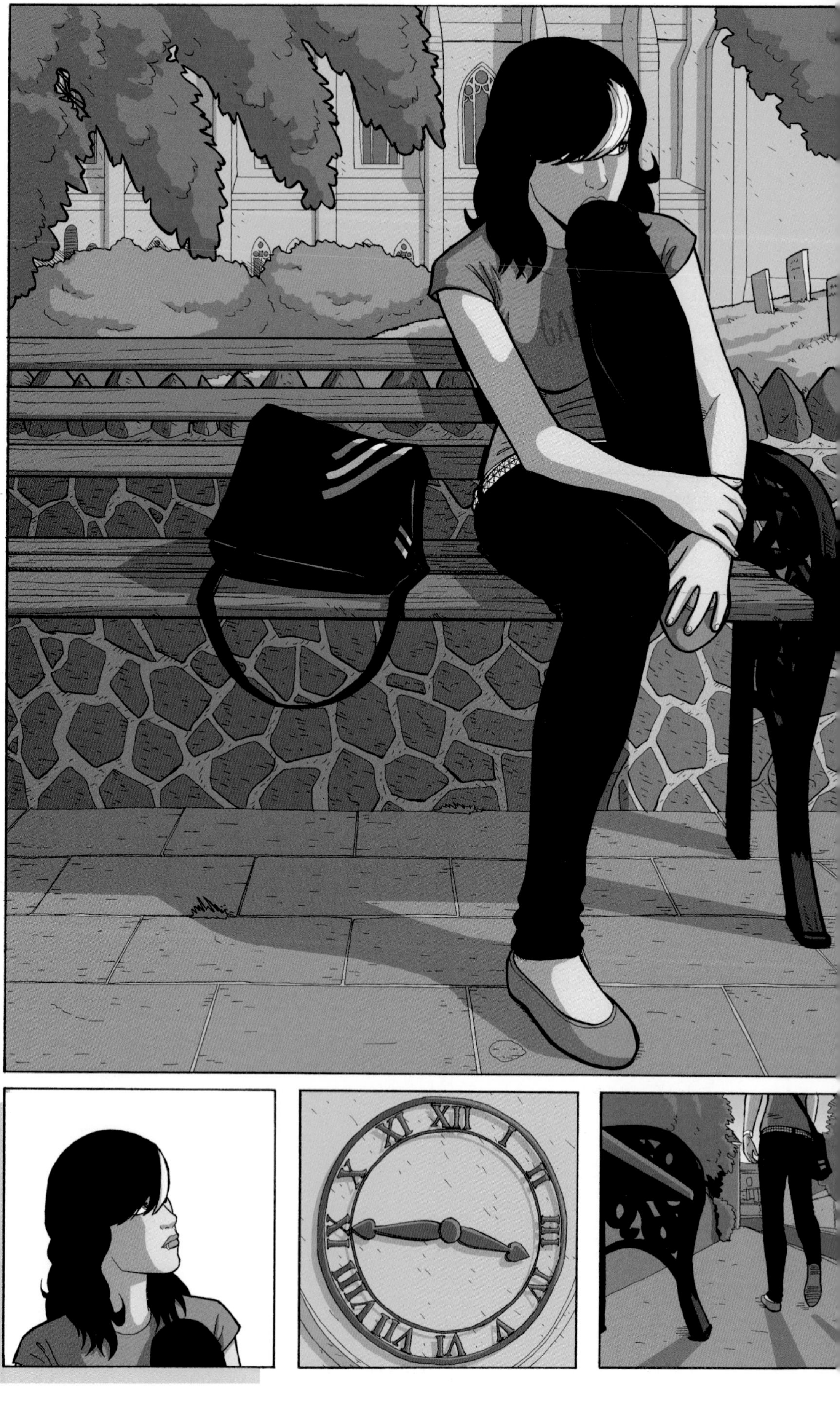

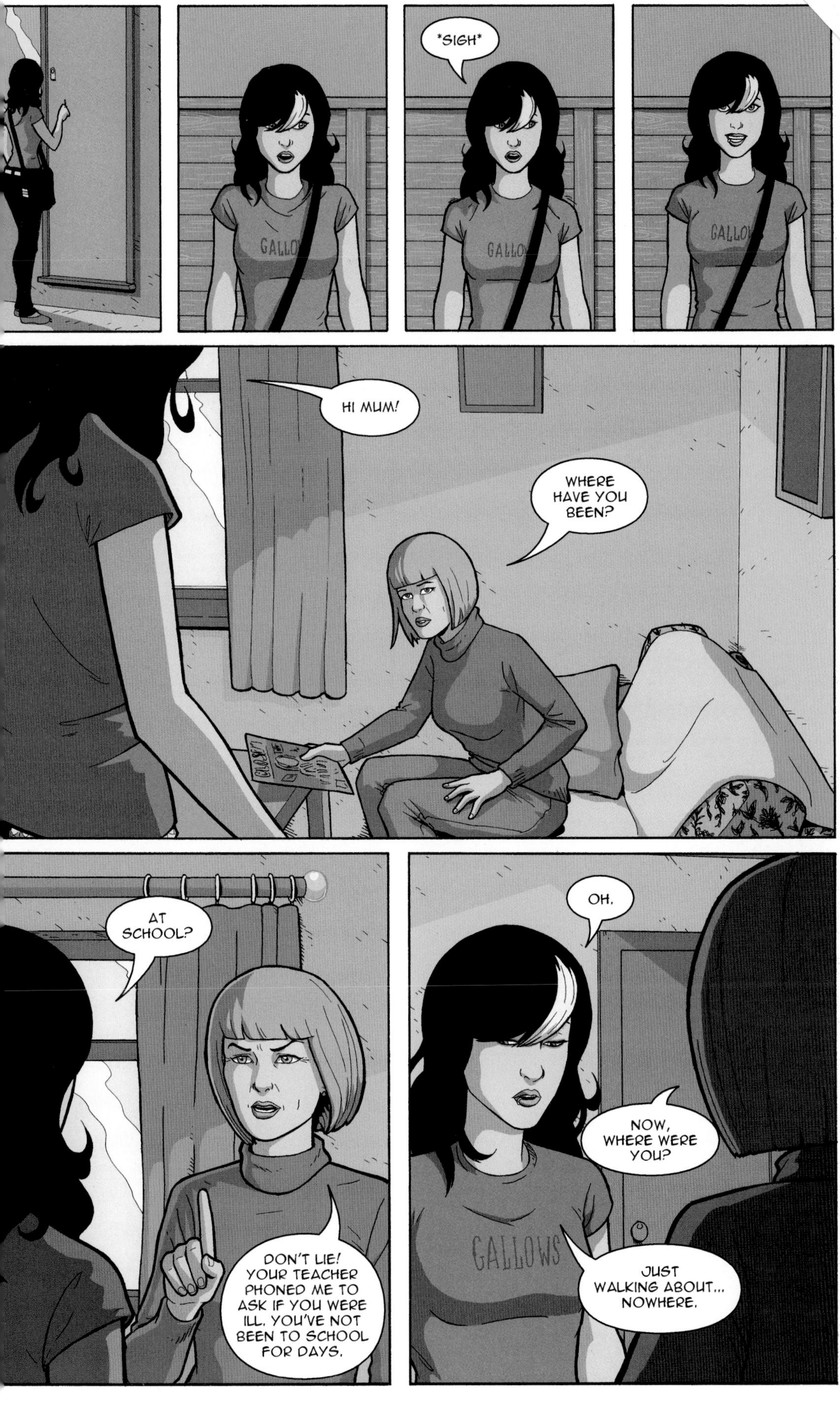
SIGH
HI MUM!
WHERE HAVE YOU BEEN?
AT SCHOOL?
DON'T LIE! YOUR TEACHER PHONED ME TO ASK IF YOU WERE ILL. YOU'VE NOT BEEN TO SCHOOL FOR DAYS.
OH.
NOW, WHERE WERE YOU?
JUST WALKING ABOUT... NOWHERE.

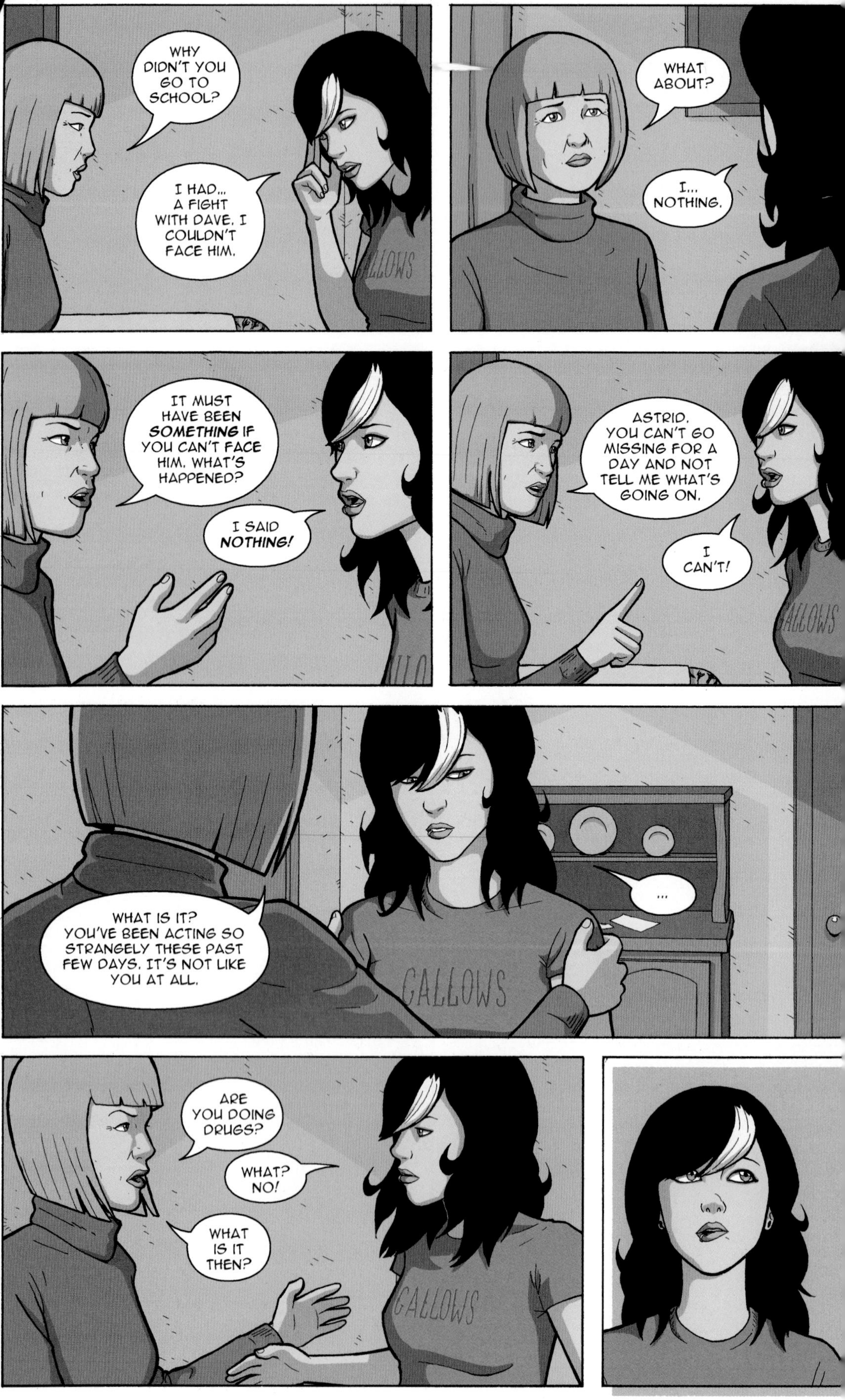
WHY DIDN'T YOU GO TO SCHOOL?
I HAD... A FIGHT WITH DAVE. I COULDN'T FACE HIM.
GALLOWS
WHAT ABOUT?
I... NOTHING.
IT MUST HAVE BEEN **SOMETHING** IF YOU CAN'T FACE HIM. WHAT'S HAPPENED?
I SAID **NOTHING!**
ASTRID. YOU CAN'T GO MISSING FOR A DAY AND NOT TELL ME WHAT'S GOING ON.
I CAN'T!
GALLOWS
...
WHAT IS IT? YOU'VE BEEN ACTING SO STRANGELY THESE PAST FEW DAYS. IT'S NOT LIKE YOU AT ALL.
GALLOWS
ARE YOU DOING DRUGS?
WHAT? NO!
WHAT IS IT THEN?
GALLOWS

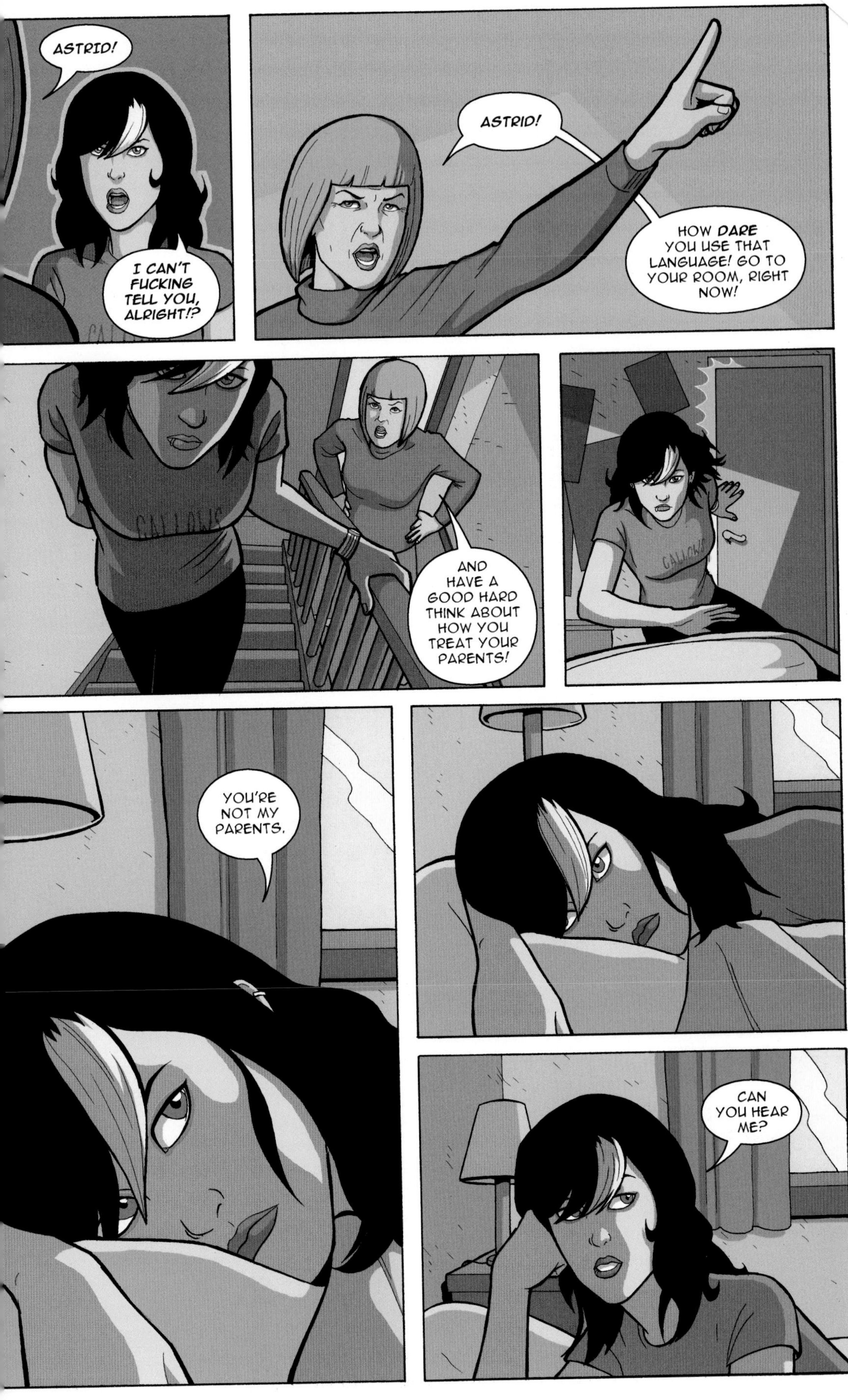
ASTRID!
I CAN'T FUCKING TELL YOU, ALRIGHT!?
ASTRID!
HOW DARE YOU USE THAT LANGUAGE! GO TO YOUR ROOM, RIGHT NOW!
AND HAVE A GOOD HARD THINK ABOUT HOW YOU TREAT YOUR PARENTS!
YOU'RE NOT MY PARENTS.
CAN YOU HEAR ME?

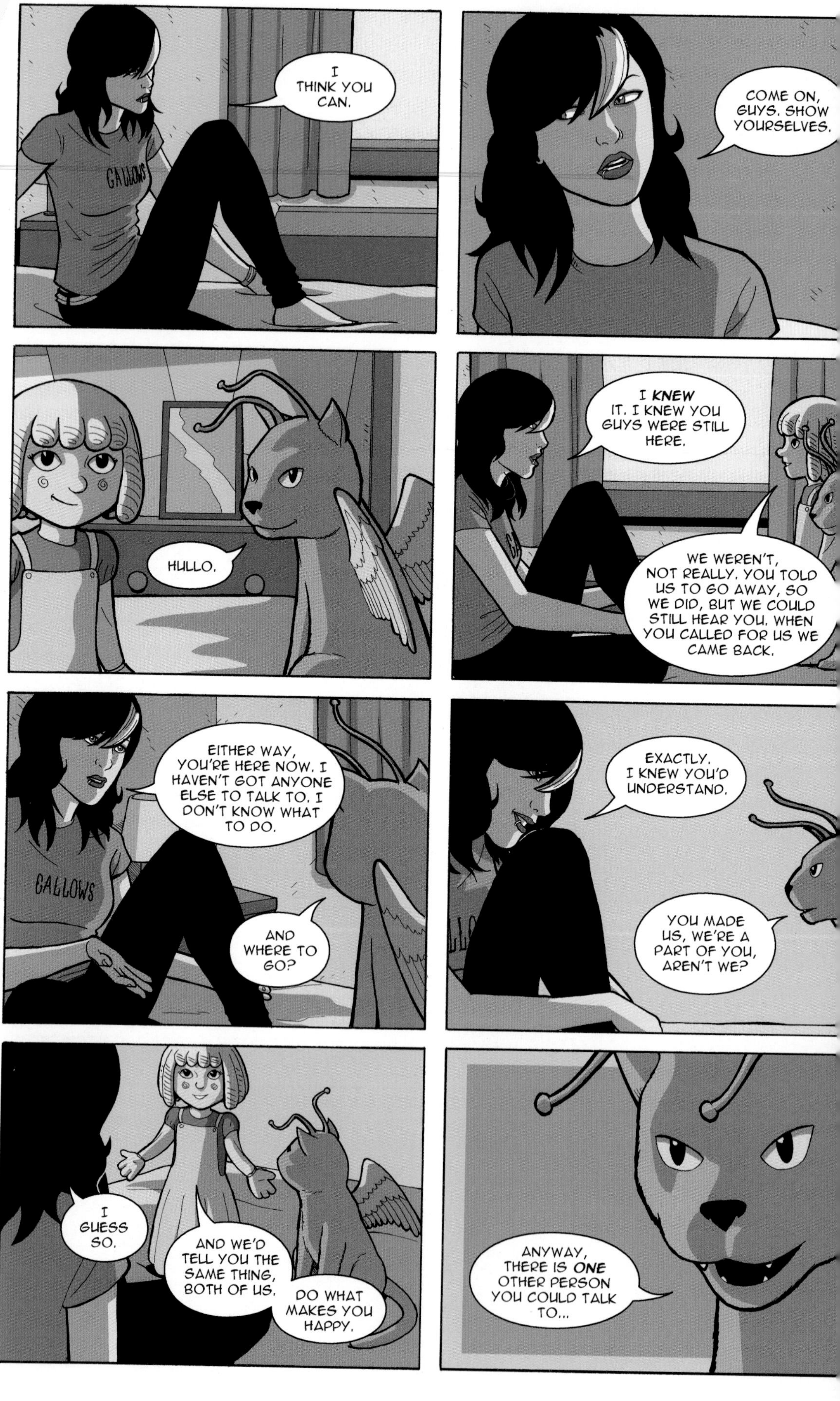
I THINK YOU CAN.
GALLOWS
COME ON, GUYS. SHOW YOURSELVES.
HULLO.
I *KNEW* IT. I KNEW YOU GUYS WERE STILL HERE.
WE WEREN'T, NOT REALLY. YOU TOLD US TO GO AWAY, SO WE DID, BUT WE COULD STILL HEAR YOU. WHEN YOU CALLED FOR US WE CAME BACK.
EITHER WAY, YOU'RE HERE NOW. I HAVEN'T GOT ANYONE ELSE TO TALK TO. I DON'T KNOW WHAT TO DO.
GALLOWS
AND WHERE TO GO?
EXACTLY. I KNEW YOU'D UNDERSTAND.
YOU MADE US, WE'RE A PART OF YOU, AREN'T WE?
I GUESS SO.
AND WE'D TELL YOU THE SAME THING, BOTH OF US.
DO WHAT MAKES YOU HAPPY.
ANYWAY, THERE IS *ONE* OTHER PERSON YOU COULD TALK TO...

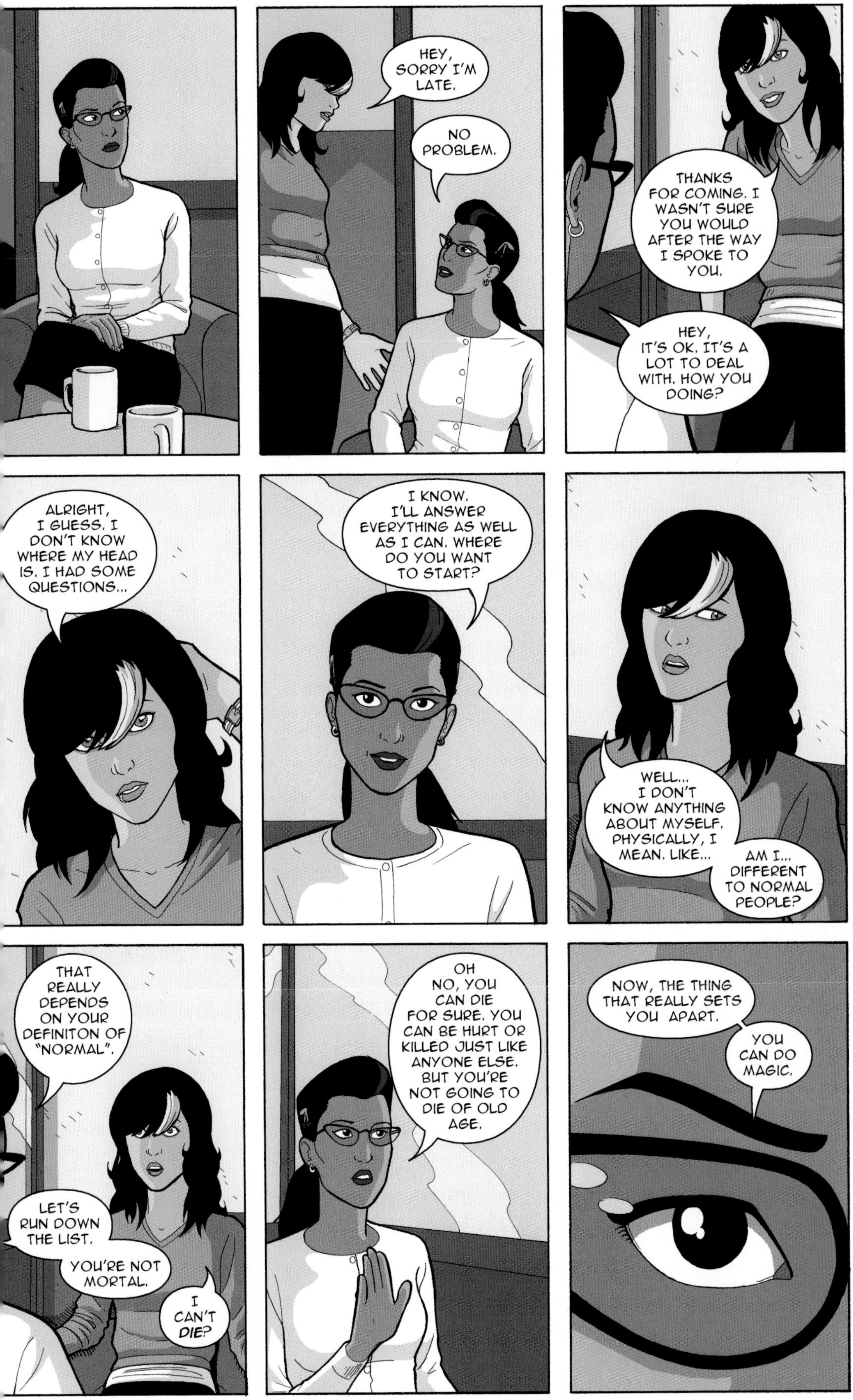
HEY, SORRY I'M LATE.
NO PROBLEM.
THANKS FOR COMING. I WASN'T SURE YOU WOULD AFTER THE WAY I SPOKE TO YOU.
HEY, IT'S OK. IT'S A LOT TO DEAL WITH. HOW YOU DOING?
ALRIGHT, I GUESS. I DON'T KNOW WHERE MY HEAD IS. I HAD SOME QUESTIONS...
I KNOW. I'LL ANSWER EVERYTHING AS WELL AS I CAN. WHERE DO YOU WANT TO START?
WELL... I DON'T KNOW ANYTHING ABOUT MYSELF. PHYSICALLY, I MEAN. LIKE...
AM I... DIFFERENT TO NORMAL PEOPLE?
THAT REALLY DEPENDS ON YOUR DEFINITON OF "NORMAL".
LET'S RUN DOWN THE LIST.
YOU'RE NOT MORTAL.
I CAN'T *DIE*?
OH NO, YOU CAN DIE FOR SURE. YOU CAN BE HURT OR KILLED JUST LIKE ANYONE ELSE. BUT YOU'RE NOT GOING TO DIE OF OLD AGE.
NOW, THE THING THAT REALLY SETS YOU APART.
YOU CAN DO MAGIC.

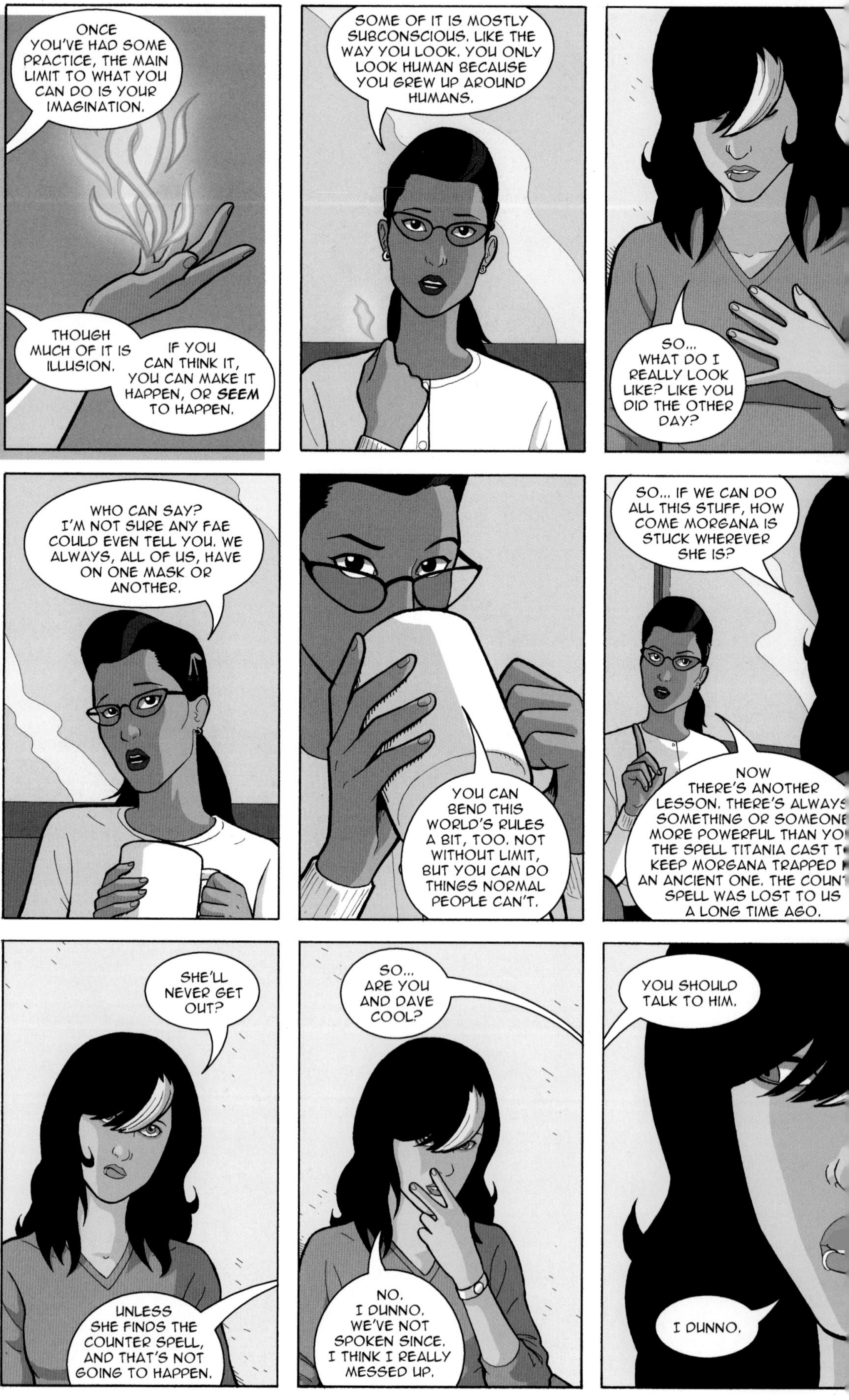
ONCE YOU'VE HAD SOME PRACTICE, THE MAIN LIMIT TO WHAT YOU CAN DO IS YOUR IMAGINATION.
THOUGH MUCH OF IT IS ILLUSION.
IF YOU CAN THINK IT, YOU CAN MAKE IT HAPPEN, OR SEEM TO HAPPEN.
SOME OF IT IS MOSTLY SUBCONSCIOUS. LIKE THE WAY YOU LOOK. YOU ONLY LOOK HUMAN BECAUSE YOU GREW UP AROUND HUMANS.
SO... WHAT DO I REALLY LOOK LIKE? LIKE YOU DID THE OTHER DAY?
WHO CAN SAY? I'M NOT SURE ANY FAE COULD EVEN TELL YOU. WE ALWAYS, ALL OF US, HAVE ON ONE MASK OR ANOTHER.
YOU CAN BEND THIS WORLD'S RULES A BIT, TOO. NOT WITHOUT LIMIT, BUT YOU CAN DO THINGS NORMAL PEOPLE CAN'T.
SO... IF WE CAN DO ALL THIS STUFF, HOW COME MORGANA IS STUCK WHEREVER SHE IS?
NOW THERE'S ANOTHER LESSON. THERE'S ALWAYS SOMETHING OR SOMEONE MORE POWERFUL THAN YO THE SPELL TITANIA CAST T KEEP MORGANA TRAPPED AN ANCIENT ONE. THE COUN SPELL WAS LOST TO US A LONG TIME AGO.
SHE'LL NEVER GET OUT?
UNLESS SHE FINDS THE COUNTER SPELL, AND THAT'S NOT GOING TO HAPPEN.
SO... ARE YOU AND DAVE COOL?
NO. I DUNNO. WE'VE NOT SPOKEN SINCE. I THINK I REALLY MESSED UP.
YOU SHOULD TALK TO HIM.
I DUNNO.

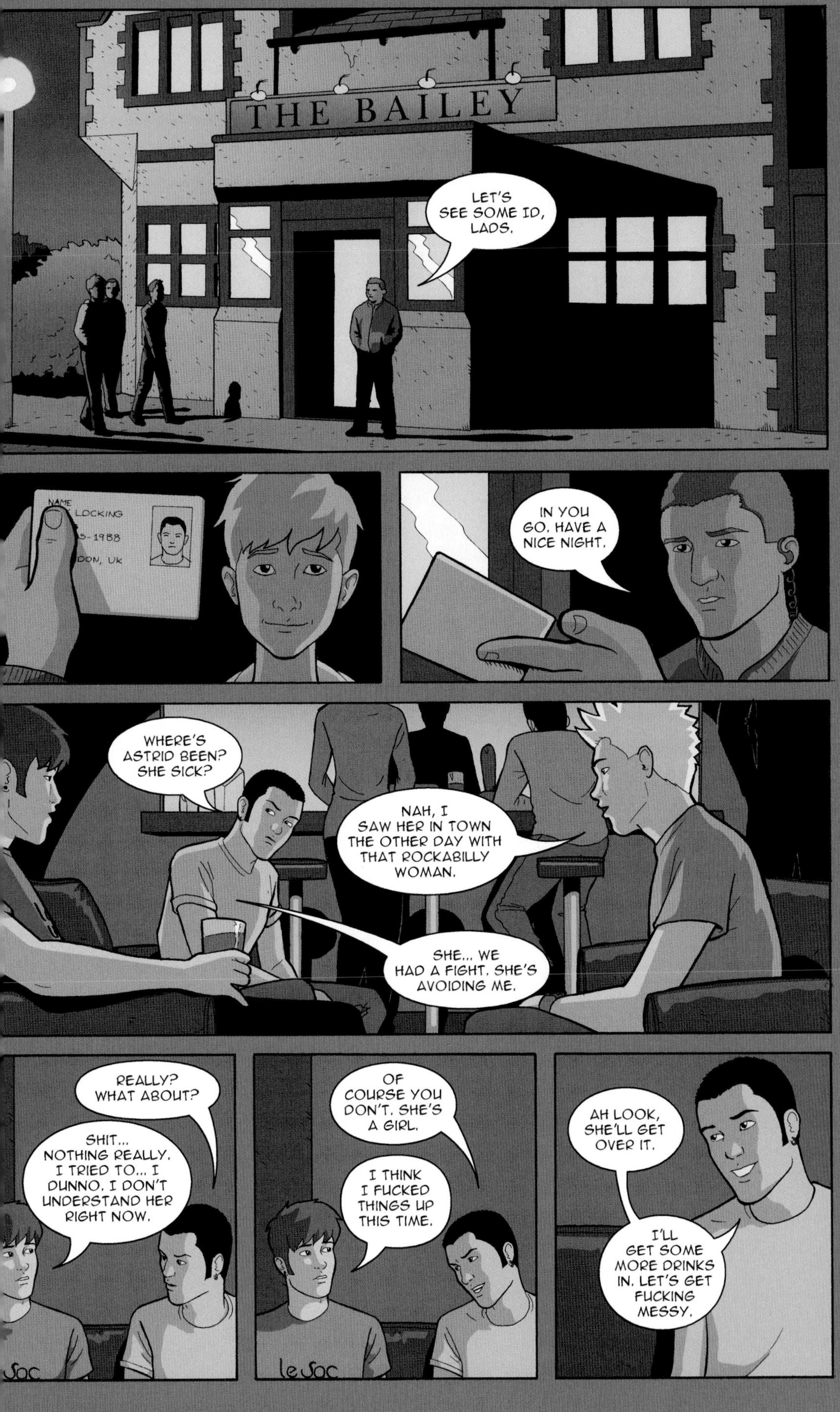
THE BAILEY
LET'S SEE SOME ID, LADS.
NAME
LOCKING
5-1988
DON, UK
IN YOU GO. HAVE A NICE NIGHT.
WHERE'S ASTRID BEEN? SHE SICK?
NAH, I SAW HER IN TOWN THE OTHER DAY WITH THAT ROCKABILLY WOMAN.
SHE... WE HAD A FIGHT. SHE'S AVOIDING ME.
REALLY? WHAT ABOUT?
SHIT... NOTHING REALLY. I TRIED TO... I DUNNO. I DON'T UNDERSTAND HER RIGHT NOW.
OF COURSE YOU DON'T. SHE'S A GIRL.
I THINK I FUCKED THINGS UP THIS TIME.
AH LOOK, SHE'LL GET OVER IT.
I'LL GET SOME MORE DRINKS IN. LET'S GET FUCKING MESSY.

ALRIGHT. BACK IN A MINUTE.

...ASTRID?

YOU'RE MUM
It's "your" you idiot

GILLEN'S A KNOB

For a good time call

YEAH, SHE'S WEIRD BUT SHE'S FIT, RIGHT.

WELL FUCKING UPTIGHT, THOUGH. I HAD TO GIVE HER SOME SPEED JUST TO LIVEN HER UP.

AND YOU STILL DIDN'T PULL HER!

MATTER OF TIME, MA—

SLAM

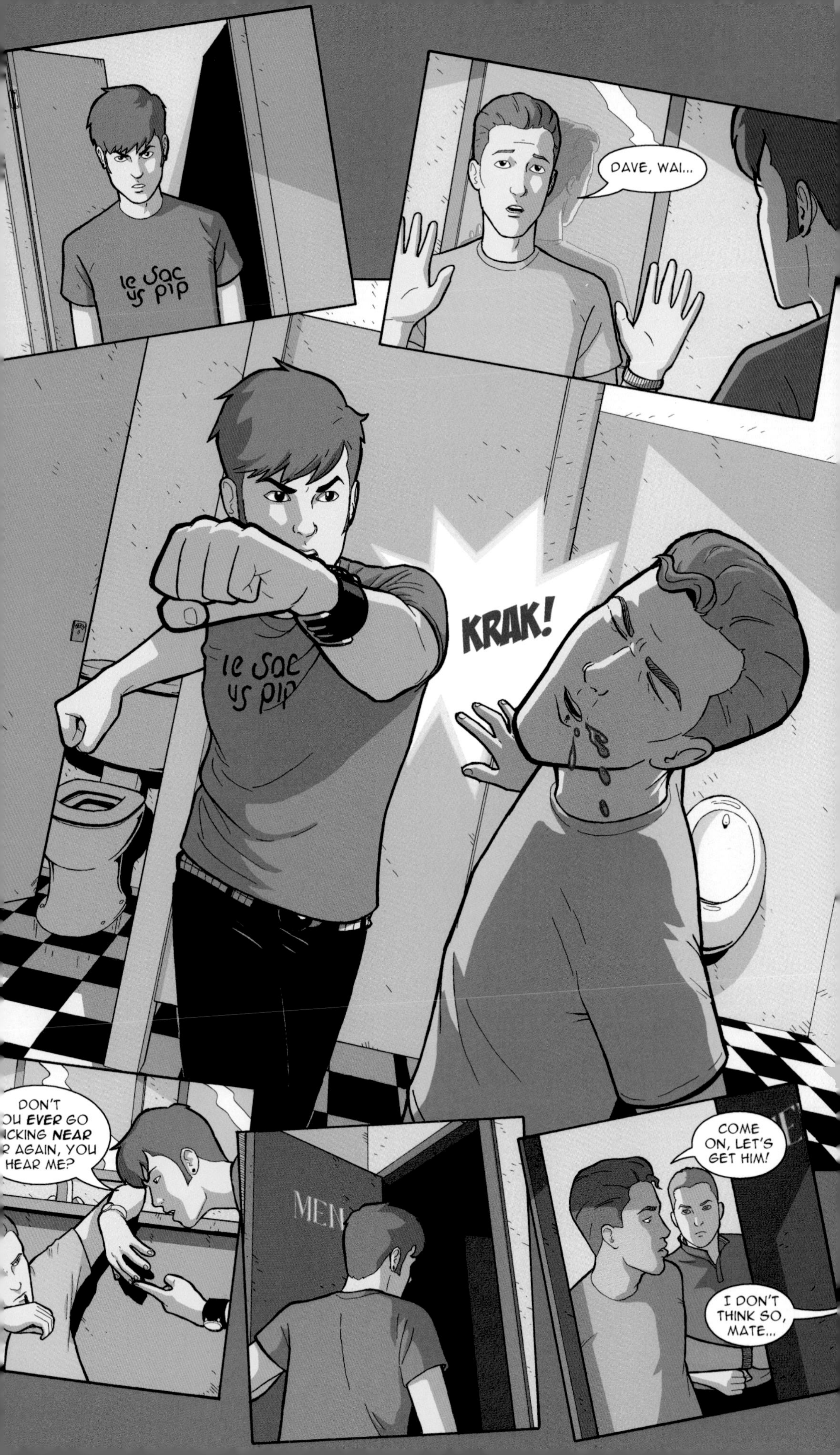
le sac
us pip
DAVE, WAI...
KRAK!
DON'T
OU EVER GO
ICKING NEAR
R AGAIN, YOU
HEAR ME?
MEN
COME
ON, LET'S
GET HIM!
I DON'T
THINK SO,
MATE...

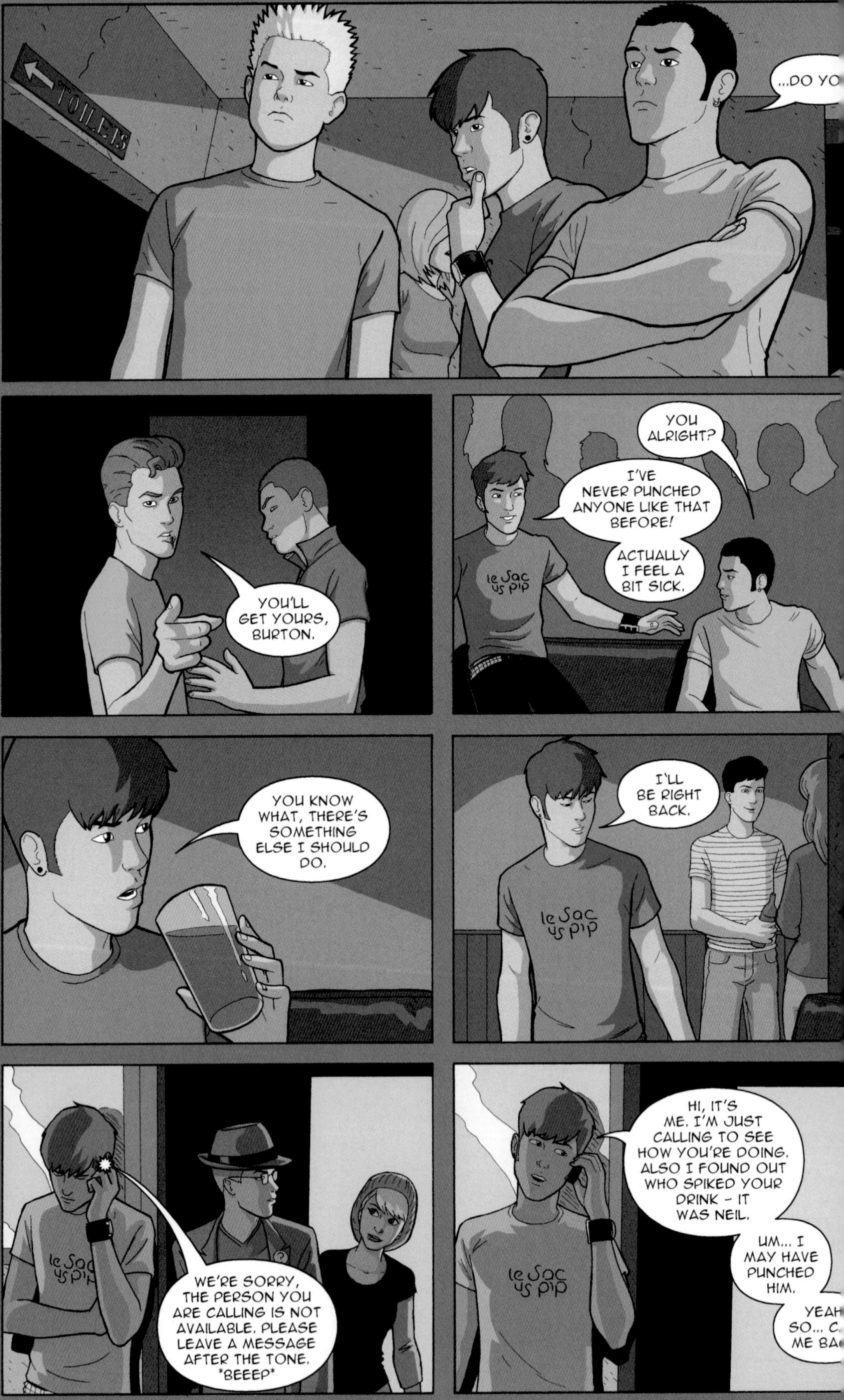
TOILETS
...DO YO
YOU'LL GET YOURS, BURTON.
YOU ALRIGHT?
I'VE NEVER PUNCHED ANYONE LIKE THAT BEFORE!
ACTUALLY I FEEL A BIT SICK.
le Sac us pip
YOU KNOW WHAT, THERE'S SOMETHING ELSE I SHOULD DO.
I'LL BE RIGHT BACK.
WE'RE SORRY, THE PERSON YOU ARE CALLING IS NOT AVAILABLE. PLEASE LEAVE A MESSAGE AFTER THE TONE. *BEEEP*
HI, IT'S ME. I'M JUST CALLING TO SEE HOW YOU'RE DOING. ALSO I FOUND OUT WHO SPIKED YOUR DRINK – IT WAS NEIL.
UM... I MAY HAVE PUNCHED HIM.
YEAH SO... C ME BA

...TO DELETE THIS MESSAGE, PRESS 3.

BEEP!

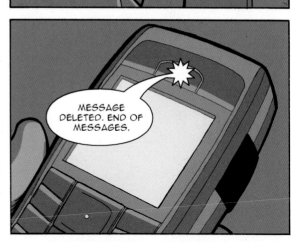

MESSAGE DELETED. END OF MESSAGES.

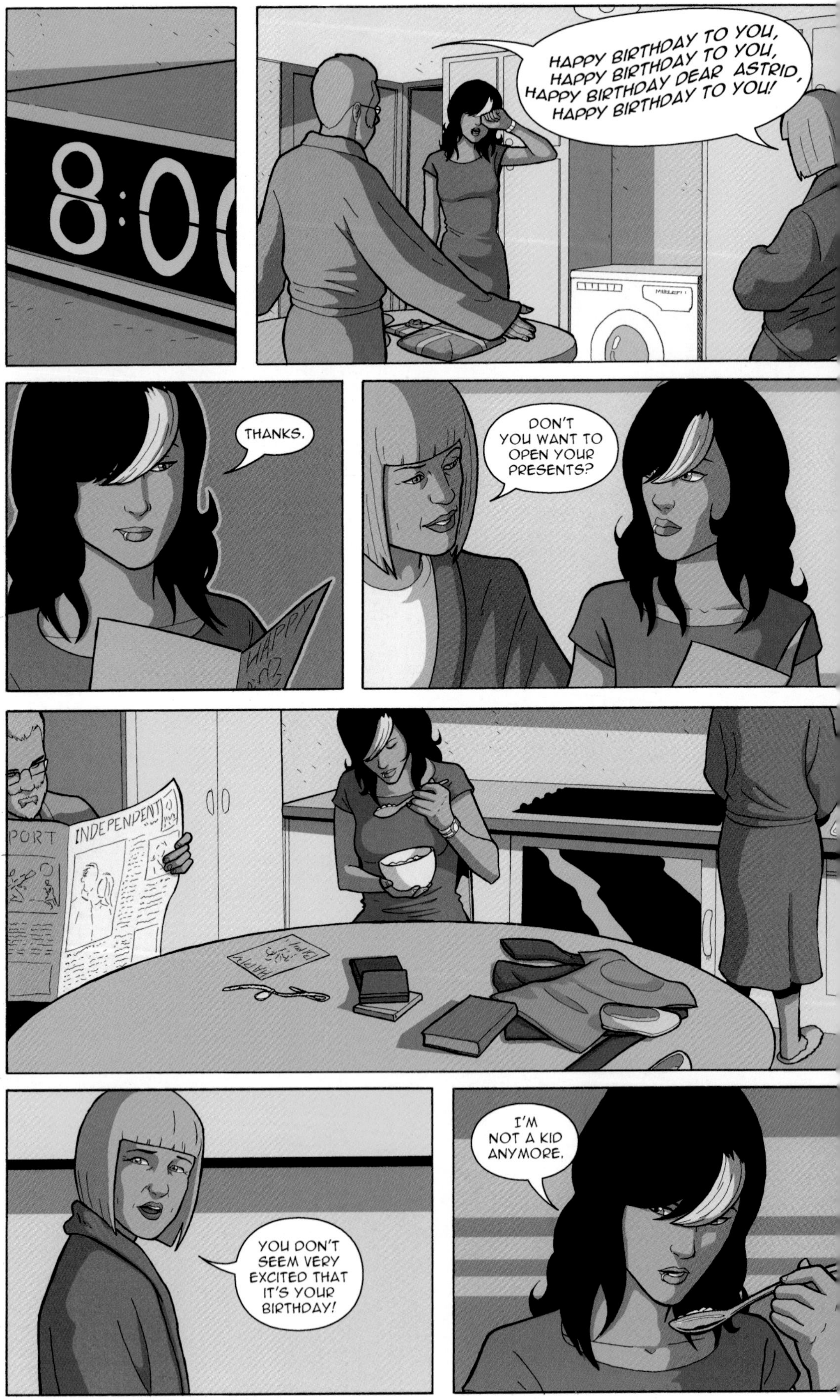
HAPPY BIRTHDAY TO YOU, HAPPY BIRTHDAY TO YOU, HAPPY BIRTHDAY DEAR ASTRID, HAPPY BIRTHDAY TO YOU!
THANKS.
DON'T YOU WANT TO OPEN YOUR PRESENTS?
INDEPENDENT
SPORT
YOU DON'T SEEM VERY EXCITED THAT IT'S YOUR BIRTHDAY!
I'M NOT A KID ANYMORE.

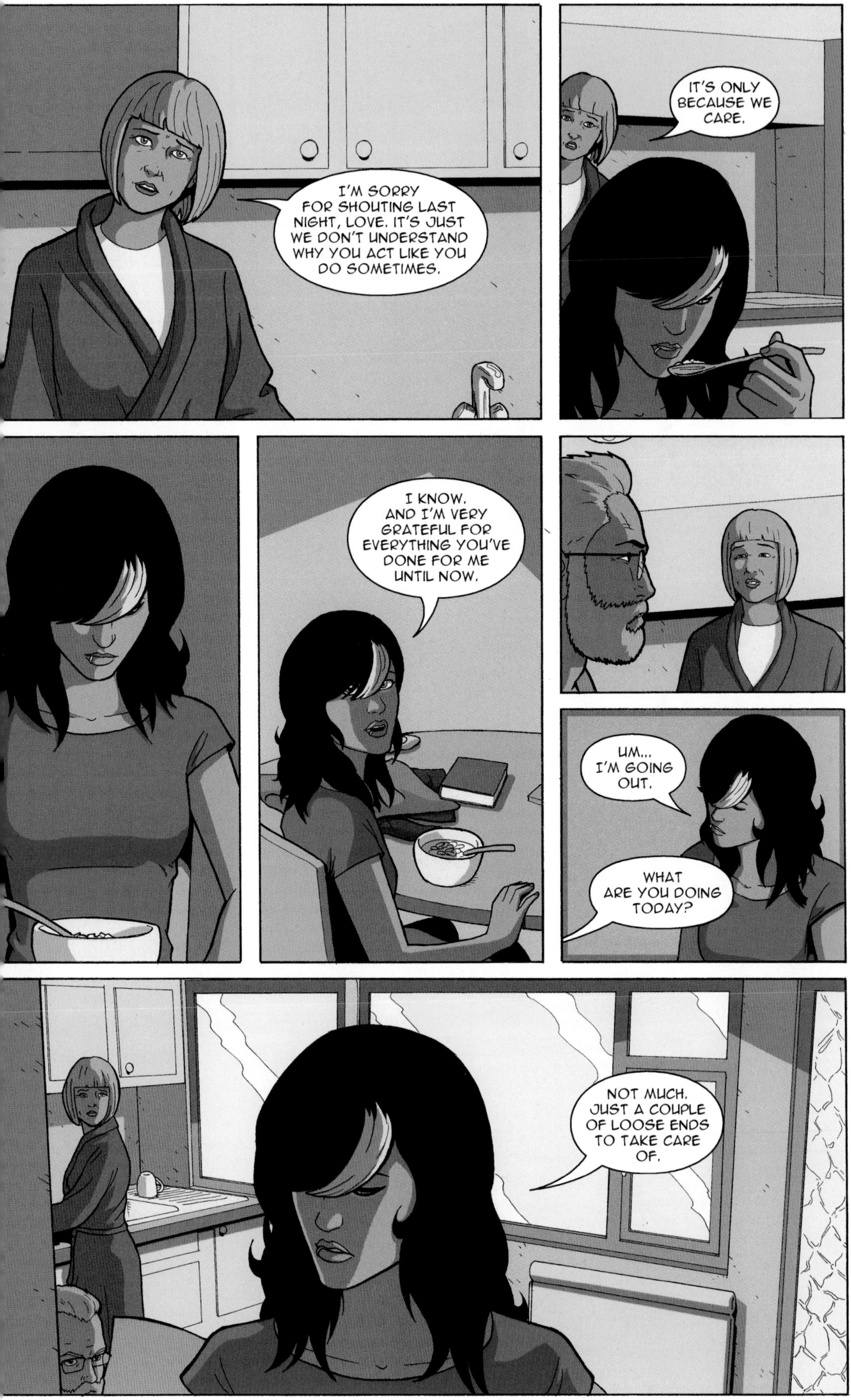
I'M SORRY FOR SHOUTING LAST NIGHT, LOVE. IT'S JUST WE DON'T UNDERSTAND WHY YOU ACT LIKE YOU DO SOMETIMES.
IT'S ONLY BECAUSE WE CARE.
I KNOW. AND I'M VERY GRATEFUL FOR EVERYTHING YOU'VE DONE FOR ME UNTIL NOW.
UM... I'M GOING OUT.
WHAT ARE YOU DOING TODAY?
NOT MUCH. JUST A COUPLE OF LOOSE ENDS TO TAKE CARE OF.

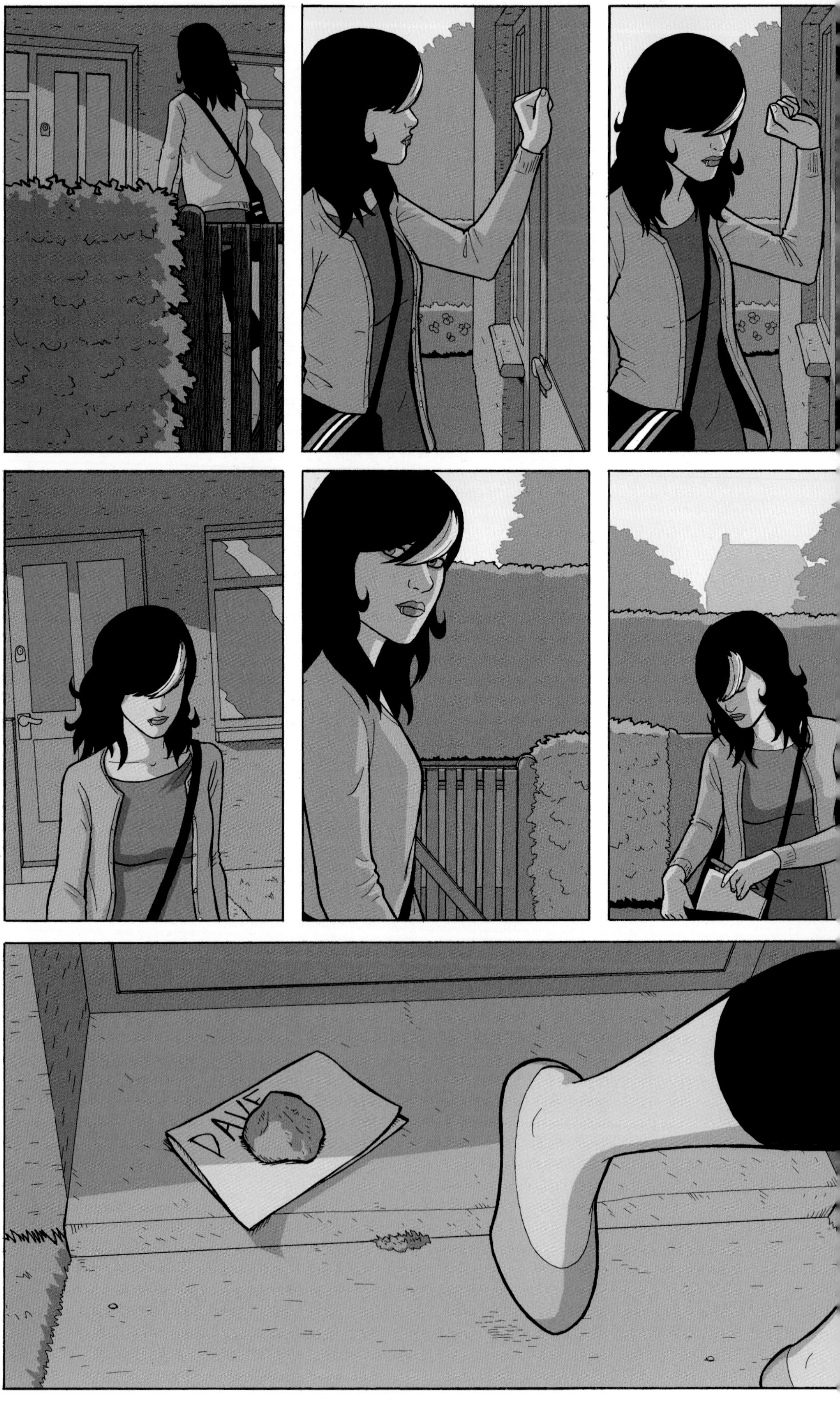
DAVE

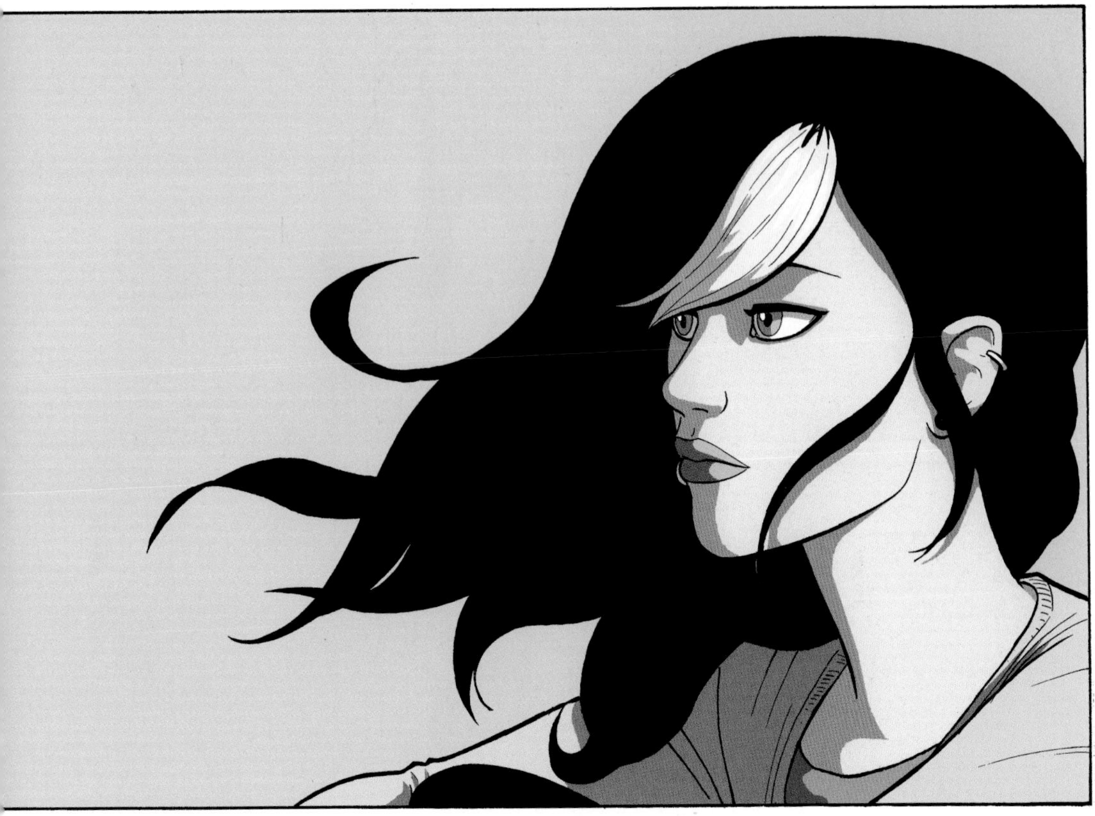

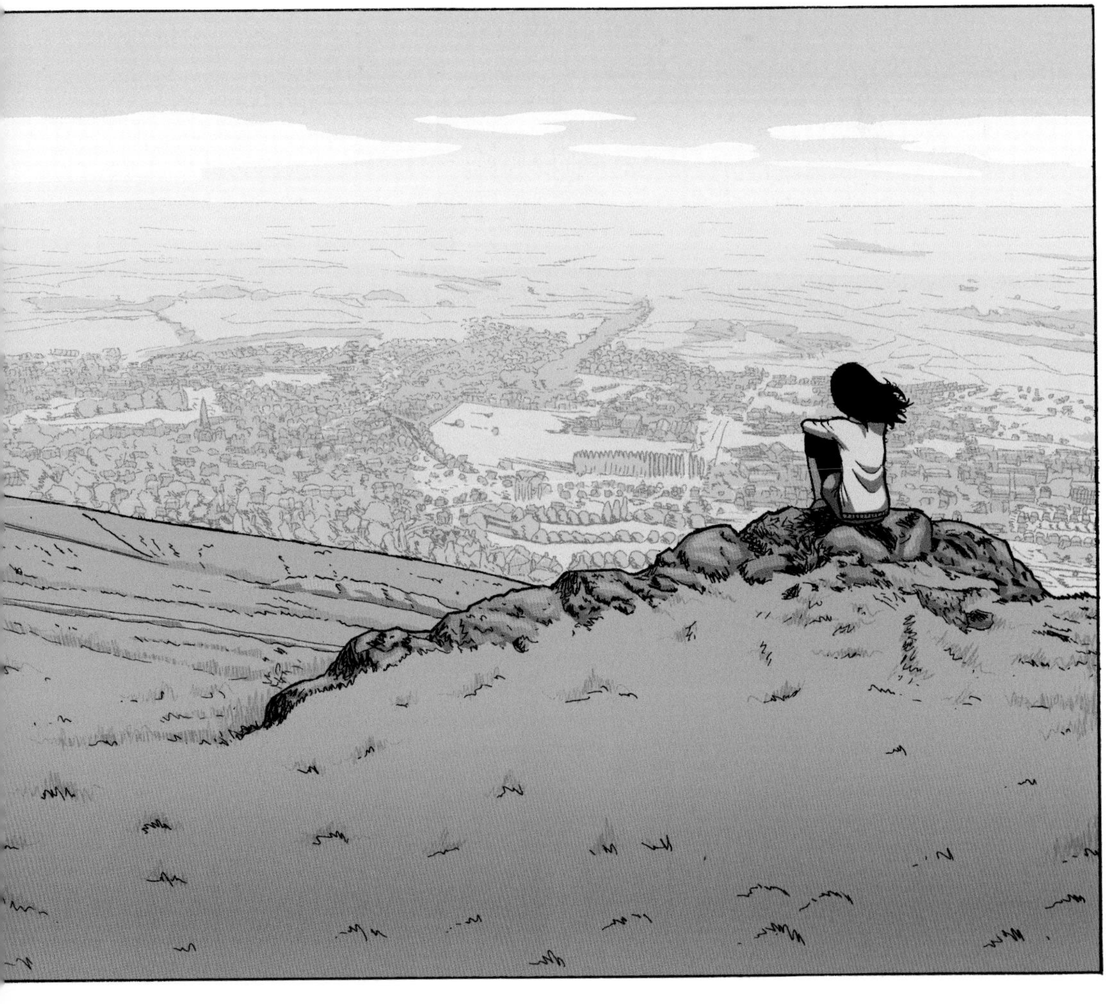

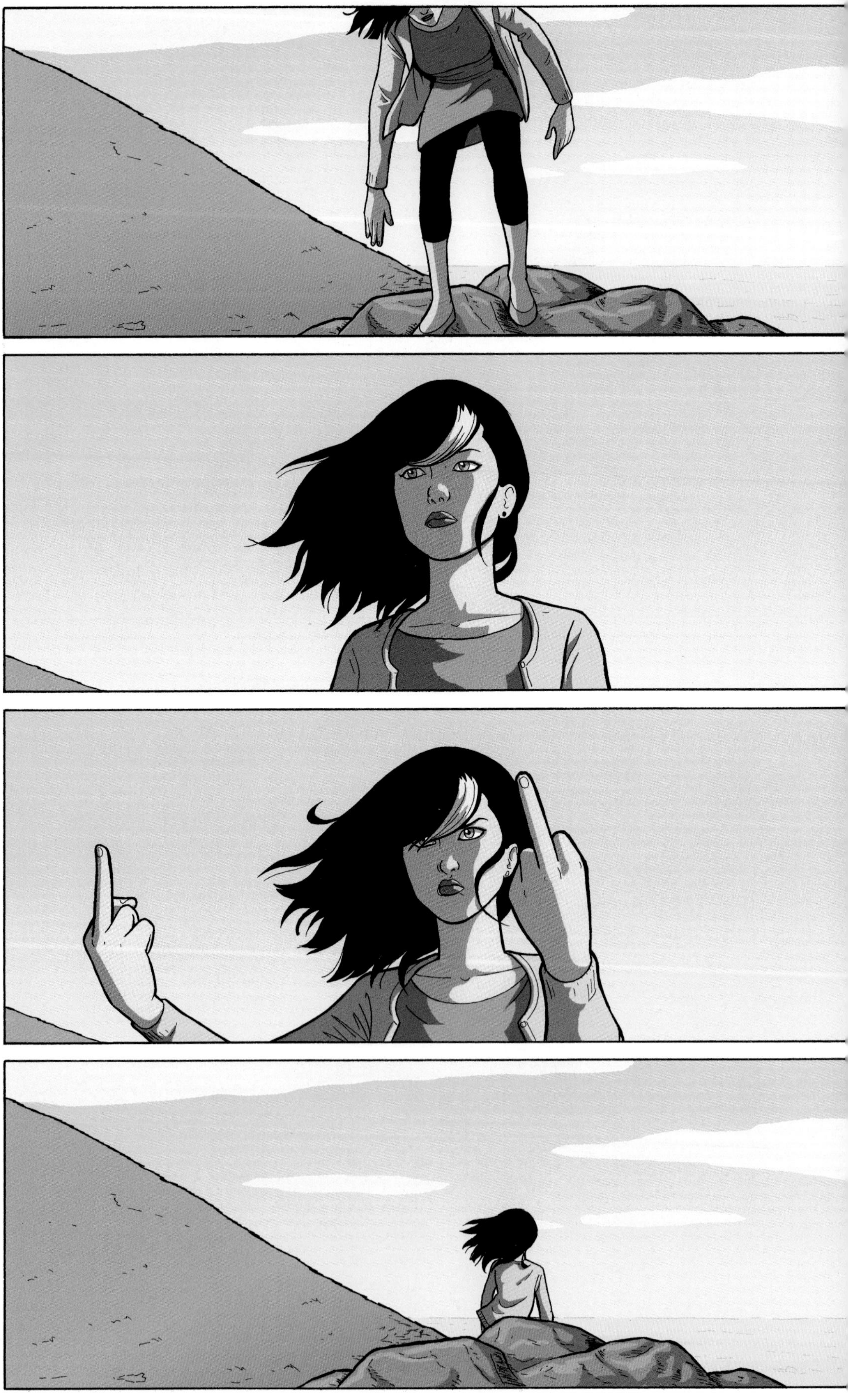

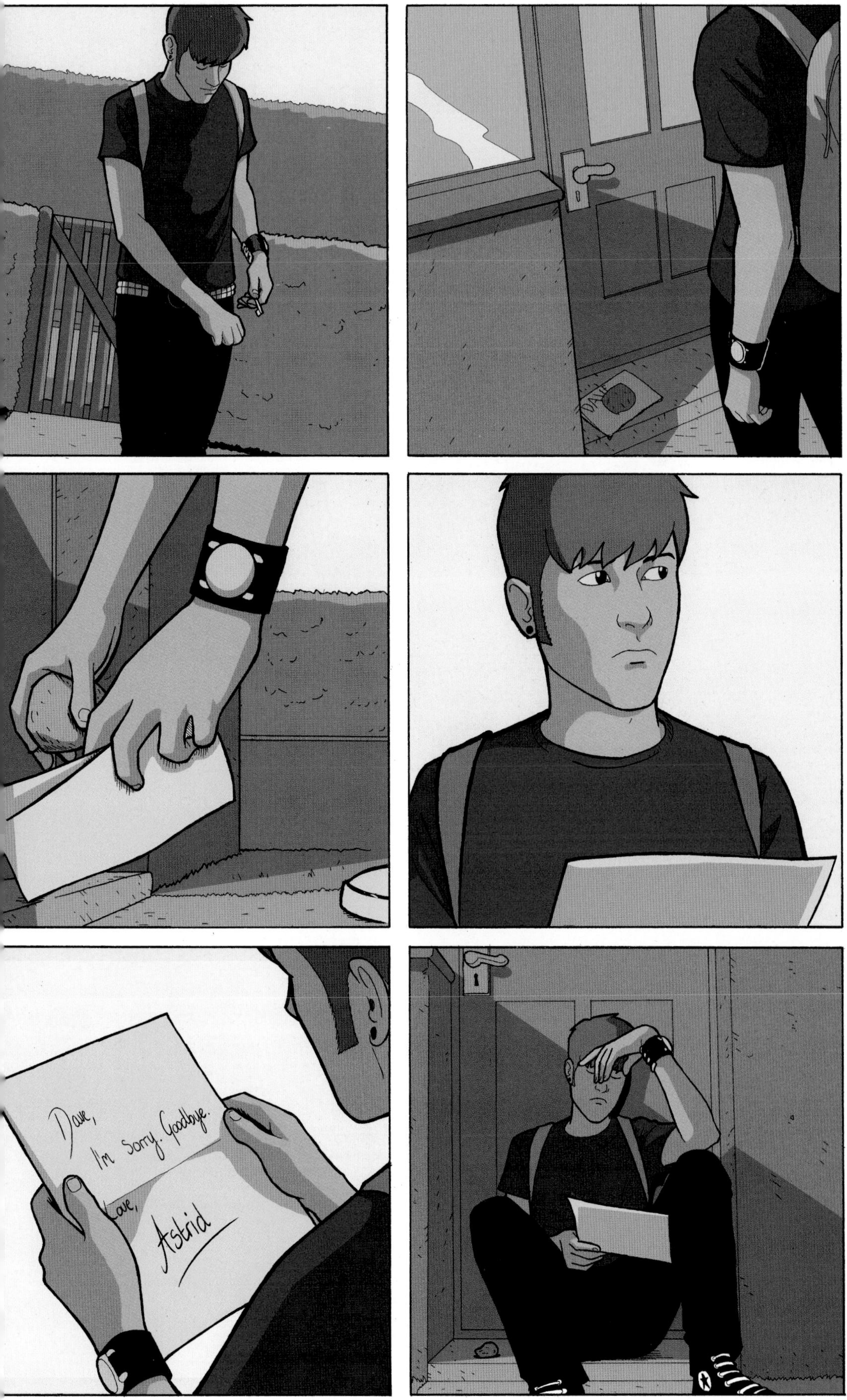
DAVE
Dave,
I'm Sorry. Goodbye.
Love,
Astrid

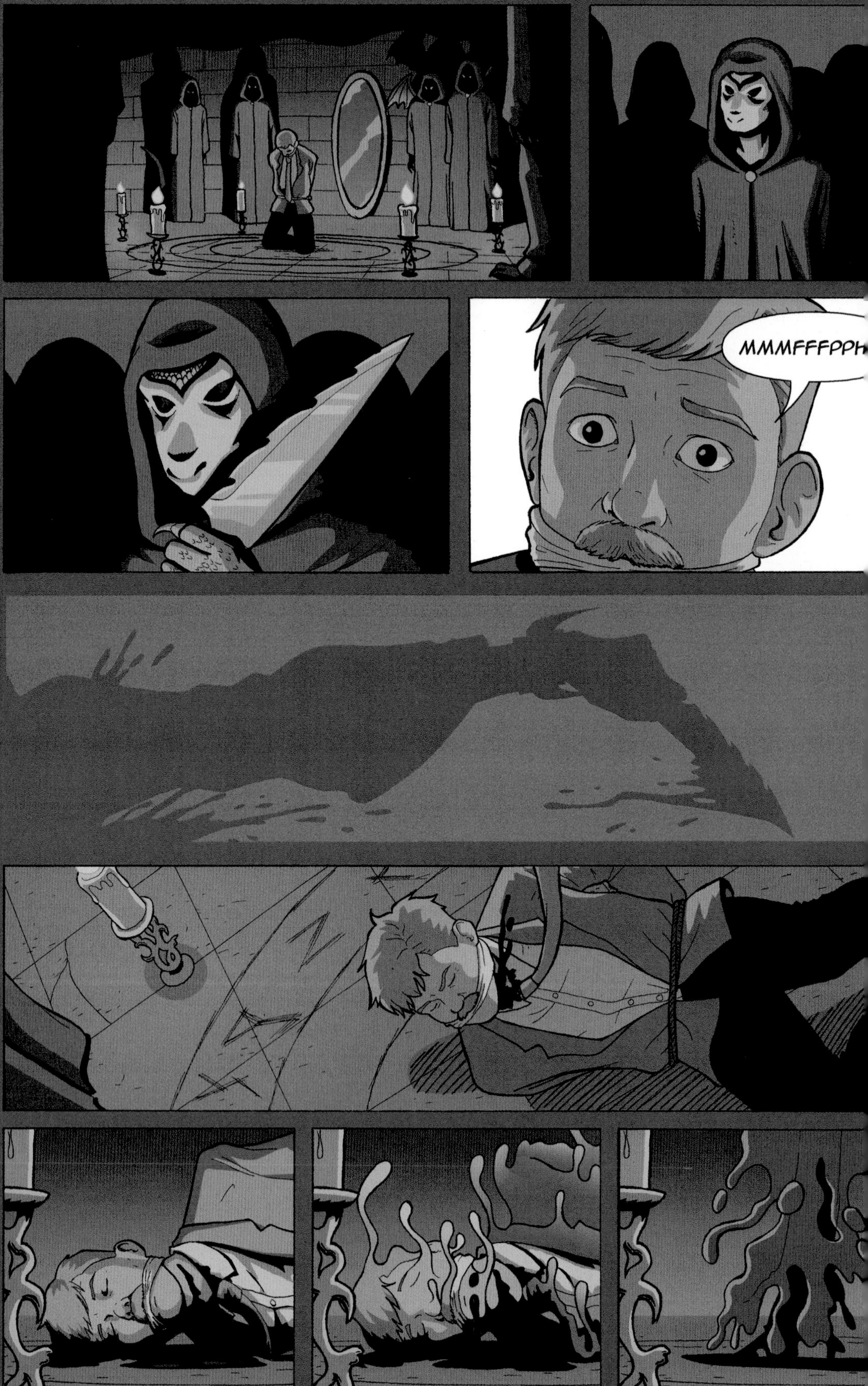
MMMFFFPPH

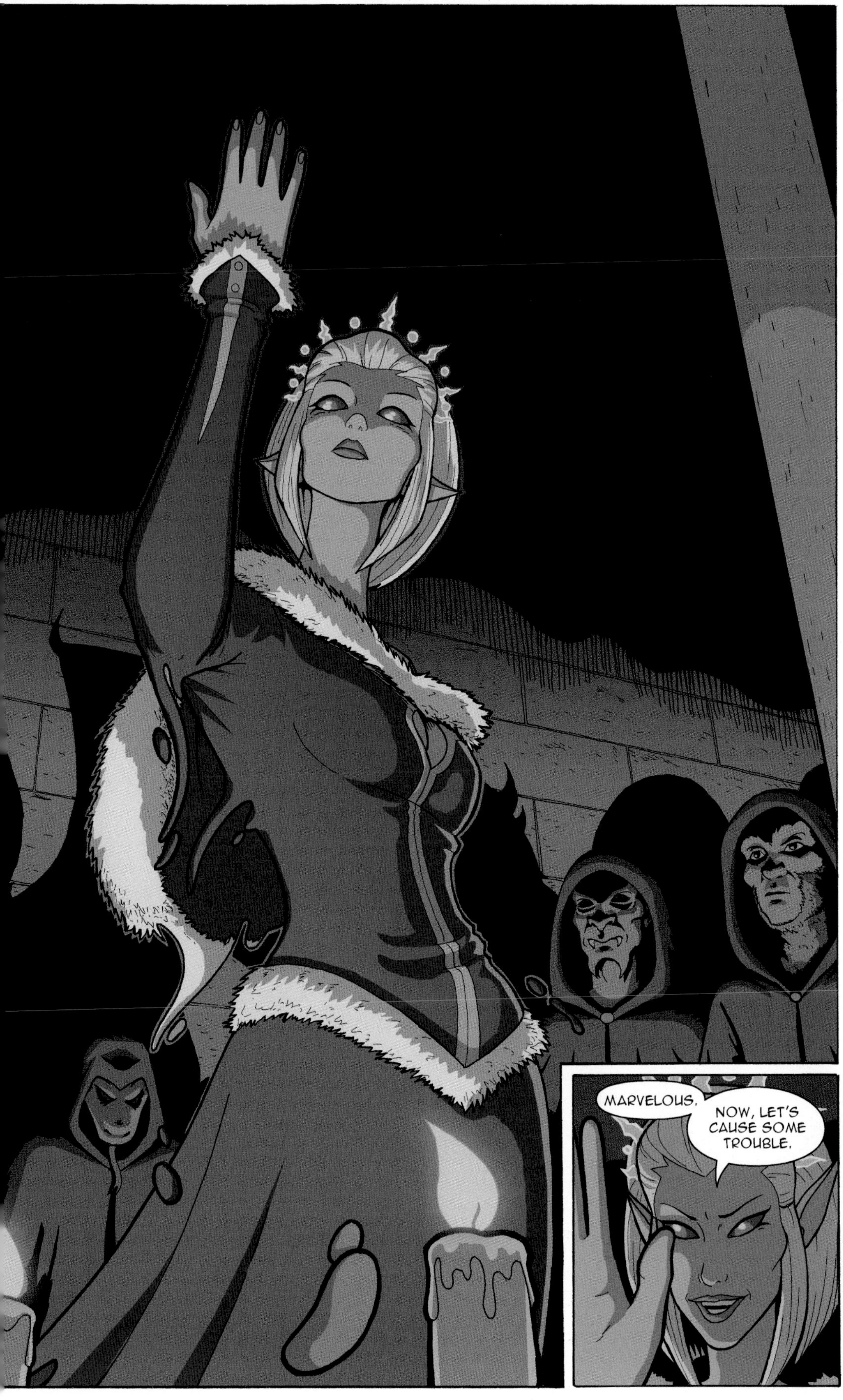
MARVELOUS.
NOW, LET'S CAUSE SOME TROUBLE.

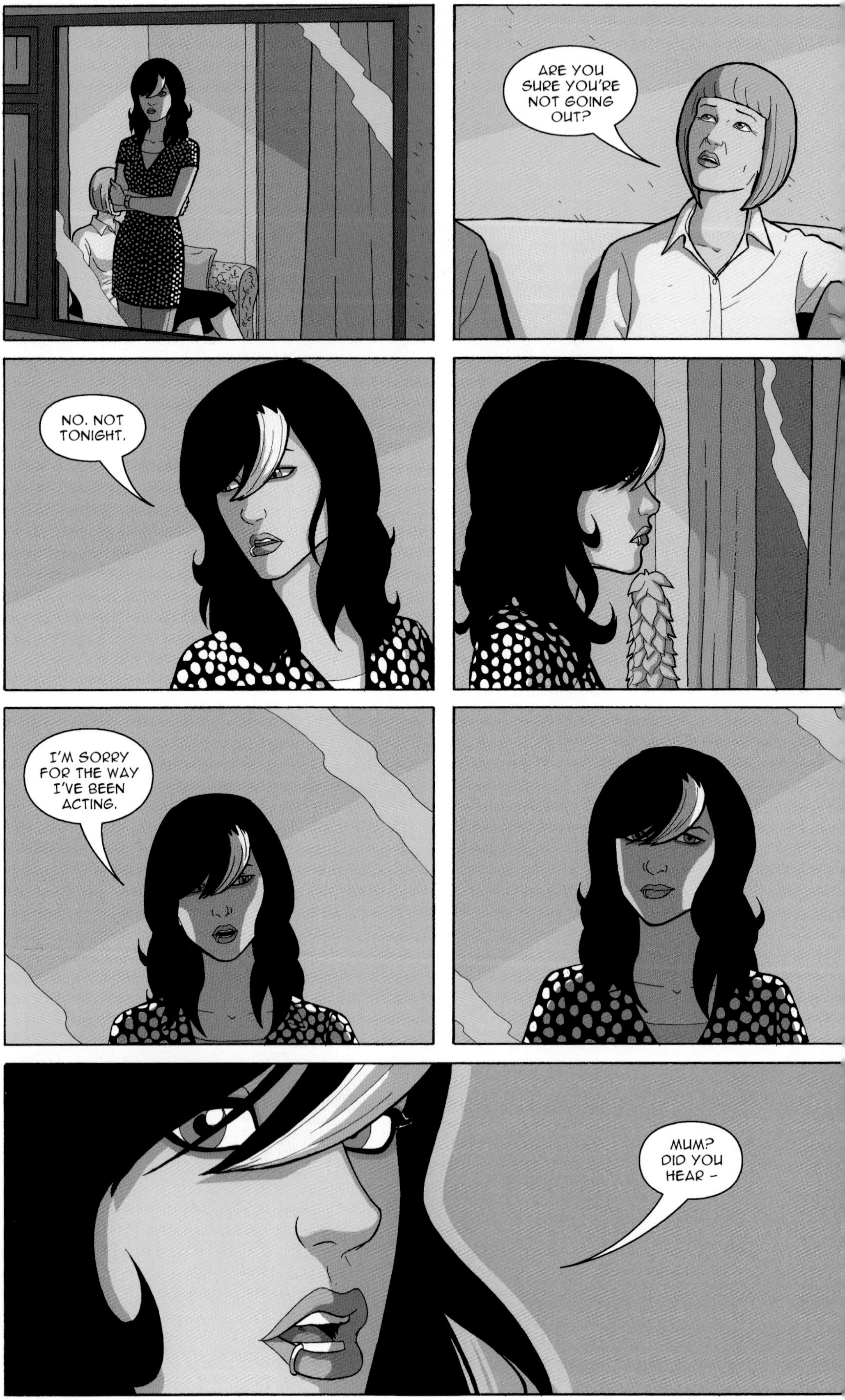

ARE YOU SURE YOU'RE NOT GOING OUT?
NO. NOT TONIGHT.
I'M SORRY FOR THE WAY I'VE BEEN ACTING.
MUM? DID YOU HEAR -

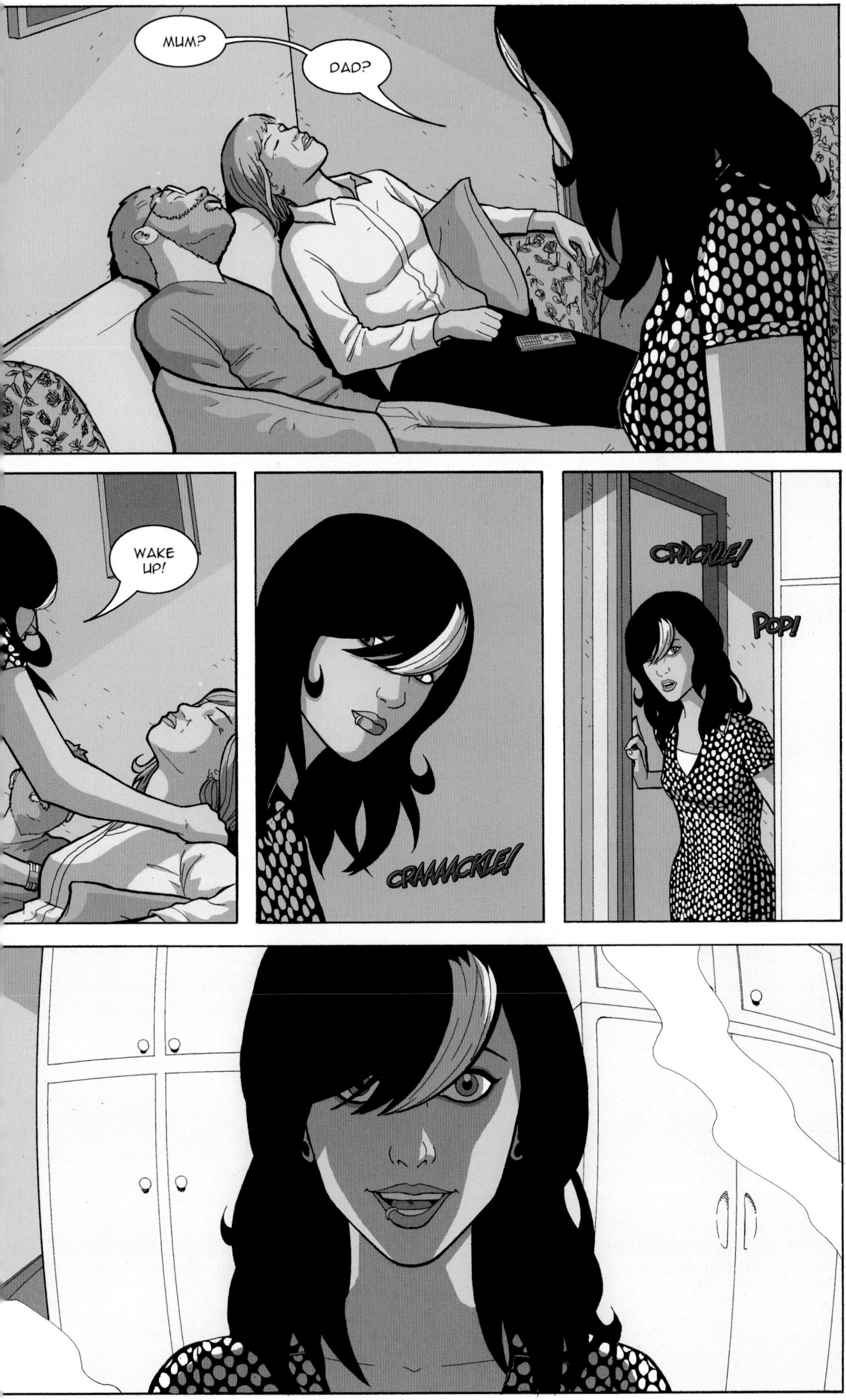
MUM?
DAD?
WAKE UP!
CRAAAACKLE!
CRACKLE!
POP!

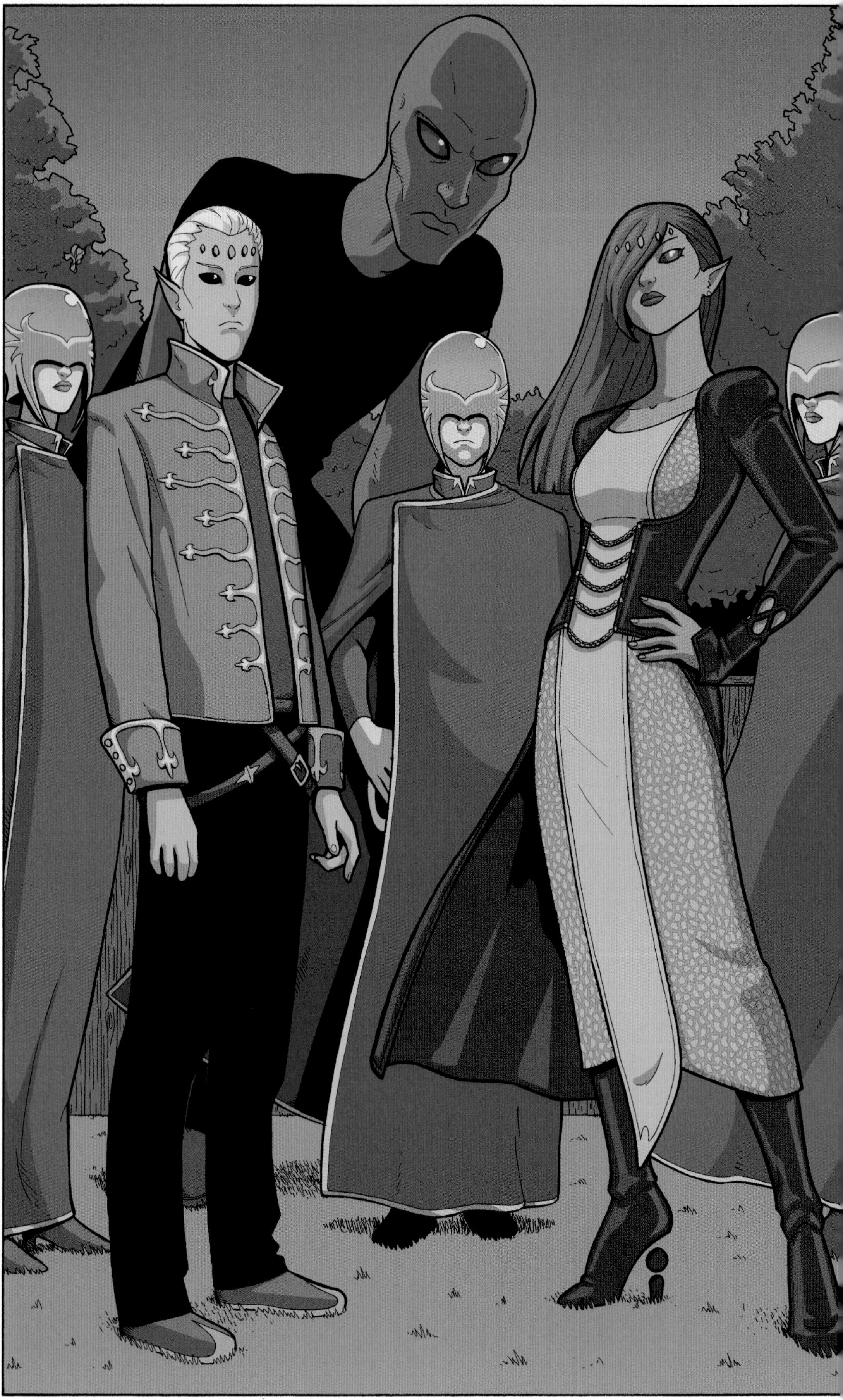

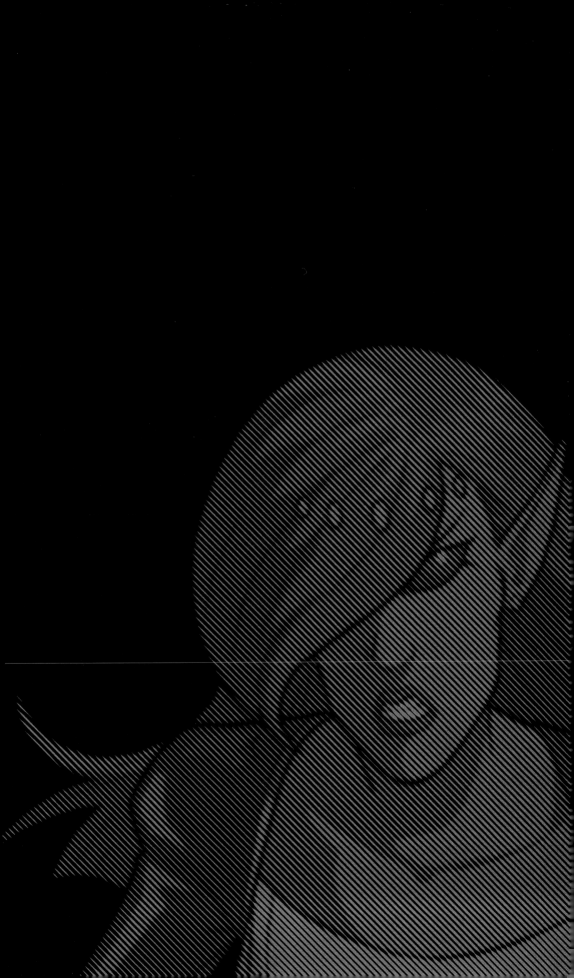

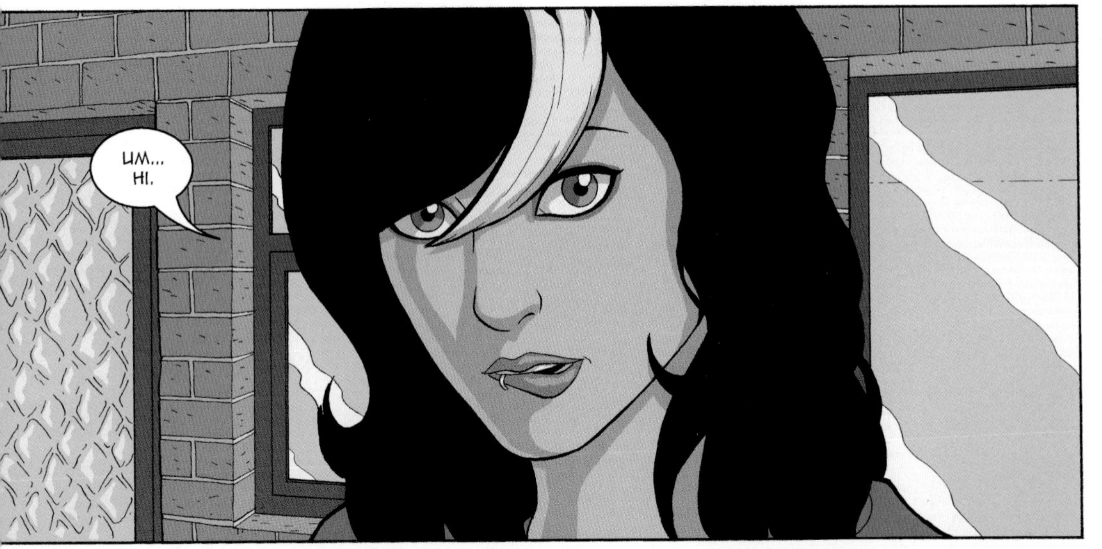
UM...
HI.

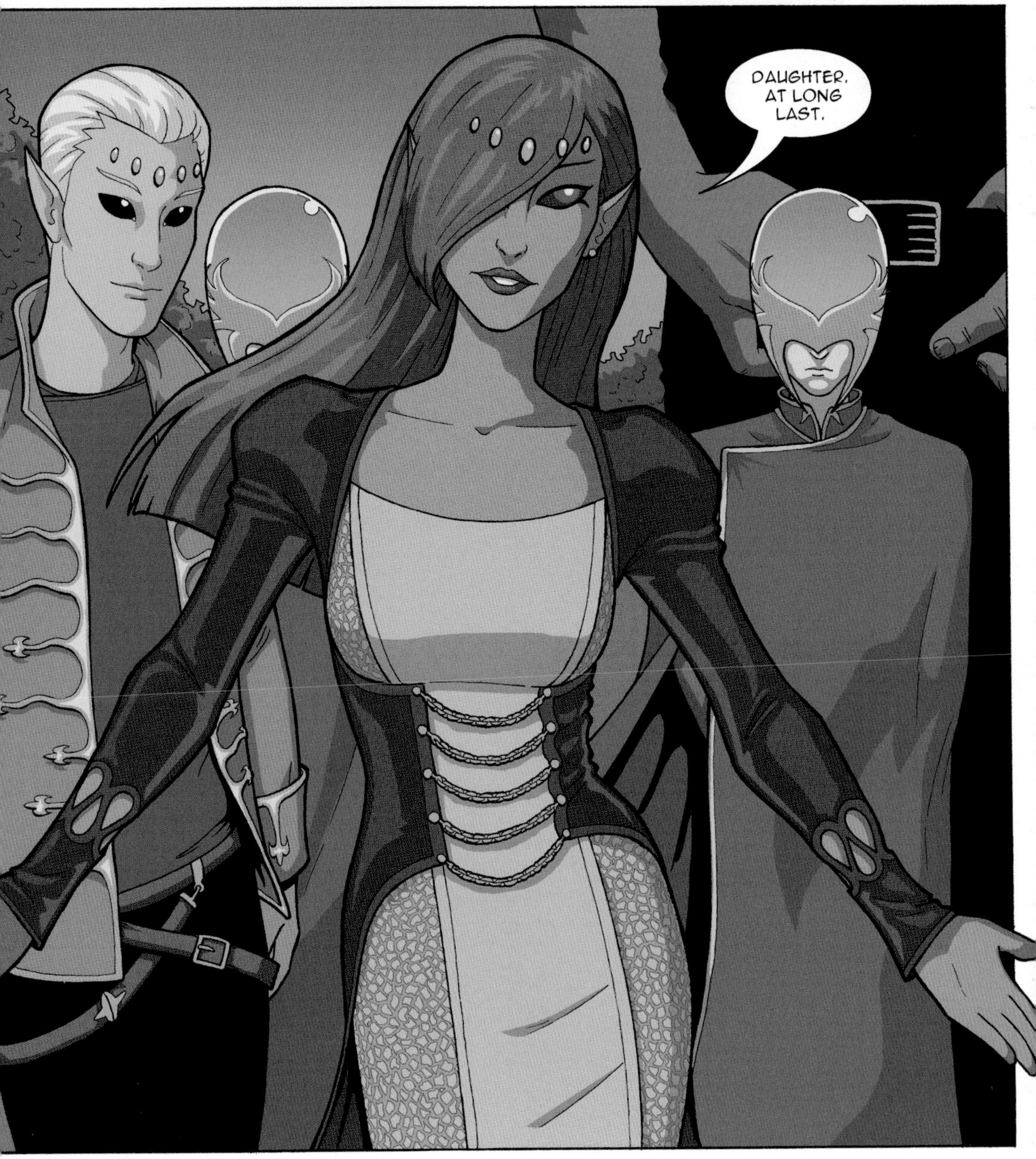
DAUGHTER.
AT LONG
LAST.

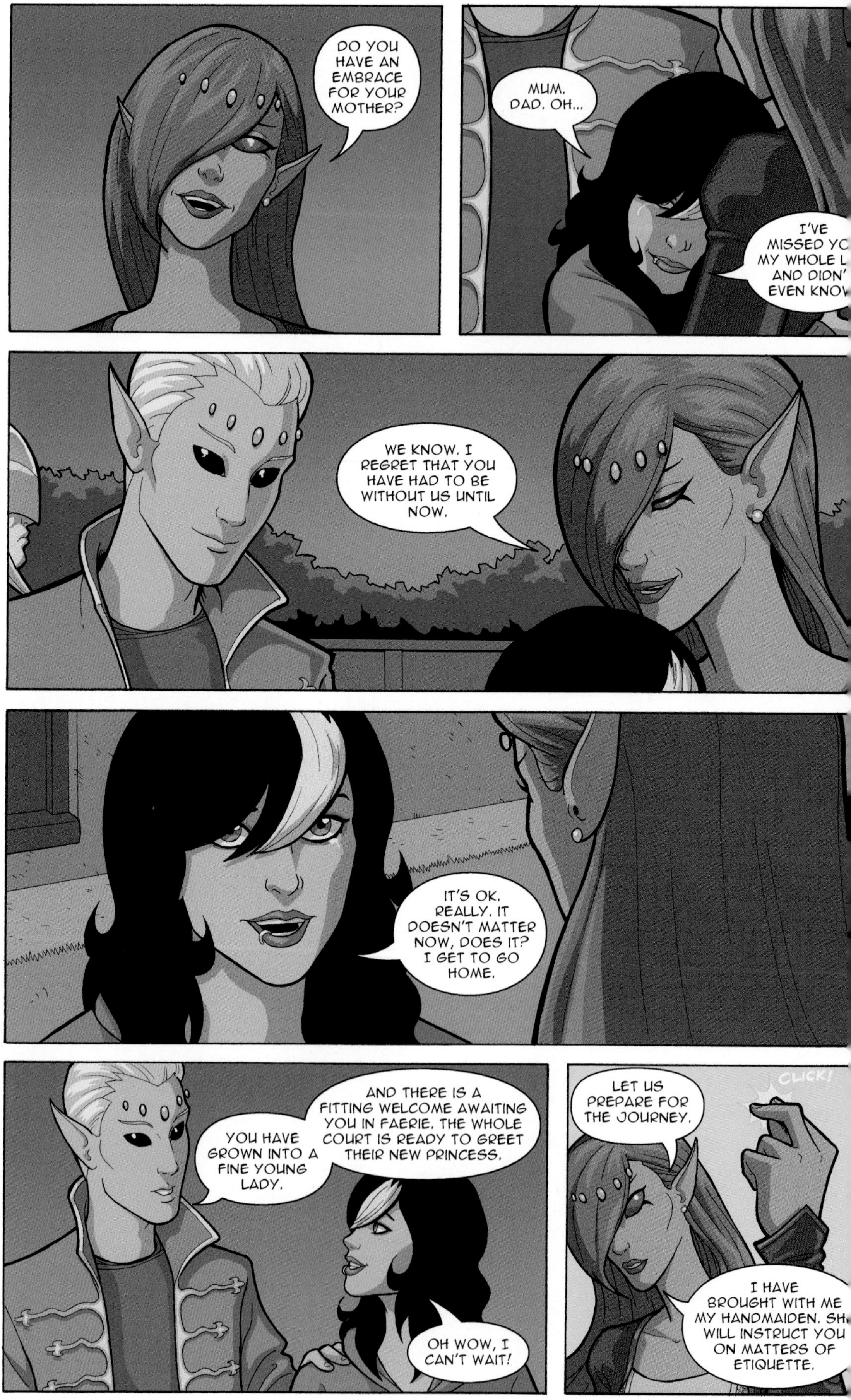
DO YOU HAVE AN EMBRACE FOR YOUR MOTHER?
MUM, DAD, OH...
I'VE MISSED YO MY WHOLE L AND DIDN' EVEN KNOW
WE KNOW. I REGRET THAT YOU HAVE HAD TO BE WITHOUT US UNTIL NOW.
IT'S OK, REALLY. IT DOESN'T MATTER NOW, DOES IT? I GET TO GO HOME.
YOU HAVE GROWN INTO A FINE YOUNG LADY.
AND THERE IS A FITTING WELCOME AWAITING YOU IN FAERIE. THE WHOLE COURT IS READY TO GREET THEIR NEW PRINCESS.
OH WOW, I CAN'T WAIT!
LET US PREPARE FOR THE JOURNEY.
CLICK!
I HAVE BROUGHT WITH ME MY HANDMAIDEN. SH WILL INSTRUCT YOU ON MATTERS OF ETIQUETTE.

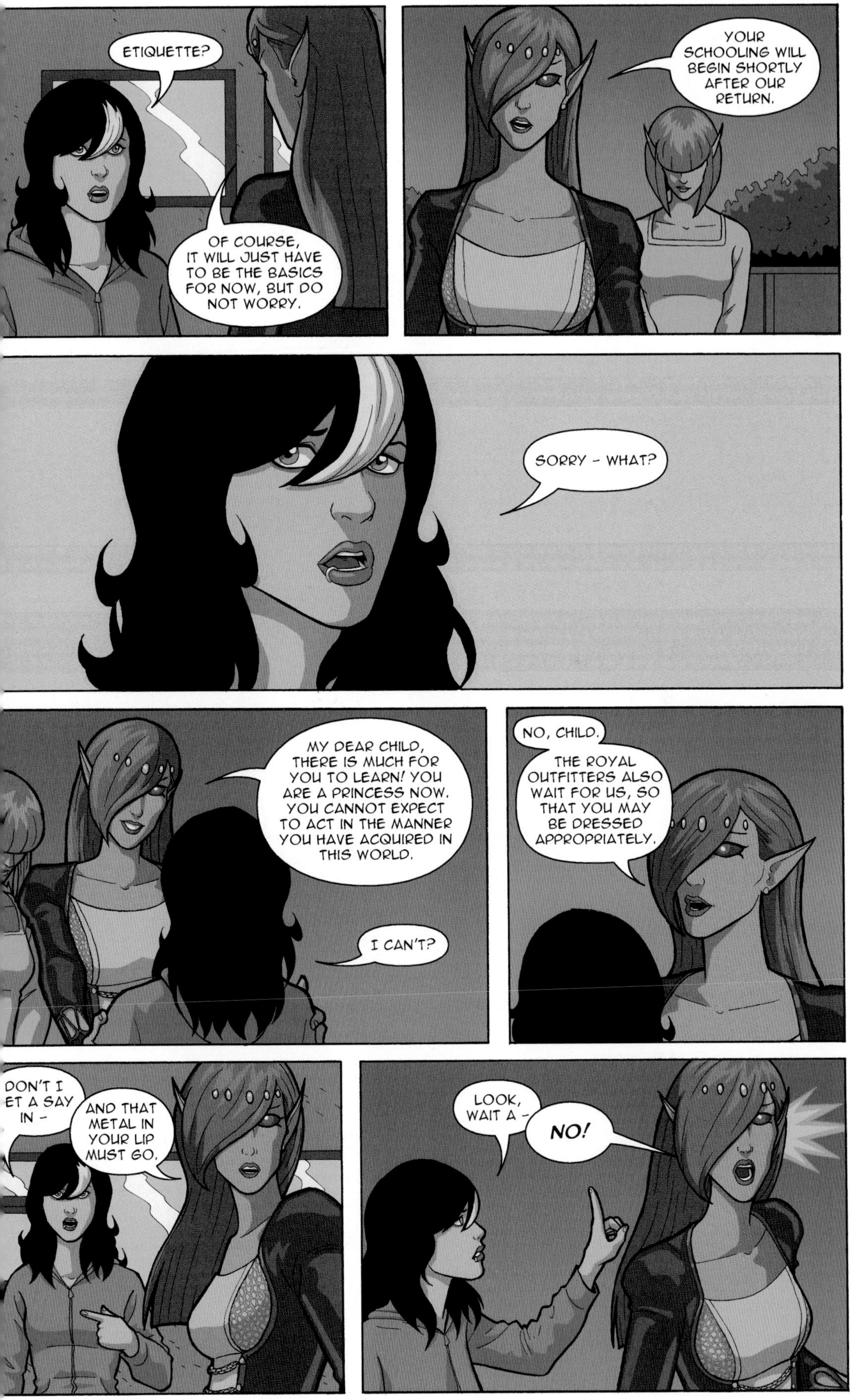
ETIQUETTE?
OF COURSE, IT WILL JUST HAVE TO BE THE BASICS FOR NOW, BUT DO NOT WORRY.
YOUR SCHOOLING WILL BEGIN SHORTLY AFTER OUR RETURN.
SORRY - WHAT?
MY DEAR CHILD, THERE IS MUCH FOR YOU TO LEARN! YOU ARE A PRINCESS NOW. YOU CANNOT EXPECT TO ACT IN THE MANNER YOU HAVE ACQUIRED IN THIS WORLD.
I CAN'T?
NO, CHILD.
THE ROYAL OUTFITTERS ALSO WAIT FOR US, SO THAT YOU MAY BE DRESSED APPROPRIATELY.
DON'T I
ET A SAY
IN -
AND THAT METAL IN YOUR LIP MUST GO.
LOOK, WAIT A -
NO!

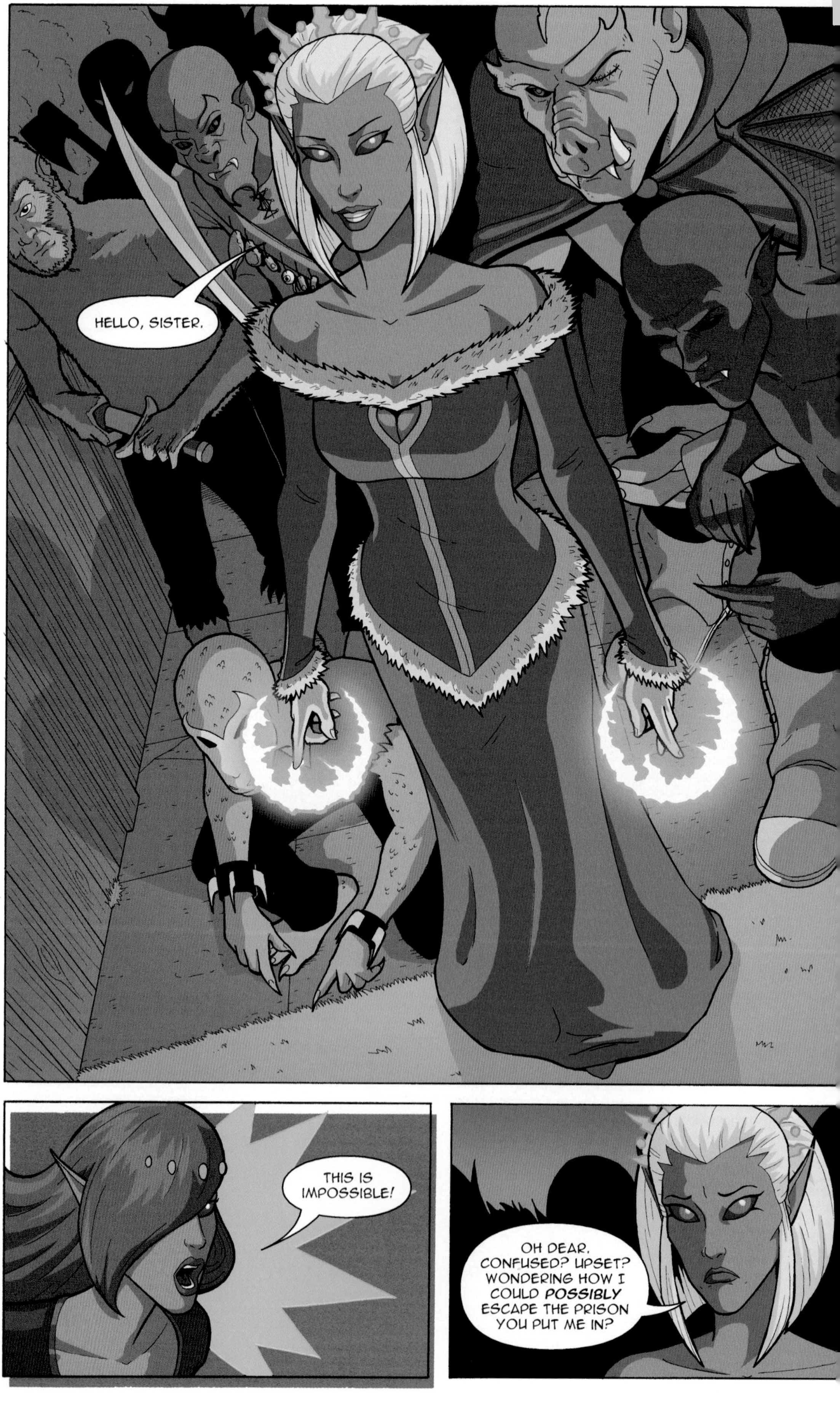
HELLO, SISTER.
THIS IS IMPOSSIBLE!
OH DEAR. CONFUSED? UPSET? WONDERING HOW I COULD **POSSIBLY** ESCAPE THE PRISON YOU PUT ME IN?

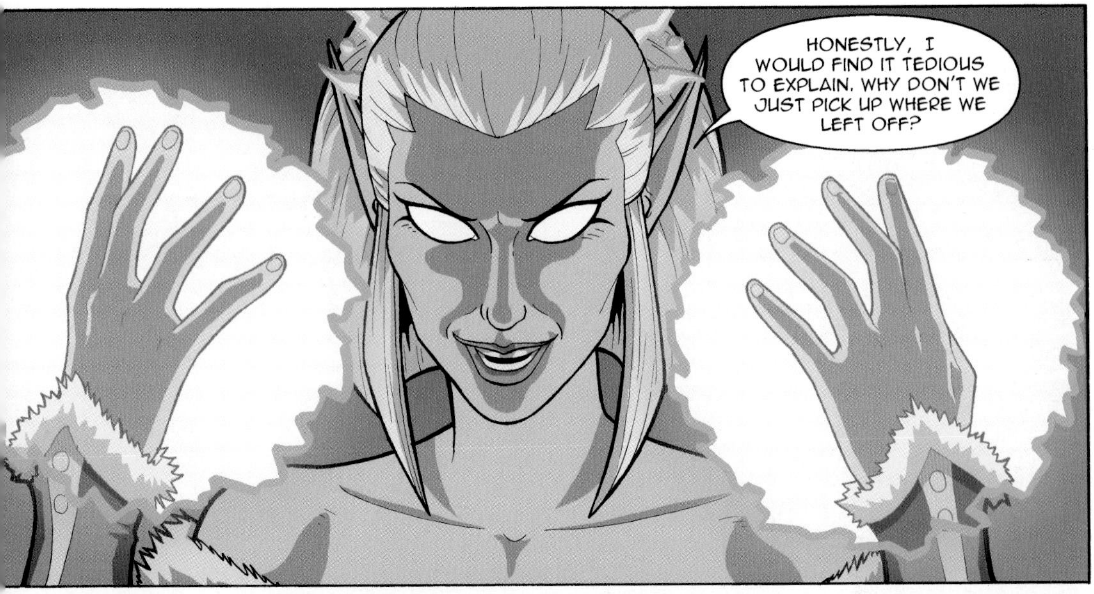
HONESTLY, I WOULD FIND IT TEDIOUS TO EXPLAIN. WHY DON'T WE JUST PICK UP WHERE WE LEFT OFF?

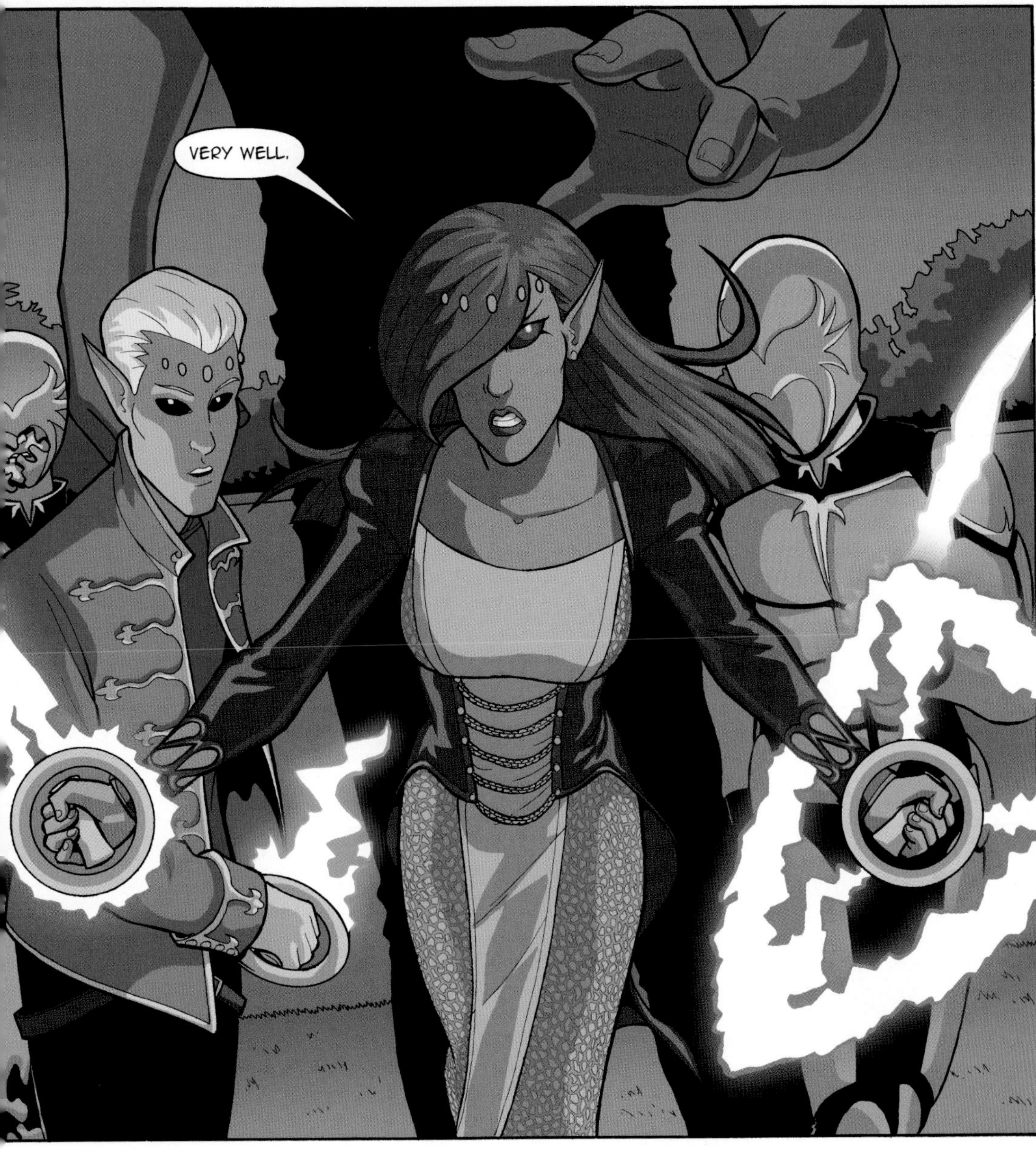
VERY WELL.

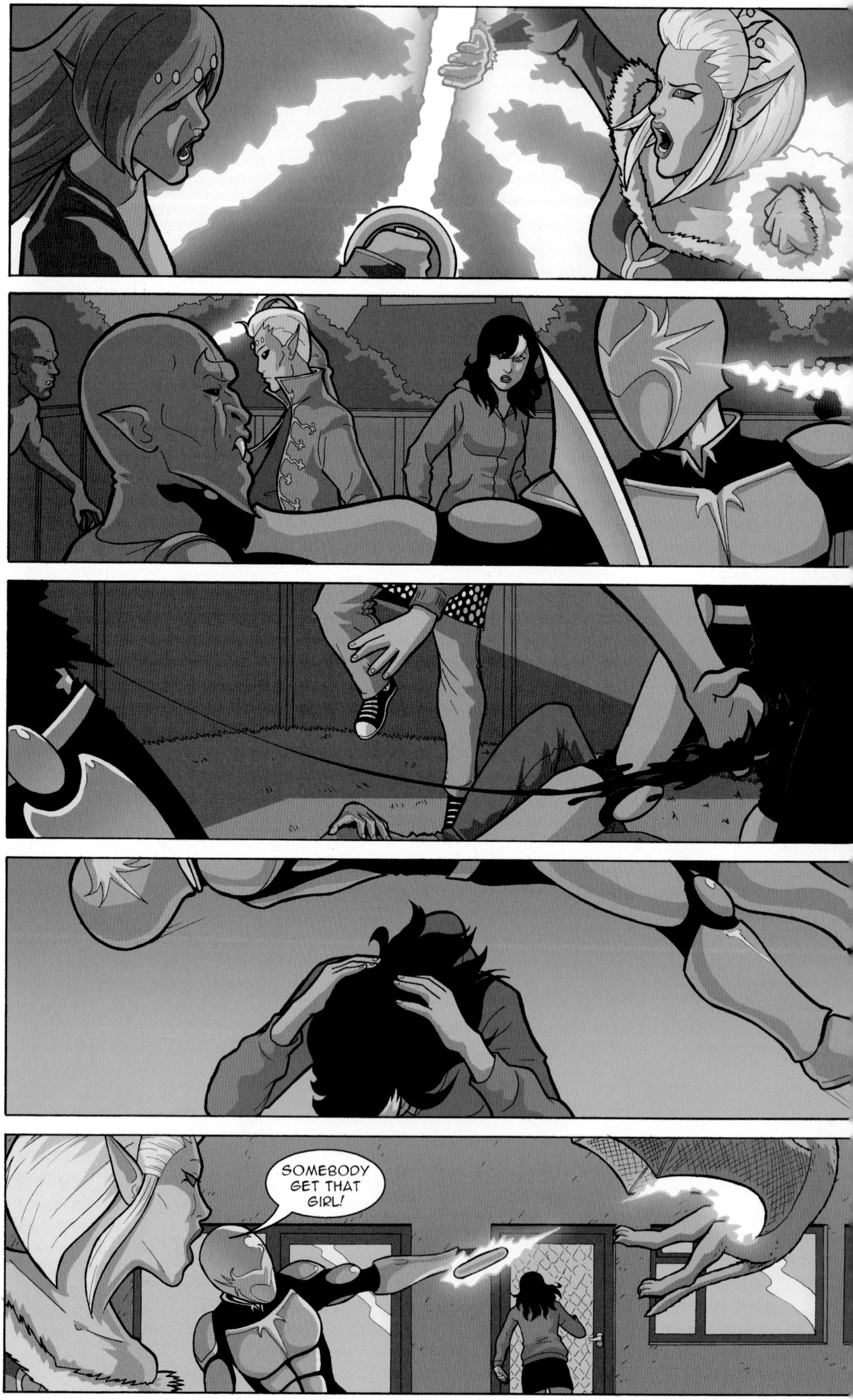
SOMEBODY GET THAT GIRL!

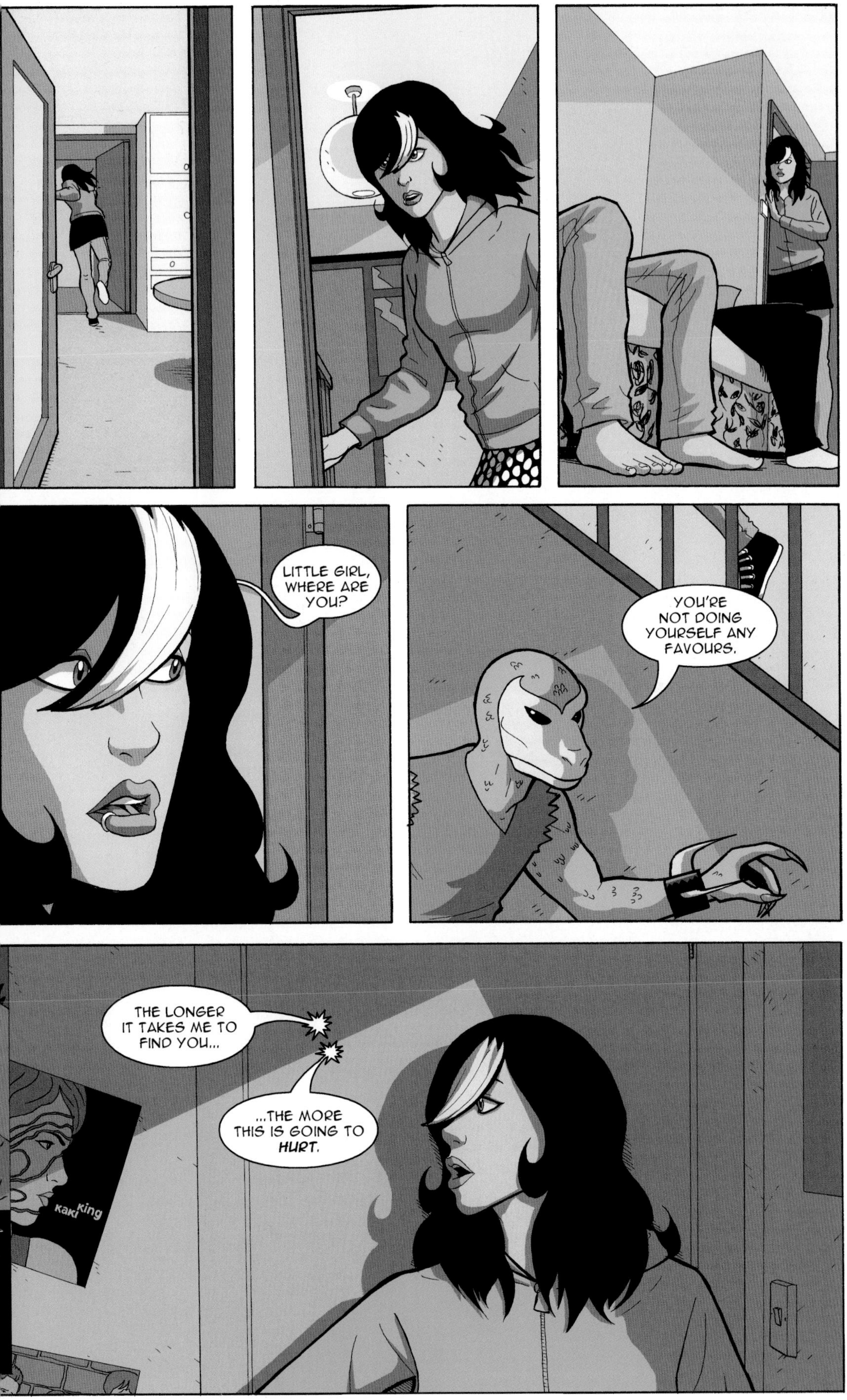
LITTLE GIRL, WHERE ARE YOU?
YOU'RE NOT DOING YOURSELF ANY FAVOURS.
THE LONGER IT TAKES ME TO FIND YOU...
...THE MORE THIS IS GOING TO *HURT*.
KAKI King

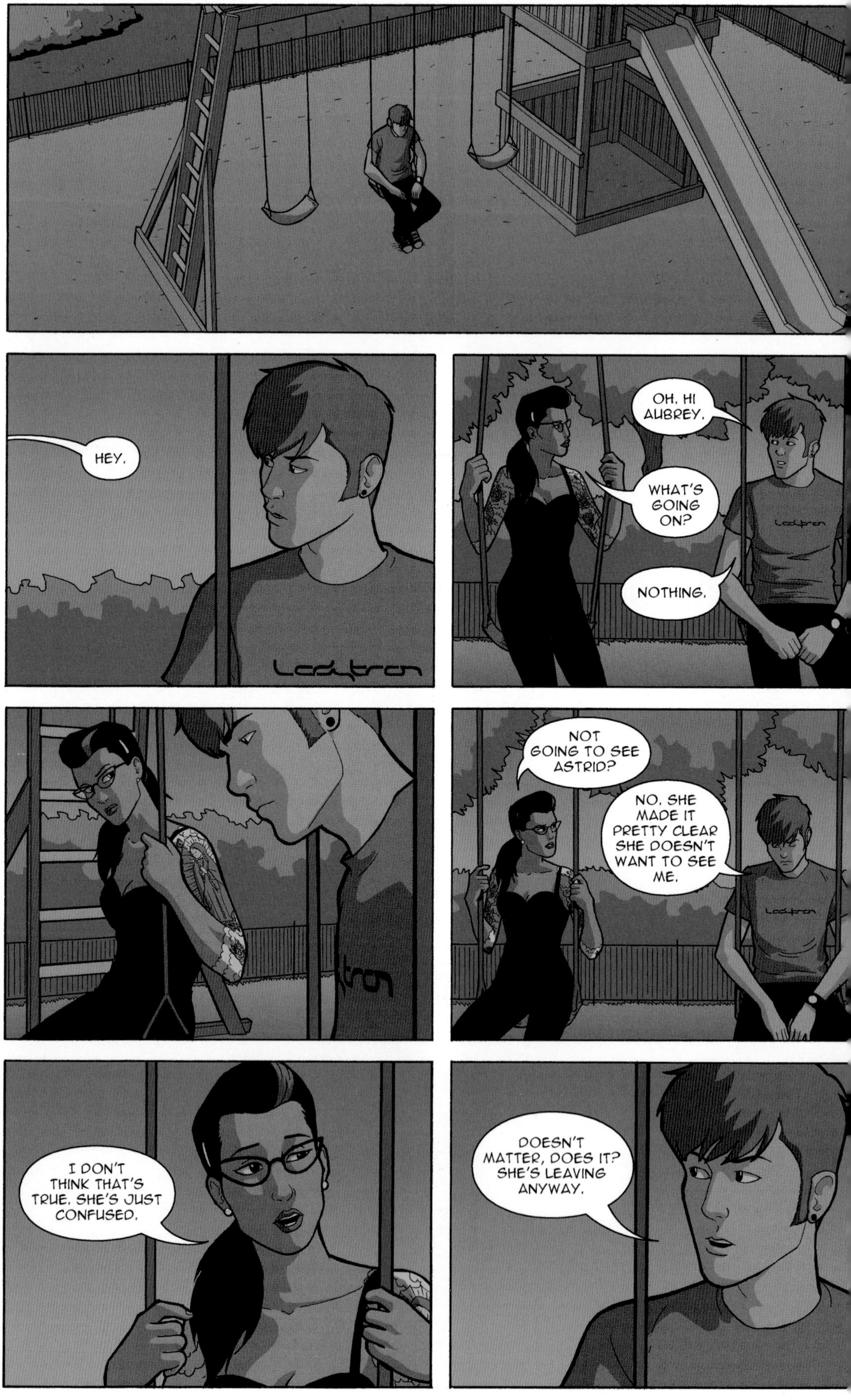
HEY.
OH, HI AUBREY.
WHAT'S GOING ON?
NOTHING.
NOT GOING TO SEE ASTRID?
NO. SHE MADE IT PRETTY CLEAR SHE DOESN'T WANT TO SEE ME.
I DON'T THINK THAT'S TRUE. SHE'S JUST CONFUSED.
DOESN'T MATTER, DOES IT? SHE'S LEAVING ANYWAY.

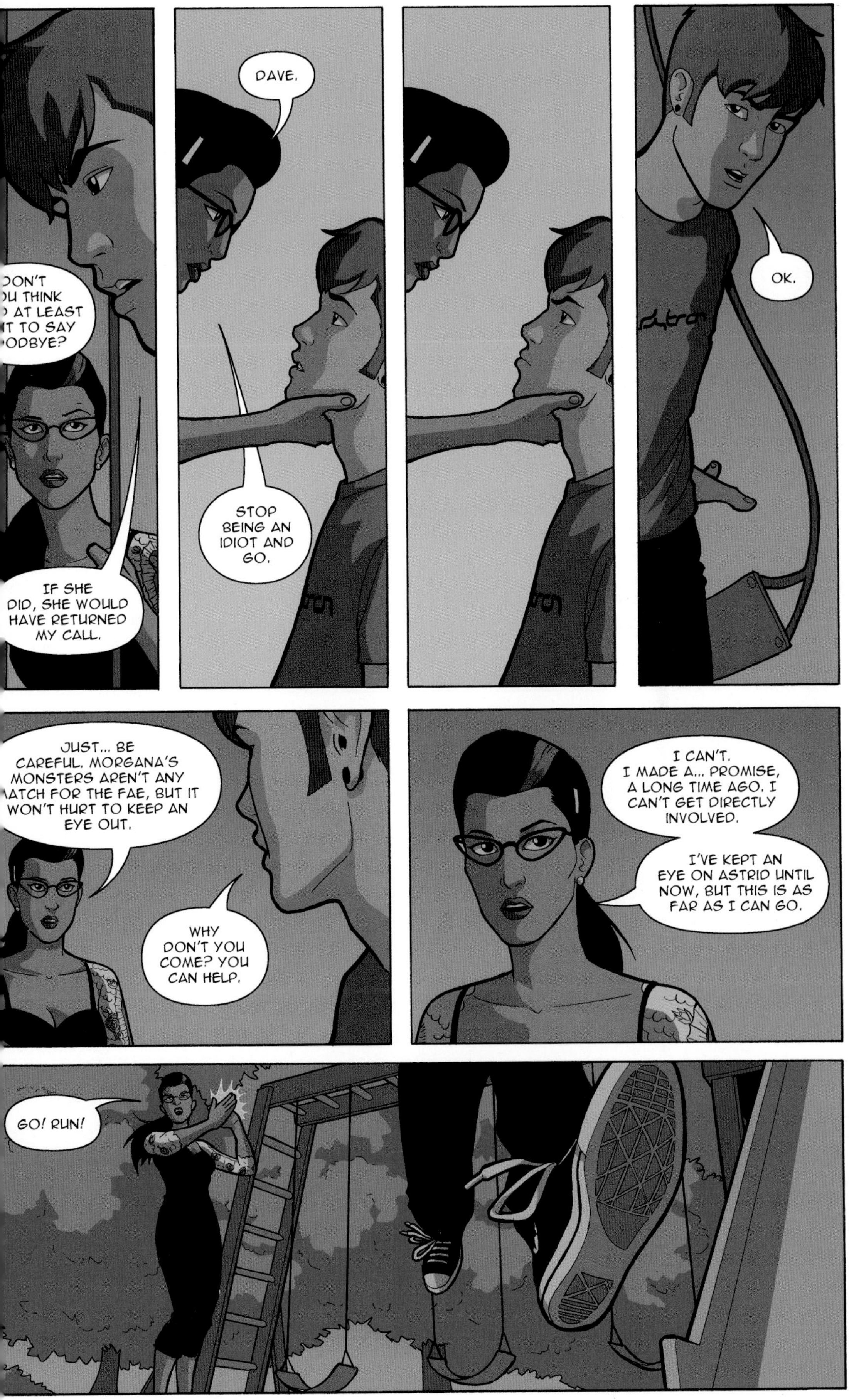

DON'T
YOU THINK
D AT LEAST
NT TO SAY
OODBYE?
IF SHE DID, SHE WOULD HAVE RETURNED MY CALL.
DAVE.
STOP BEING AN IDIOT AND GO.
OK.
JUST... BE CAREFUL. MORGANA'S MONSTERS AREN'T ANY
MATCH FOR THE FAE, BUT IT WON'T HURT TO KEEP AN EYE OUT.
WHY DON'T YOU COME? YOU CAN HELP.
I CAN'T. I MADE A... PROMISE, A LONG TIME AGO. I CAN'T GET DIRECTLY INVOLVED.
I'VE KEPT AN EYE ON ASTRID UNTIL NOW, BUT THIS IS AS FAR AS I CAN GO.
GO! RUN!

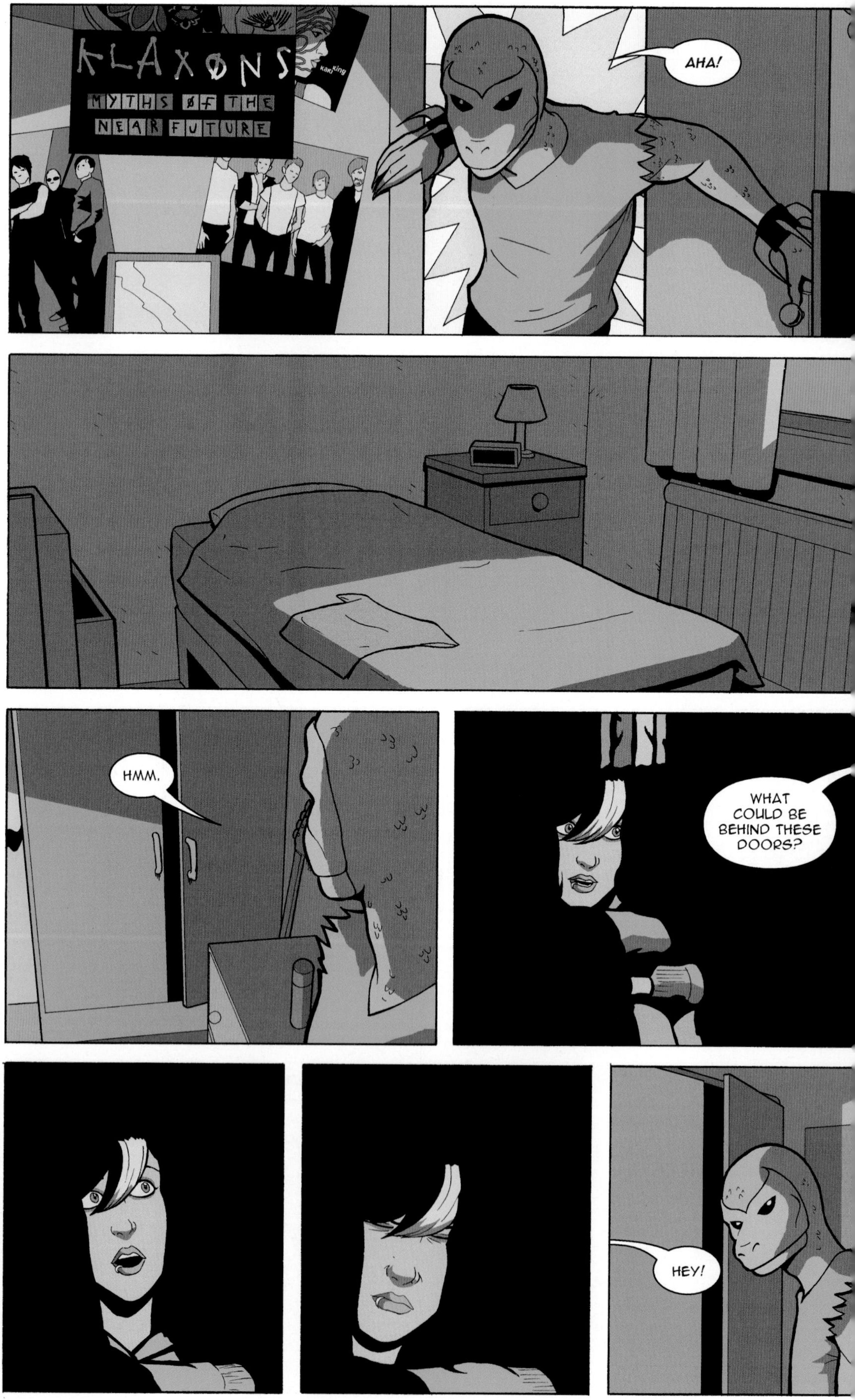
KLAXØNS
MYTHS ØF THE NEAR FUTURE
AHA!
HMM.
WHAT COULD BE BEHIND THESE DOORS?
HEY!

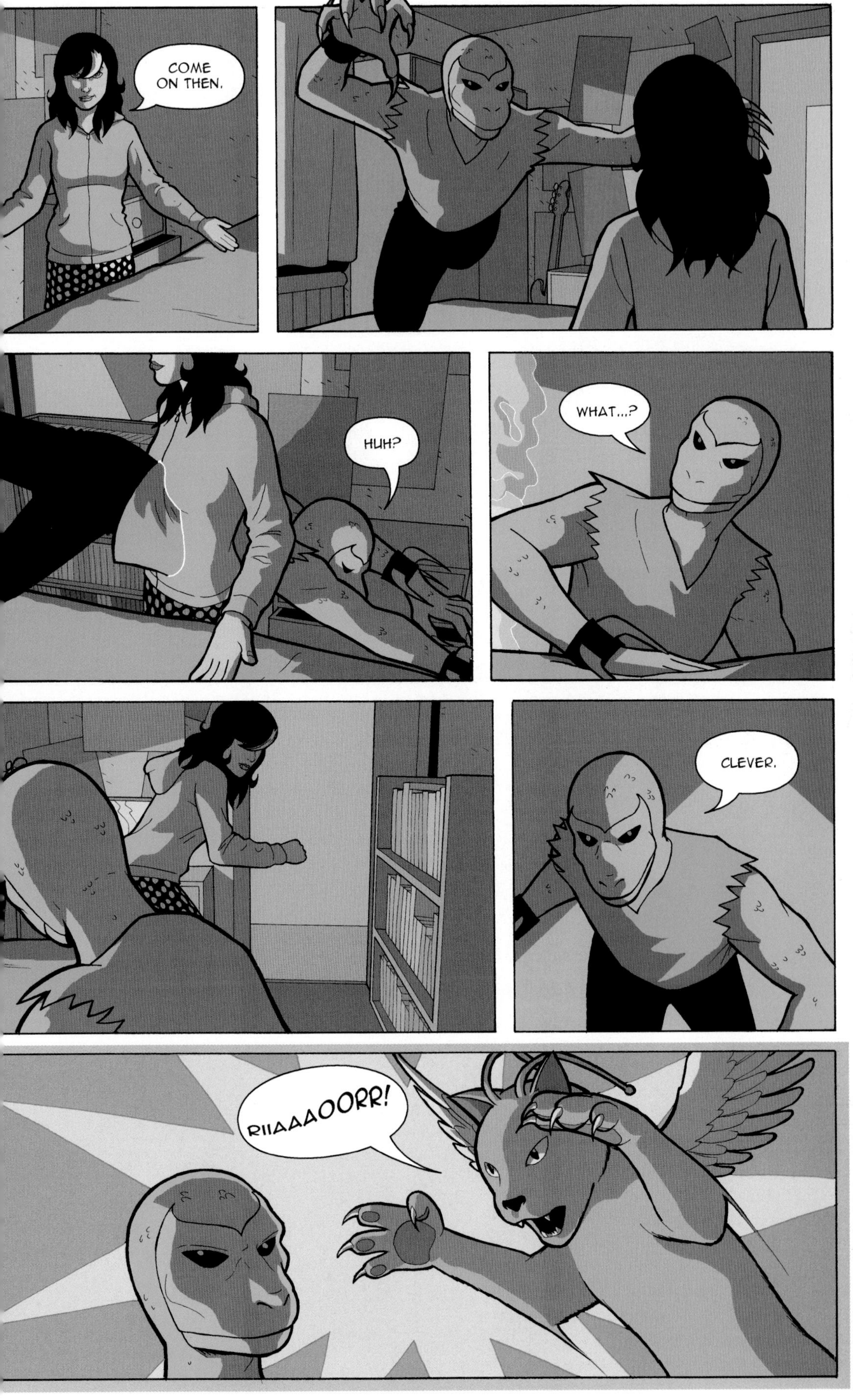
COME ON THEN.
HUH?
WHAT...?
CLEVER.
RIIAAAOORR!

RAARGH! GET...
...OFF!
NOW, BACK TO Y-
THWACK!
YEAH, YOU THINK TWICE ABOUT PICKING A FIGHT WITH US, BUDDY!
COME O
I NEED T
SORT TH
OUT.

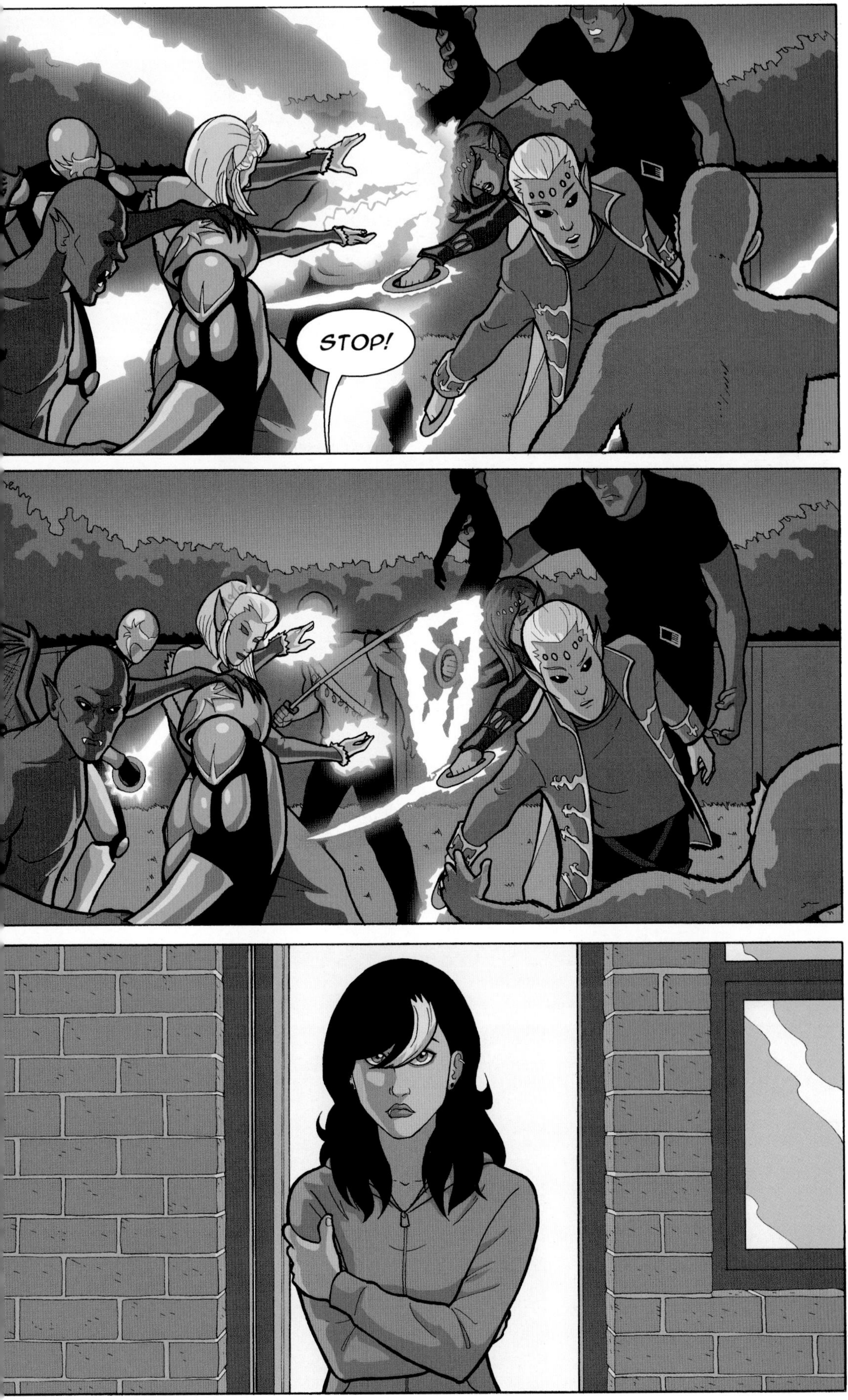
STOP!

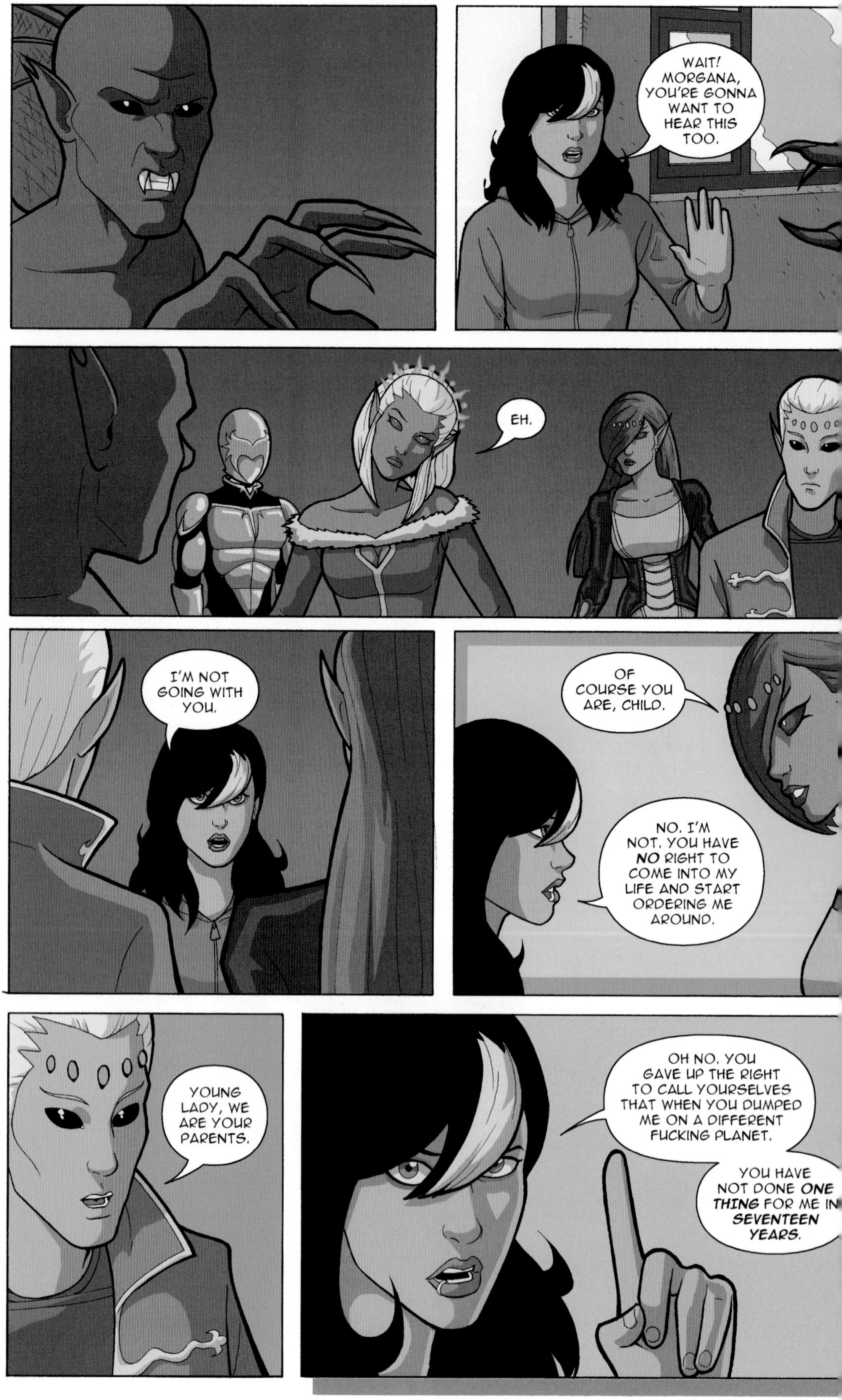
WAIT! MORGANA, YOU'RE GONNA WANT TO HEAR THIS TOO.
EH.
I'M NOT GOING WITH YOU.
OF COURSE YOU ARE, CHILD.
NO. I'M NOT. YOU HAVE **NO** RIGHT TO COME INTO MY LIFE AND START ORDERING ME AROUND.
YOUNG LADY, WE ARE YOUR PARENTS.
OH NO. YOU GAVE UP THE RIGHT TO CALL YOURSELVES THAT WHEN YOU DUMPED ME ON A DIFFERENT FUCKING PLANET.
YOU HAVE NOT DONE ***ONE THING*** FOR ME IN ***SEVENTEEN YEARS***.

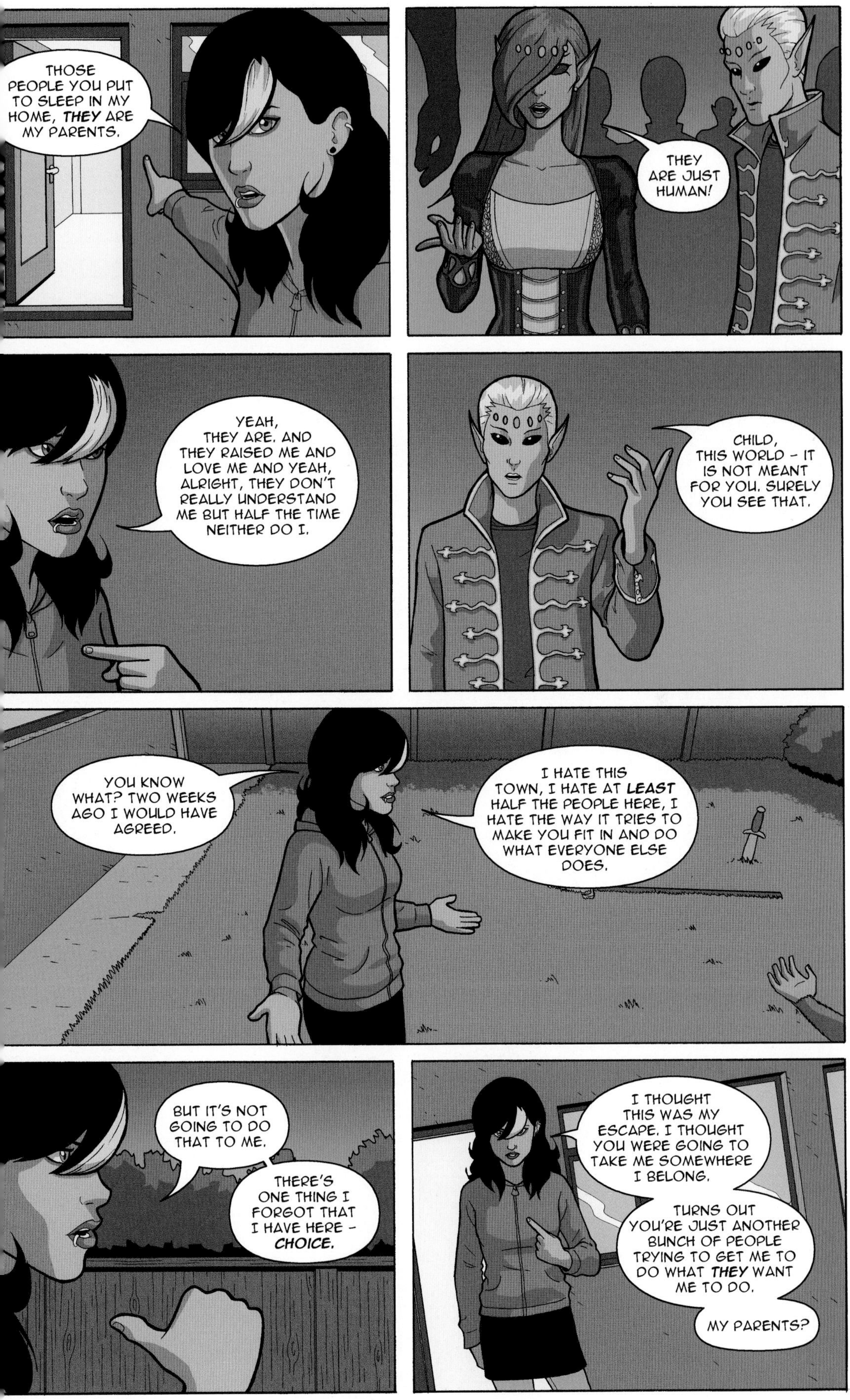

THOSE PEOPLE YOU PUT TO SLEEP IN MY HOME, ***THEY*** ARE MY PARENTS.
THEY ARE JUST HUMAN!
YEAH, THEY ARE. AND THEY RAISED ME AND LOVE ME AND YEAH, ALRIGHT, THEY DON'T REALLY UNDERSTAND ME BUT HALF THE TIME NEITHER DO I.
CHILD, THIS WORLD - IT IS NOT MEANT FOR YOU. SURELY YOU SEE THAT.
YOU KNOW WHAT? TWO WEEKS AGO I WOULD HAVE AGREED.
I HATE THIS TOWN, I HATE AT ***LEAST*** HALF THE PEOPLE HERE, I HATE THE WAY IT TRIES TO MAKE YOU FIT IN AND DO WHAT EVERYONE ELSE DOES.
BUT IT'S NOT GOING TO DO THAT TO ME.
THERE'S ONE THING I FORGOT THAT I HAVE HERE - ***CHOICE.***
I THOUGHT THIS WAS MY ESCAPE. I THOUGHT YOU WERE GOING TO TAKE ME SOMEWHERE I BELONG.
TURNS OUT YOU'RE JUST ANOTHER BUNCH OF PEOPLE TRYING TO GET ME TO DO WHAT ***THEY*** WANT ME TO DO.
MY PARENTS?

YOU DON'T *DESERVE* TO BE MY PARENTS.

NOW GET THE FUCK OUT OF MY GARDEN.

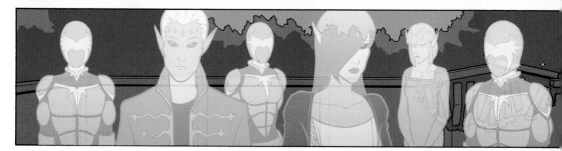

NO!

THAT WAS QUITE THE PERFORMANCE, NIECE.

I HAD INTENDED TO KILL YOU. I SHOULD STILL DO SO, FOR WASTING MY TIME.

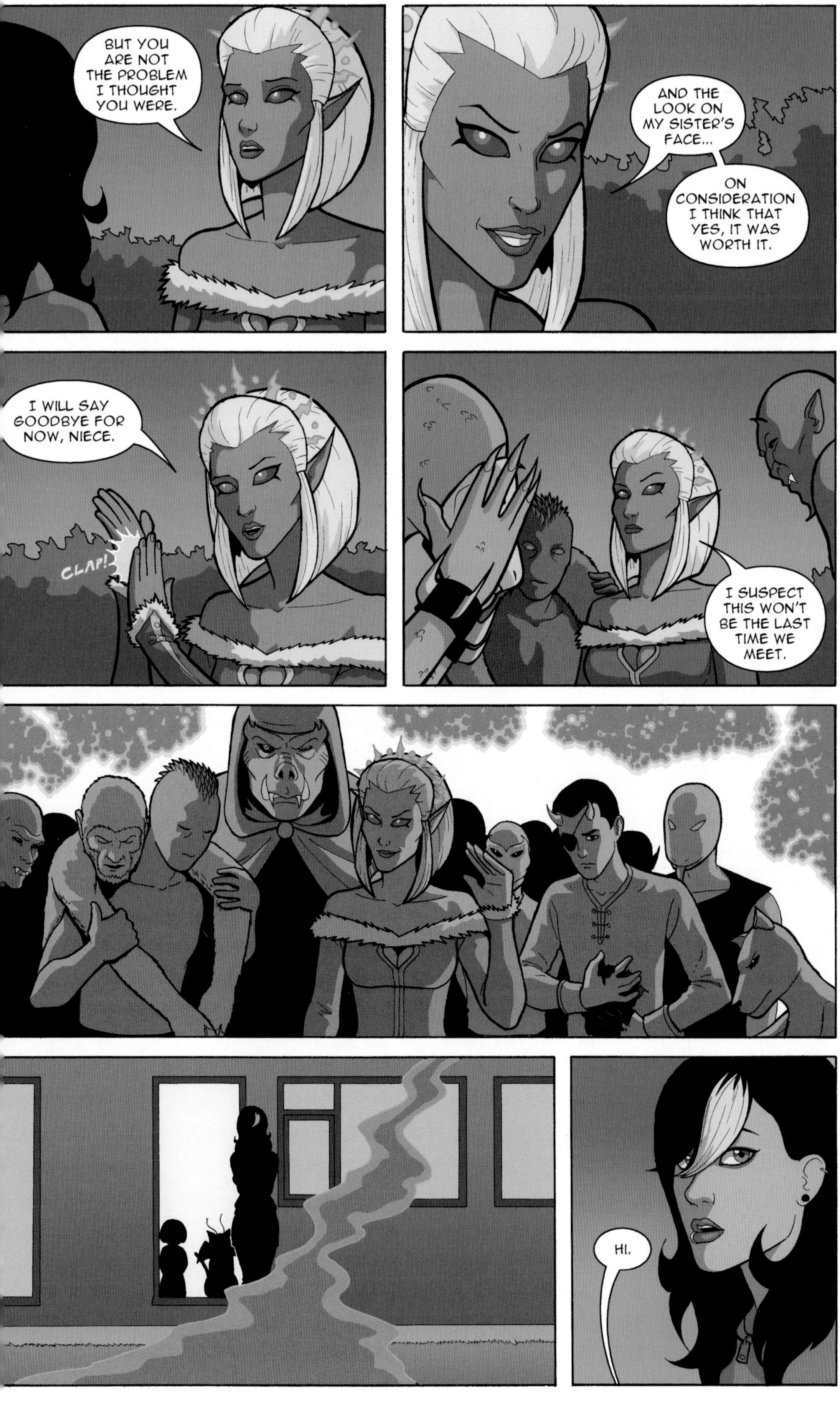
BUT YOU ARE NOT THE PROBLEM I THOUGHT YOU WERE.
AND THE LOOK ON MY SISTER'S FACE...
ON CONSIDERATION I THINK THAT YES, IT WAS WORTH IT.
I WILL SAY GOODBYE FOR NOW, NIECE.
CLAP!
I SUSPECT THIS WON'T BE THE LAST TIME WE MEET.
HI.

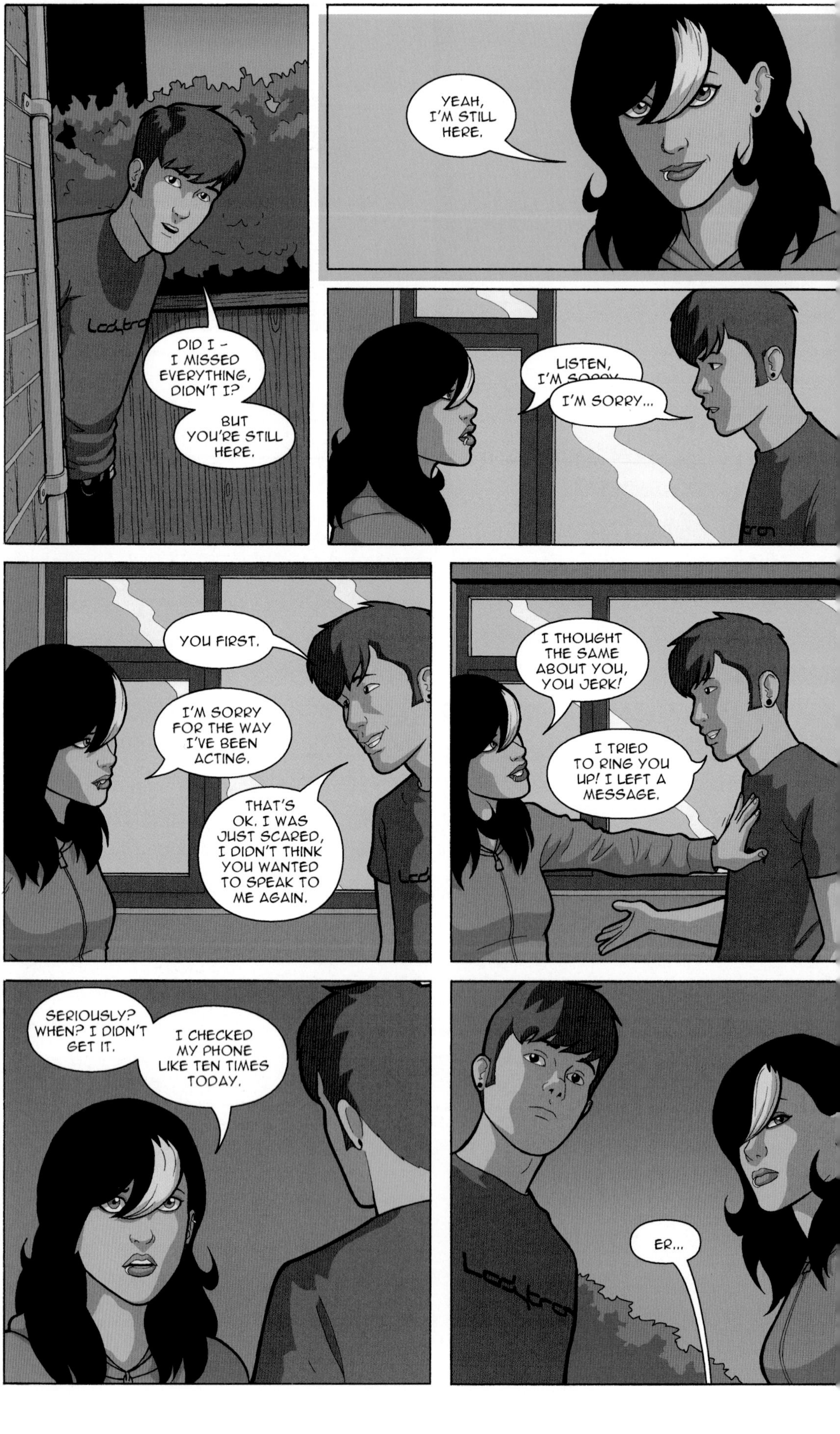
DID I - I MISSED EVERYTHING, DIDN'T I?
BUT YOU'RE STILL HERE.
YEAH, I'M STILL HERE.
LISTEN,
I'M SORRY...
YOU FIRST.
I'M SORRY FOR THE WAY I'VE BEEN ACTING.
THAT'S OK. I WAS JUST SCARED, I DIDN'T THINK YOU WANTED TO SPEAK TO ME AGAIN.
I THOUGHT THE SAME ABOUT YOU, YOU JERK!
I TRIED TO RING YOU UP! I LEFT A MESSAGE.
SERIOUSLY? WHEN? I DIDN'T GET IT.
I CHECKED MY PHONE LIKE TEN TIMES TODAY.
ER...

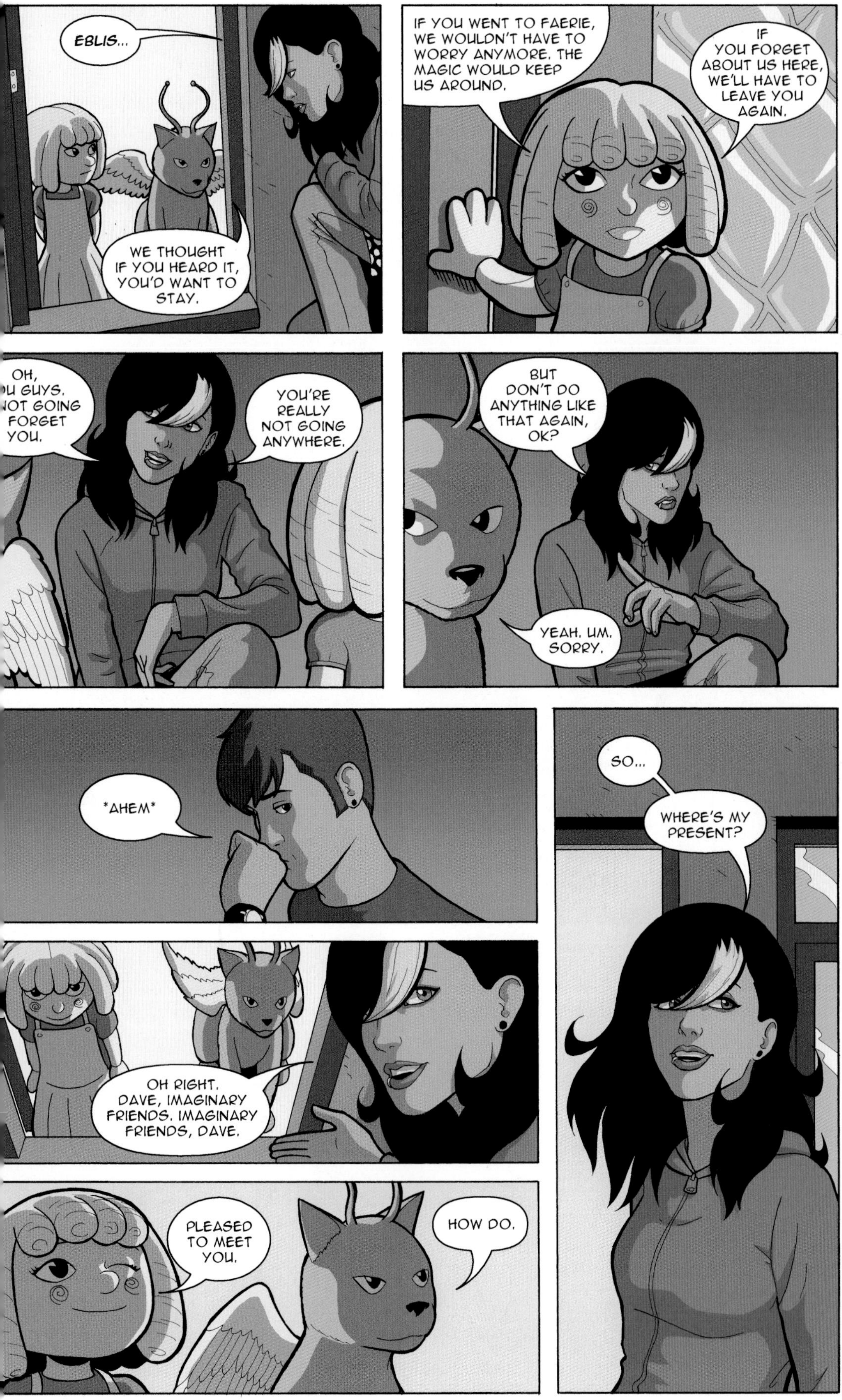
EBLIS...
WE THOUGHT IF YOU HEARD IT, YOU'D WANT TO STAY.
IF YOU WENT TO FAERIE, WE WOULDN'T HAVE TO WORRY ANYMORE. THE MAGIC WOULD KEEP US AROUND.
IF YOU FORGET ABOUT US HERE, WE'LL HAVE TO LEAVE YOU AGAIN.
OH, U GUYS. NOT GOING FORGET YOU.
YOU'RE REALLY NOT GOING ANYWHERE.
BUT DON'T DO ANYTHING LIKE THAT AGAIN, OK?
YEAH. UM. SORRY.
AHEM
SO...
WHERE'S MY PRESENT?
OH RIGHT. DAVE, IMAGINARY FRIENDS. IMAGINARY FRIENDS, DAVE.
PLEASED TO MEET YOU.
HOW DO.

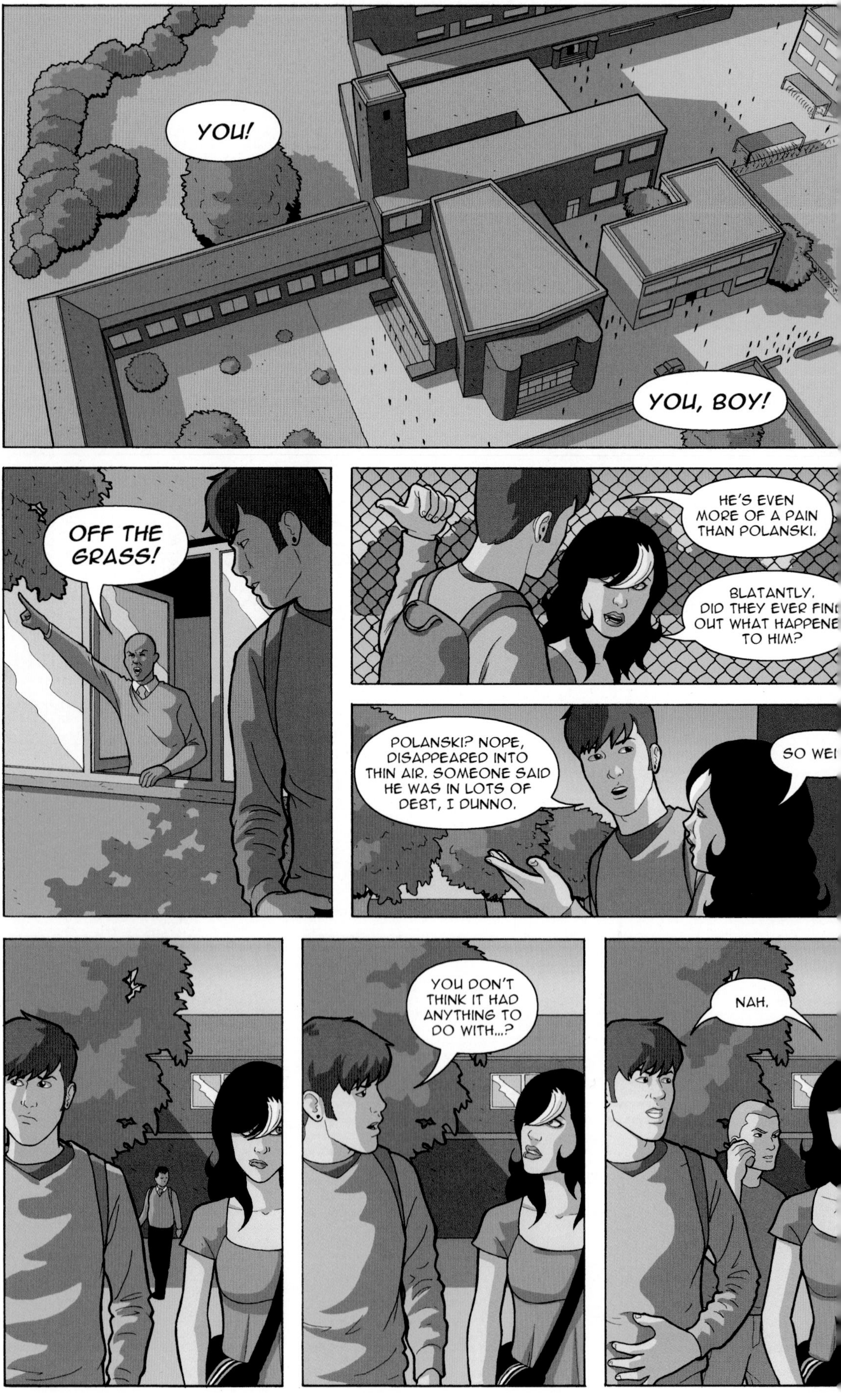
YOU!
YOU, BOY!
OFF THE GRASS!
HE'S EVEN MORE OF A PAIN THAN POLANSKI.
BLATANTLY. DID THEY EVER FIN
OUT WHAT HAPPENE
TO HIM?
POLANSKI? NOPE, DISAPPEARED INTO THIN AIR. SOMEONE SAID HE WAS IN LOTS OF DEBT, I DUNNO.
SO WEI
YOU DON'T THINK IT HAD ANYTHING TO DO WITH...?
NAH.

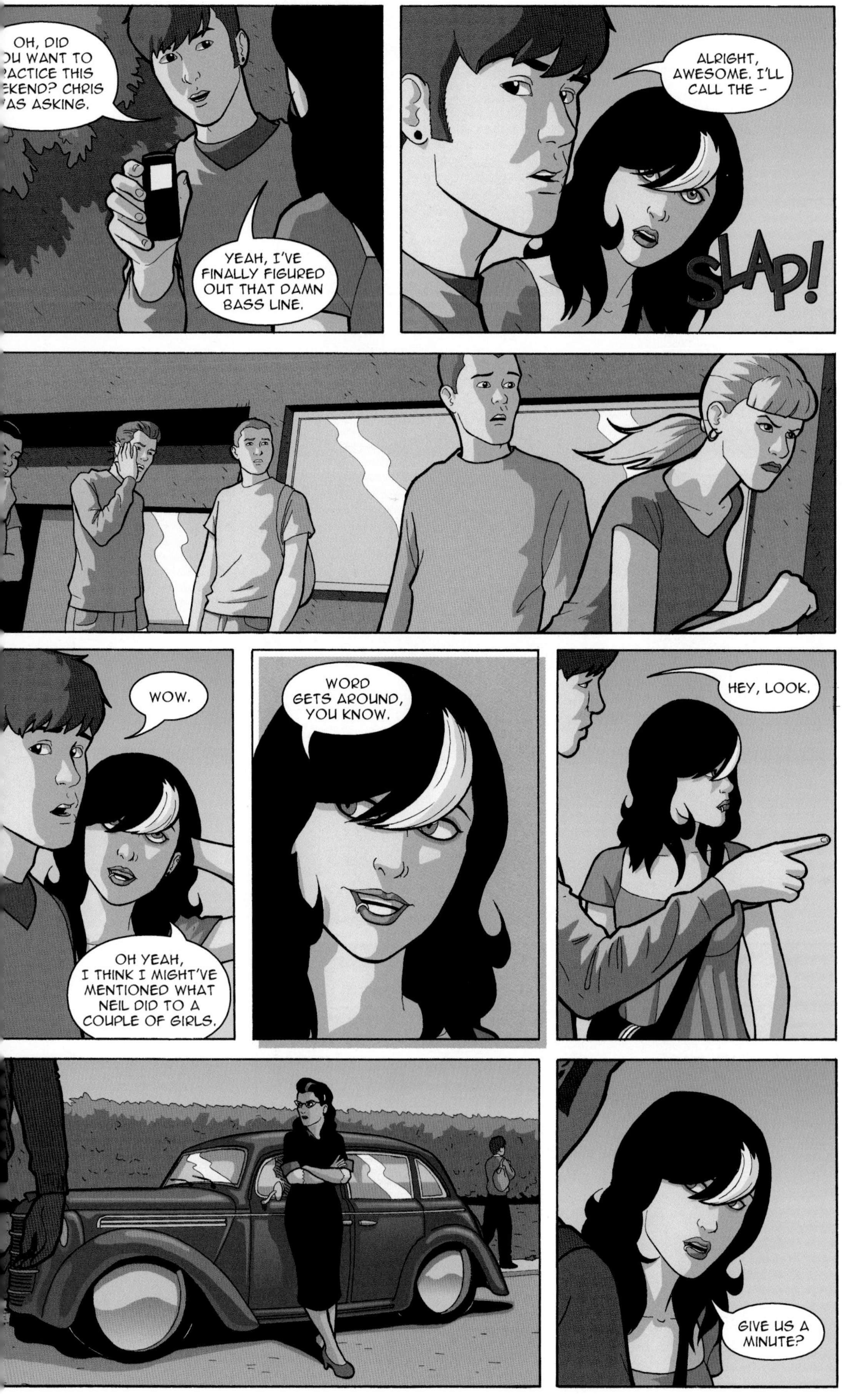
OH, DID
OU WANT TO
RACTICE THIS
EKEND? CHRIS
AS ASKING.
YEAH, I'VE FINALLY FIGURED OUT THAT DAMN BASS LINE.
ALRIGHT, AWESOME. I'LL CALL THE –
SLAP!
WOW.
OH YEAH, I THINK I MIGHT'VE MENTIONED WHAT NEIL DID TO A COUPLE OF GIRLS.
WORD GETS AROUND, YOU KNOW.
HEY, LOOK.
GIVE US A MINUTE?

HI.

HOW'S IT GOING?

PRETTY GOOD. I THINK I MADE THE RIGHT DECISION.

YOU DID.

YOU DON'T THINK I MADE A MISTAKE?

EVEN IF YOU DID, IT'S YOUR MISTAKE TO MAKE. THAT'S THE POINT.

SO... WHAT ABOU YOU? NOW I ALL OVER, WH ARE YOU GO TO DO?

WELL, THE SHOP'S DOING GOOD BUSINESS. AND I'M ENJOYING THE FRESH AIR.

IT'D BE A SHAME TO LEAVE NOW.

ESPECIAL AS YOU'V GOT FAMI HERE, RIGH

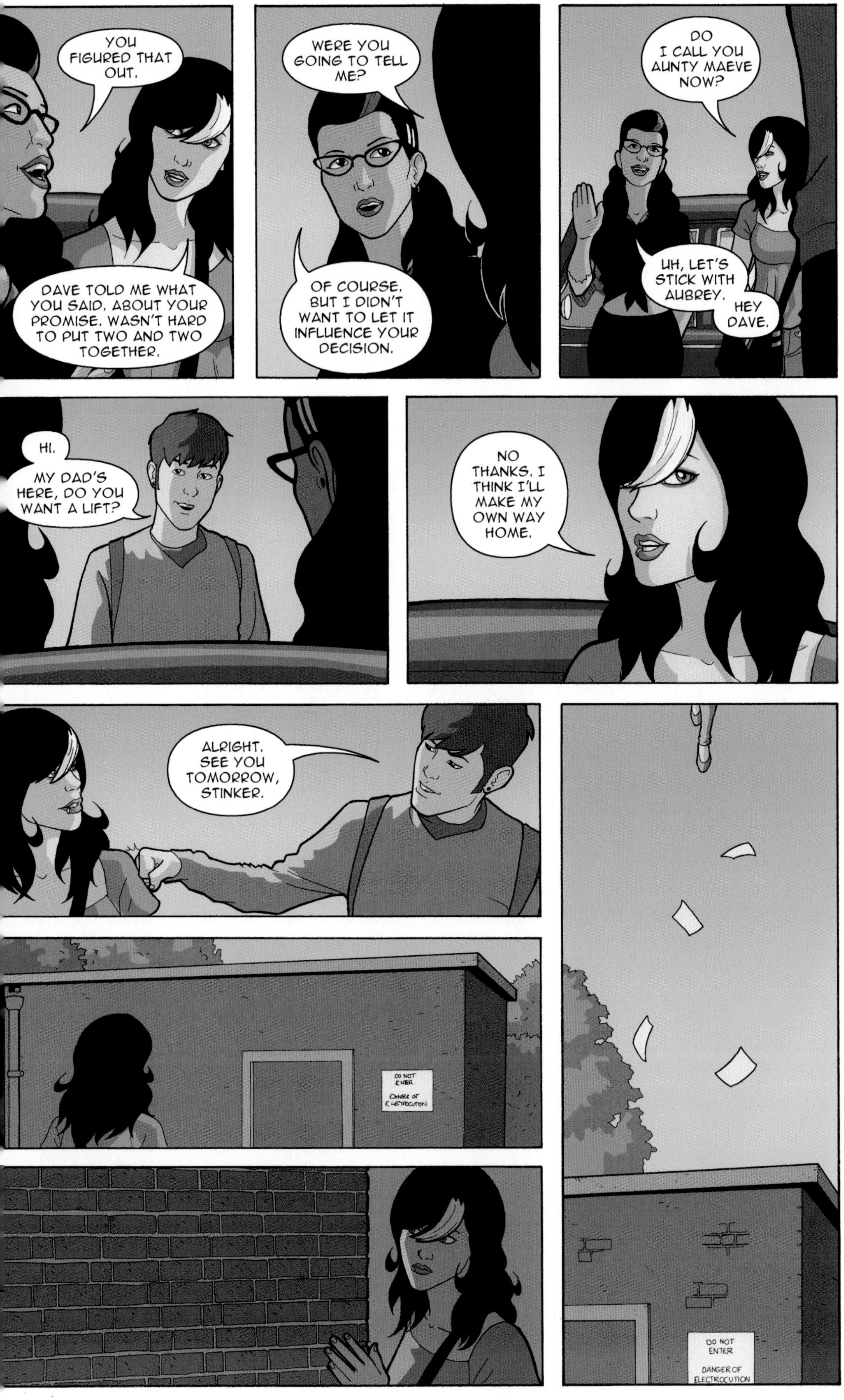
YOU FIGURED THAT OUT.
DAVE TOLD ME WHAT YOU SAID. ABOUT YOUR PROMISE. WASN'T HARD TO PUT TWO AND TWO TOGETHER.
WERE YOU GOING TO TELL ME?
OF COURSE. BUT I DIDN'T WANT TO LET IT INFLUENCE YOUR DECISION.
DO I CALL YOU AUNTY MAEVE NOW?
UH, LET'S STICK WITH AUBREY.
HEY DAVE.
HI.
MY DAD'S HERE, DO YOU WANT A LIFT?
NO THANKS. I THINK I'LL MAKE MY OWN WAY HOME.
ALRIGHT. SEE YOU TOMORROW, STINKER.
DO NOT ENTER
DANGER OF ELECTROCUTION
DO NOT ENTER
DANGER OF ELECTROCUTION

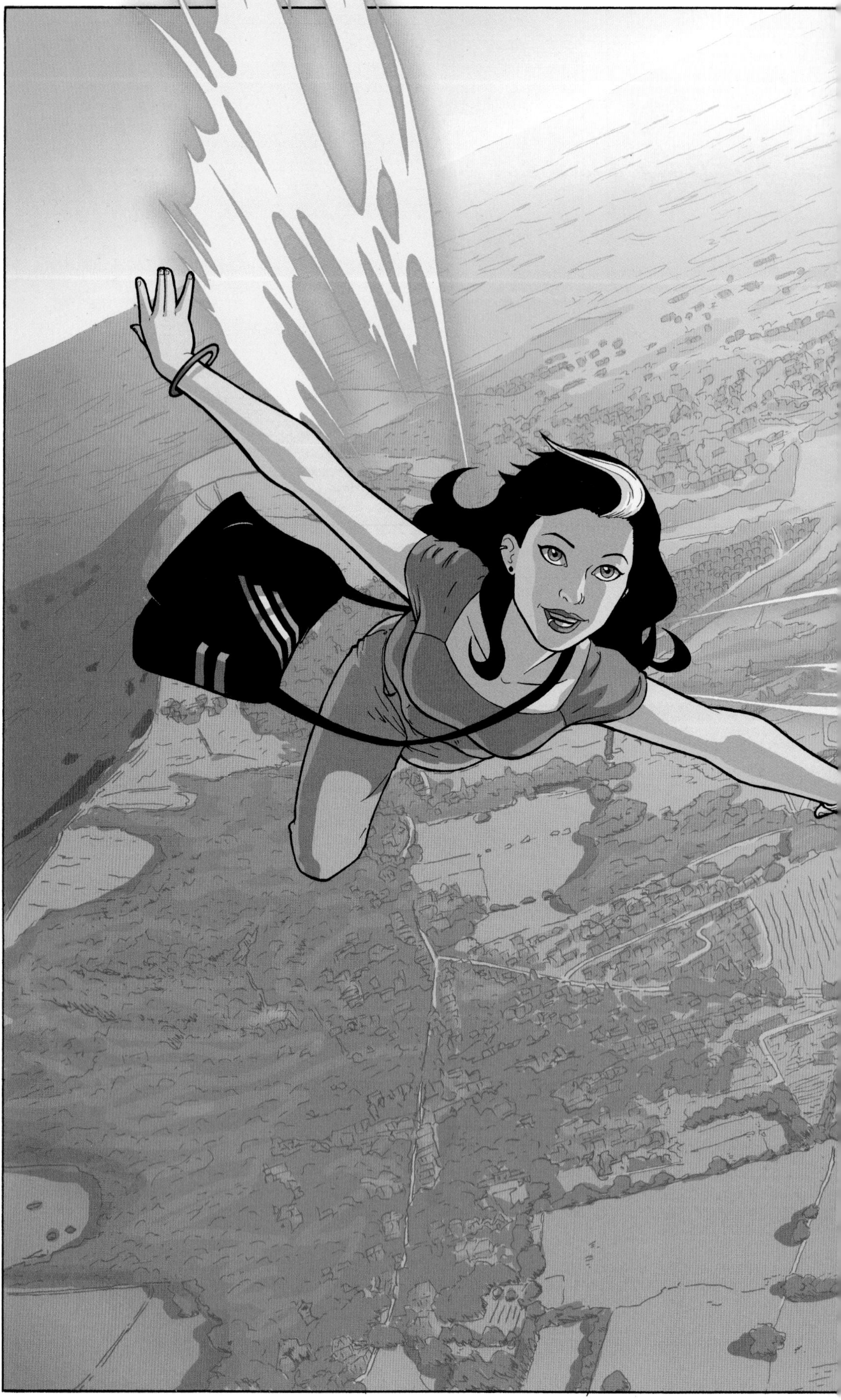